"The World's Best Books"

STUDIES IN PRINT CULTURE AND THE HISTORY OF THE BOOK

EDITORIAL ADVISORY BOARD

Roger Chartier
Robert A. Gross
Joan Shelley Rubin
Michael Winship

THE WORLD'S BEST BOOKS

*Taste, Culture,
and the
Modern Library*

JAY SATTERFIELD

UNIVERSITY OF MASSACHUSETTS PRESS
AMHERST AND BOSTON

Copyright ©2002 by University of Massachusetts Press

All rights reserved

Printed in the United States of America

First paperback printing 2010

LC 2001008665

ISBN 978-1-55849-791-7

Designed by Dean Bornstein

Set in Granjon and Didot

Printed and bound by Lightning Source, Inc.

Library of Congress Cataloging-in-Publication Data

Satterfield, Jay, 1964–
  The world's best books : taste, culture, and the Modern Library / Jay Satterfield.
    p. cm. — (Studies in print culture and the history of the book)
Includes bibliographical references and index.
  ISBN 1-55849-353-0 (alk. paper)
  1. Modern Library (Firm)—History. 2. Modern library of the world's best books—History. 3. Publishers and publishing—New York (State)—New York—History—20th century. 4. Monographic series. 5. Literature publishing—United States—History—20th century. 6. Books and reading—United States—History—20th century.   I. Title. II. Series.
  Z473 .M79 S28 2002
  070.5'09—dc21

2001008665

British Library Cataloguing in Publication data are available.

Contents

Illustrations . . . vii

Acknowledgments . . . ix

Introduction . . . 1

CHAPTER ONE
Establishing the World's Best Books . . . 10

CHAPTER TWO
Advertising the World's Best Books . . . 38

CHAPTER THREE
Booming the World's Best Books . . . 65

CHAPTER FOUR
Packaging the World's Best Books . . . 88

CHAPTER FIVE
Selecting the World's Best Books . . . 119

CHAPTER SIX
Closing the World's Best Books . . . 142

Epilogue . . . 172

Notes . . . 177

Selected Bibliography . . . 217

Index . . . 227

ILLUSTRATIONS

1. Advertisement, *New Republic,* 17 November 1917 . . . 21

2. Advertisement, *New York Times Book Review,* 18 November 1928 . . . 48

3. Advertisement, *New York Times Book Review,* 19 May 1940 . . . 62

4. Advertisement, *Publishers' Weekly,* 14 May 1932 . . . 79

5. Everyman's Library title page, 1925 . . . 91

6. Modern Library title page, 1925 . . . 92

7A. Colophon used by Boni & Liveright, 1917 . . . 108

7B. Colophon used by Boni & Liveright, 1924 . . . 108

7C. Colophon designed by Lucian Bernhard, 1925 . . . 108

7D. Colophon designed by Rockwell Kent, 1929 . . . 108

8. Endpapers designed by Horace Brodzky, 1919 . . . 109

9. Endpapers designed by Rockwell Kent, 1929 . . . 110

10. Advertisement, *New Yorker,* 5 October 1998 . . . 175

Acknowledgments

There are many people I wish to thank for their help on this project. David Schoonover, Shirley Wajda, Kathleen Diffley, and Ken Cmiel all provided early critical readings and supportive good humor. I am especially grateful to John Raeburn, whose comments and suggestions guided this project from its inception.

The book is stronger for the insights of Gordon Neavill of Wayne State University and Fred Antzcak, whose workshop in the Project on the Rhetoric of Inquiry at the University of Iowa helped me refine ideas while giving me confidence to move forward. Sidney Gissman of the University of Iowa Libraries shared her collection of the Little Leather Library with me.

The Bibliographical Society of America, the University of Iowa Seashore Fellowship Committee, and the University of Iowa American Studies Program all contributed financial support. At the University of Chicago, thanks are due to Alice Schreyer for giving me the time I needed for revisions.

Jean Ashton of the Rare Book and Manuscript Library at Columbia University granted permission to quote from the Random House Archives and the Bennett A. Cerf Papers. Random House also gave permission to quote from their archives. Ron Greeley granted permission to quote materials from the Oral History Collection at Columbia University, and Phyllis Wagner Cerf provided access to her late husband's oral history. The University of Chicago Library allowed me to reproduce materials from its collections, expertly photographed by Ted Lacey. John Montag of Nebraska Wesleyan University kindly permitted me to reproduce an image from the Cochrane-Woods Library.

I thank my parents, Leon and Mary Ann Satterfield, on whose bookshelves I first discovered the Modern Library when I was a teenager and decided that *Walden* must be a good book because it looked just like *Catcher in the Rye*. Finally, I thank my wife, Jen, who makes everything worthwhile.

J. S.

"The World's Best Books"

Introduction

On October 13, 1930, a Gimbels department store advertisement in the *New York Times* urged customers to "take the case of the Modern Library" as proof that Gimbels would not be undersold. Gimbels had to do a little fancy work with numbers to show it offered a better bargain than Macy's. The previous Saturday Macy's had thrown down the gauntlet by charging only nine cents for a single Modern Library volume (eighty-six cents under the suggested retail price), then fifty cents for each subsequent book. Gimbels responded by offering unlimited volumes at a dime apiece, making it the better value for the customer developing a home library.

The Modern Library's precipitous price fall began when Macy's featured the inexpensive reprint series as a loss leader to lure midtown shoppers. Gimbels's response initiated a full-fledged price war that saw both stores losing over forty cents on each book sold. Crowds gathered and students formed cooperative shopping groups to combat initial limits on books sold at sale price.[1] Under the headline "Merchants Gone Mad" *Publishers' Weekly* reported a fifty-yard-long line at Macy's book counter, and both stores stamped their books to deter area booksellers from acquiring stock at a price far less than the publisher's discount.[2] After a week, Gimbels had to admit: "Due to the extraordinary demand for these books, our usually complete stocks have been depleted. As today is Columbus Day, we do not know whether we will be able to replenish our stocks immediately. However, as long as copies of the Modern Library are obtainable, Gimbels expects to sell them."[3]

A loss leader's deviation from a well-known standard price attracts attention, but unless the product is coveted by the store's target market, the marketing ploy will be ineffective. Incredible as it may seem, these two stores catering to middle-class shoppers attracted crowds to buy serious literature at a time when many cultural critics were decrying the public's unwillingness to support American publishing. Industry analysts had become resigned to the sobering prospect that serious literature appealed only to a small cultural elite.[4] Yet the Modern Library included some of the most challenging modern literature to be had in the United

States by authors such as Proust, Dostoyevsky, Henry James, and Virginia Woolf. Each Modern Library title was a notable literary endeavor that most Macy's shoppers might have passed over as beyond them had they encountered the original edition in a bookstore. Furthermore, many authors represented in the series thought their writings unsuited to the intellectual and aesthetic capabilities of an unsophisticated American public. But once established in "The Modern Library of the World's Best Books" a book promised both to stimulate and amuse; skillful marketing, careful selection, and close attention to packaging contrived to suggest it was no longer "highbrow" literature only for the intellectual elite, but quality literature sure to please a substantial audience.[5]

In the 1920s the Modern Library achieved an honorific cultural status unparalleled in reprint publishing, equivalent to that enjoyed simultaneously by America's "intellectual" magazines and experimental theater troupes. Pundits as well as a significant number of middle-class Americans lauded this series of inexpensive reprints as an invaluable cultural enterprise, one that effectively brought challenging literary works to a large readership. The Modern Library's high repute with both readers and cultural critics inspired the *Modern Quarterly* to proclaim, "It is today by far the best of all series of books of its type upon the market." The owners of the series were characteristically more commercially forthright: "The Modern Library is today the biggest selling series of its kind in the world," they blustered.[6]

Commercial success and cultural prestige had rarely gone hand in hand, especially in the publishing world.[7] Critics panned or ignored most best-sellers, and they ridiculed marketing ventures such as the Book-of-the-Month Club and Dr. Eliot's Five-Foot Shelf of Harvard Classics. But commercial success the Modern Library indubitably had: despite the deepening Depression, in 1930 it sold over a million books. What had begun in 1917 as a publishing venture designed for self-consciously "modern" bohemian intellectuals found an extensive new audience after Bennett Cerf and Donald Klopfer bought the series from Horace Liveright in 1925. They combined high production standards with modern marketing techniques and distribution methods to quadruple sales in just five years while also assiduously building the series' reputation for editorial excellence.

The Modern Library's origin as a self-consciously subversive literary purveyor to America's fledgling Greenwich Village intelligentsia established its early critical success, but Cerf and Klopfer risked the prestige of the series when they aggressively sought expanded markets. The 1920s saw a vociferous group of young critics fight to establish themselves as the nation's arbiters of taste.[8] Firmly embracing modernism, this disparate group held forth in dozens of "little magazines" and liberal periodicals such as the *New Republic, New Masses,* and the *Modern Quarterly,* and by the 1930s, the *Nation*. These young critics questioned America's capacity for achieving cultural maturity under the onslaught of twentieth-century commercialism, and most attempts to market serious literature beyond a limited audience attracted their ire. The anti-intellectualism they saw rampant in the U.S. middle class compelled them to shun the "general reader's" aesthetic sensitivity. As a result, they questioned the motives and methods of publishers who tried to reach such readers and assailed them for falsifying culture by selling it like "patent medicine."[9] "Culture," they feared, would soon become just another mass-produced commodity devoid of artistic expression; and publishers' advertising and new distribution schemes were telltale signs of the standardization to come and the subsequent destruction of literary values.

No publishing venture designed to reach new markets received more negative attention than the Book-of-the-Month Club, which mailed out its first books in 1926. Its unique distribution system and panel of "experts" who selected each month's "outstanding" book, left critics fretting about America's "literary dictatorship."[10] Janice Radway theorizes that hostility to the club's methods represented only one battle in a broader conflict over cultural hegemony between America's affluent middle class and critics alienated by modern commercialism. The Book-of-the-Month Club's "failure to maintain the fences cordoning off culture from commerce, the sacred from the profane, and the low from the high" offended both young modernists for kowtowing to a philistine sensibility and traditionalists for its dilution of their revered "Culture." The club threatened all of these critics because it created, in Radway's words, "a permeable space between regions and forces otherwise kept conceptually distinct," while it blurred the "distinction between those who were cultured and those who were not." Taste arbiters reacted to protect their own cultured status by mapping out a new infernal region, "middlebrow culture," to reestablish the barrier separating culture from commerce.[11]

Building on Joan Shelley Rubin's history of "middlebrow culture," Radway suggests that a loose consortium of critics purposefully attempted to marginalize "middlebrow culture" to preserve the authority of their own cultured status and to defend their position as the nation's taste arbiters. But "middlebrow" was not the only cultural category dismissed by modern critics: highbrows were characterized as ineffectual, pretentious snobs, and lowbrows as dullards in an ignorant herd.[12] Many young critics sought to escape the limits of taste categories by defining a new, "genuine" culture represented and practiced by thoughtful, independent individuals who embodied the nation's spirit.[13] "Good taste," or the appreciation of "genuine" culture, was unconfined by the labels of "a standardizing age": a person or cultural artifact designated as highbrow or lowbrow betokened a constricted purview antithetical to an organic, integrated cultural ideal.[14] Critics hoped to expand "culture" beyond Matthew Arnold's "the best which has been thought and said in the world" to include an anthropological concept of national spirit.[15] Arnold's view of culture continued to have its defenders, but most analysts of culture were set on revising it by moving the term away from an established canon of great artistic creation to a description of art that expressed and advanced the nation's values and beliefs.[16]

The process of repositioning culture had been under way in intellectual circles for some time. Randolph Bourne had fired the first volley in the 1910s. He criticized Americans' "strict accord with Arnold's definition" of culture, which demanded "contact with the treasures of Europe," because it represented an "alien standard of the classics" and provided "a resting-point" for Americans' "lazy taste." In contrast, Bourne dreamed of a "genuine culture," a living, organic adaptation to the environment that embraced "American ideals and qualities, our pulsating democracy, the vigor and daring of our pioneer spirit, our sense of *camaraderie,* our dynamism, the big-heartedness of our scenery, our hospitality to all the world."[17] Bourne still saw culture as artistic production, but one that reflected a national spirit and embodied a capacious worldview: it was not merely the best, as Arnold would have it, but an ideal expression of a nation's psyche.

Even the leading "great books" champion, John Erskine, wanted to reinvigorate Arnoldian culture with a living national spirit. Calling culture "an interplay of life and ideas," he berated the "false culture" subscribed to by academics, whose air of cultivation was merely a "false, echoing culture." "True culture" was integrated with everyday practical life, adapting traditions to fit the needs of the present: "The true culture would involve as much of the past, but it would circle through the moment in which we now breathe, it would be a putting forth of modern energies, it would take the color of the earth out of which it is now springing." Erskine thought Arnold "had in him too much imitative culture, too strong an affection for patterns," but true culture organically adapts to changing environments. He asserted "the Puritan in New England was cultured" as was "the Cavalier in the South," because both "converted their past into new accomplishments" in accordance with their "different ideas" and "different landscapes." Citing eating habits, modes of living, and values of personal propriety, Erskine showed how the Puritans and Cavaliers modified their pasts to form new "cultures." Culture, while it always had its roots in the great ideas of the past, became for Erskine a "working up" of the past and the present "into new values" expressing the spirit of a people.[18]

By 1930, John Dewey could unapologetically dismiss the idea that "interest in art, science and philosophy" constituted the entirety of culture; instead, this limited view was superseded by "genuine culture," denoting "the type of emotion and thought that is characteristic of a people and epoch as a whole, an organic intellectual and moral quality."[19] His devaluation of discrete artistic monuments in favor of an organic worldview was exemplified by the *New Republic* columnist Stark Young's anecdotal rejoinder to a Columbia University professor who proclaimed that Texas had no culture "except a little opera now and then." Young recalled a serendipitous traveling encounter with a matronly Texas woman whose unpretentious manner and active intellectual curiosity showed a refreshing openness to new ideas and experiences. The woman's "clear humanity" was a more authentic expression of culture than the professor's "drool" about the "opera," "classic poets," and "imported music," because it encapsulated "the wide, generous ways and new energies of this life in such a country, and the accumulation of knowledge and feeling that grows from them."[20] For Young, the Texan woman's display of the best qualities of the American spirit represented culture far better than the professor's foreign and arid canon.[21]

To most of these critics who dreamed of the nation's promise unleashed by an organic culture, the modern industrial state loomed as a menace. Standardization, commercialism, and materialism might repress the vigorous, romantic side of the American spirit to produce a race of intellectually dull, conforming automatons.[22] Edward Sapir contrasted "spurious" culture with "genuine" culture not necessarily "high" or "low," when he warned that there was no necessary correlation between the evolution of civilization and "the relative genuineness of the culture which forms its spiritual essence." He defined "genuine culture" as "inherently harmonious, balanced, self-satisfactory," and continued: "It is the expression of a richly varied and yet somehow unified and consistent attitude towards life, an attitude that sees the significance of any one element of civilization in relation to all others." Industrialism, he charged, created the "telephone girl" who spent her day harnessed to a machine. Lost in high-efficiency technical manipulations and alienated from the organic whole, she trudged through life without "creative and emotional impulses." The mechanized nature of industrial civilization led to its spiritual poverty: "Part of the time we are dray-horses; the rest of the time, if such time is vouchsafed us, we are listless consumers of goods that have received no least impress of our own personality. In other words, our spiritual selves go hungry, for the most part, pretty much all of the time."[23] Modern industrialism favored a "spurious culture" and mass-produced consumer goods sapped the "vitality of culture" observed in aboriginal civilizations where the individual, "far from a passive pawn," could creatively integrate life and ideas.

Cultural critics, like Sapir, believed commercial interests threatened to starve genuine culture and spoonfeed a faux culture to an anesthetized, ignorant mass.[24] Lewis Mumford worried about Americans who would only buy cultural products cheapened by "book-club ballyhoo," and critic Robert Duffus suggested culture lost its genuineness when purveyed by modern marketing techniques.[25] He contrasted "culture" set off by quotation marks with culture able to stand alone. According to Duffus, when "culture" first appeared with Dr. Eliot's Five-Foot Shelf of Harvard Classics, its publishers presented it as "fetish worship, pure and simple." People who purchased "culture" failed to understand "that it is the grinding that is important, not the grist." Preselected sets of "the best" or simplified outlines were "culture," not culture:

> I wish to advance the thesis that culture cannot be attained in fifteen minutes a day or in a minute less than every minute of one's waking time. It cannot be attained easily, it cannot be attained altogether joyously. It has its austere and terrible moments. It demands that we confront unflinchingly a number of bitter facts about the relation between

ourselves and the universe. It is an adventure which requires courage and serenity at times when we feel more like whimpering in the dark. It is joining forces with Ahuramazda in the eternal struggle to bring light, meaning, and loveliness to the sunless chaos.

Culture had to be discovered individually—not in a prescriptive product—by cultivating an intimate relationship between life and the infinite in art. Like Arnold, Duffus thought culture radiated "sweetness and light" but, contradicting another Arnoldian notion, he said culture was found "nearly always where one is not looking for it": it could be experienced "halfway up a cliff or halfway down a mine or quarter way through Plato's 'Republic.'"[26]

Duffus was a keen observer of the country's book trade. In 1929, he published an extended critique of the industry, *Books: Their Place in a Democracy,* which discussed the impact of book production and distribution on America's cultural health. For Duffus, reading books developed intellectual habits that could nurture a strong democratic populace capable of self-rule. Americans were under constant siege by materialism, but books offered a strong defense. The act of reading "serious" literature developed the individual's critical capabilities and unleashed the best quality of the American spirit: a wide embrace of new ideas that could propel the nation to new heights of artistic and social excellence. His vision was shared by James Truslow Adams who first coined the phrase "the American dream" in 1931 to describe the pinnacle of American cultural achievement. When the nation looked beyond its materialism toward its spiritual values, it dreamed not of "motor cars and high wages merely," but of a "land in which life should be better and richer and fuller for every man, with opportunity for each according to his ability or achievement." Adams believed the egalitarian ideal was subverted for the most part by materialism and a misguided adoration of Ford cars and other products of mass production. "In the struggle to 'make a living'" Americans "forgot how to *live.*" All was not bleak, however. Adams found "a perfect working out in a concrete example of the American dream" one day when looking down upon the reading room of the Library of Congress: "One sees the seats filled with silent readers, old and young, rich and poor, black and white, the executive and the laborer, the general and the private, the noted scholar and the schoolboy, all reading at their own library provided by their own democracy." Seated at their desks, Adams saw a handful of Americans cultivating intellectual and spiritual growth devoted "to the good of the whole."[27] In the repressed American spirit lay the seeds for the American dream—an egalitarian republic of letters capable of intelligent self-rule—books could hasten their germination and overcome the stunting effects of selfish materialism.

Significantly, while Adams bemoaned the threat of mass production and Duffus criticized publishing ventures such as the Harvard Classics as ersatz "culture," in *Books* the latter saw the Modern Library as representing concrete proof "that the public outside the traditional bookstore system is not unanimously Philistine or mentally sub-normal."[28] Unlike other publishing ventures that targeted a broad, middle-class audience and had a negative "standardizing" effect for Duffus, the Modern Library was clearly a first-rate example of culture—and one that could evoke the best qualities of the American character to facilitate Adams's American dream. Marketed as the "World's Best Books," displaying pragmatic ingenuity in design, parading a cosmopolitan outlook, and devoting itself to personal choice and democratic pricing, the Modern Library resonated with the dreams of American culture as formulated in the inter-war period. It successfully presented itself as culture by representing the national spirit's most positive characteristics.

Ironically, however, as a product employing modern marketing techniques and name-brand advertising, made commercially attractive through standardized packaging, and affordably priced through mass production, the Modern Library also seems to embody many of the evils of industrialized civilization identified by critics such as Sapir and Adams. Yet the Modern Library's cultural success is legendary. Malcolm Cowley thought the Modern Library's founding was one of the more significant literary events of the World War I era, and the intellectual historian Henry May claimed that the small volumes "started the personal libraries of a generation's poor intellectuals" and helped generate the intellectual revolt of the 1920s.[29] The series, avidly read in their youth by such intellectuals as Susan Sontag, Annie Dillard, and Saul Bellow, as well as by Hemingway, Faulkner, and Dos Passos, was, as Charles Scribner Jr. put it, "sure to appeal to anyone with a spark of intellectual curiosity and love of literature."[30] More recently, the *New York Times Book Review* placed the Modern Library's inauguration on its timeline of epochal literary events, flanked by T. S. Eliot and the first Pulitzer Prize.[31]

Introduction 9

Bennett Cerf and Donald Klopfer were adept players in the publishing world. They treated literature as other manufactures treated their products: aggressively marketing it to produce substantial profits. As ambitious modern businessmen who were as concerned with material success as cultural prestige, they successfully tacked between a commercial stance and a more refined posture as bookmen concerned with developing American culture. This tacking, or playing both sides of Radway's fence "cordoning off culture and commerce," allowed them to hide their raw commercialism from ballyhoo-wary critics yet still present their series with enough commercial zeal to capture significant markets.[32] Exploiting "culture" flattered their own notions of their role in one of the nation's most revered professions, but it also made good business sense when dealing with a product seen by many intellectuals as the surest path toward the creation of a "genuine culture."

From 1925, when Cerf and Klopfer took control of the series and began to apply new marketing strategies, to the start of World War II, the Modern Library sustained a period of healthy growth as it rapidly expanded into new markets. Its distribution and sales methods in the early 1930s foreshadowed the era of the mass-market paperback, and it became the cornerstone of Random House, perhaps the most financially successful publishing firm of the twentieth century. This period was crucial in the development of the modern concept of culture and it saw a dramatic reformulation of the country's book trade as publishers came to see their books as commodities demanding modern sales methods. But unlike other similarly conceived publishing ventures, the Modern Library became a revered cultural entity even as it treated its wares as mass-produced merchandise. What kept the Modern Library from opprobrium? Why was its blend of culture and commerce not only inoffensive but hailed as a cultural triumph? Accepting the Gimbels challenge to "take the case of the Modern Library," a critical history of the series must explore the book trade's interactions with intellectual and popular taste as it examines the effects of advertising, distribution, manufacturing, and selection of titles on the perceived cultural reputation of books.

CHAPTER ONE

Establishing the World's Best Books

The story of the Modern Library's unlikely success as "genuine culture" begins with Boni & Liveright's entrance into the social matrix of the New York publishing world. The publishing industry had long been dominated by conservative, family-run publishing houses. But in the first decades of the twentieth century, three Jewish publishing firms, Ben W. Huebsch, Alfred Knopf, and Boni & Liveright, rose up to challenge traditional publishing methods, to welcome modernist authors spurned by other houses, and, in time, to change the nature of American book production. The Modern Library emerged in 1917 from one of these upstarts ostracized by mainstream "Christian" publishers. Its parent firm, Boni & Liveright, married a romantic vision of art and literature with a modern commercial sensibility to understand books as intellectual creations *and* as commodities.

In its first eight years the Modern Library became a modest financial success, but more important, it earned critics' respect by conforming to the burgeoning definition of "genuine culture." Under Boni & Liveright's management, the series established a network of allies in the intellectual world and became an important cultural entity. It was not exciting enough to hold Boni & Liveright's original attention, though, and by the midtwenties it suffered from neglect. In 1925, Horace Liveright sold the series to two aspiring businessmen, Donald Klopfer and Bennett Cerf, who were determined to realize its financial potential and cultivate its cultural prestige.

JEWISH PUBLISHING: AMERICAN BOOK PRODUCTION, 1917

At the turn of the century, fiscally and socially conservative, Protestant, family-run firms dominated the publishing industry. As obstinate about editorial decisions as about book distribution and promotion, they partitioned the book-buying public into two groups: serious gentlemen scholars who pursued disinterested knowledge, and a larger, feminized public attracted to light novels. Wary of offending either group, publishers' lists heavily featured moralistic tales for popular consumption and genteel essays for easy-chair reading. The few readers aware of the changes taking place in European writing were largely ignored. Some unconventional American authors such as Upton Sinclair, Jack London, and Theodore Dreiser managed to find their way into print, but, as Horace Liveright's biographer Walker Gilmer points out, "Literary revolt in substance or style, like outspokenness in sex and politics, met inflexible timidity in established firms."[1] Publishers known for their religious affiliations such as Lippincott and Harper's were not likely to produce books blatantly antireligious or morally questionable. Financial security lay in safe literary and philosophical writings that would neither upset conventional pieties nor catch the censor's eye.

The 1890s were a period of rationalization in the publishing industry. In 1891 the first major international copyright law cut off the supply of unprotected English novels and shut down many small reprint publishers. That law eliminated competing editions of new titles and consolidated holdings of literary rights. A deep economic depression in 1893 made capital scarce, and larger firms, with their well-developed backlists and formidable financial assets, tightened their grip on the industry. Even profitable dime novels published by nontraditional firms had to scale back production when Congress raised postal rates in 1901. Although the old family-run firms, several of which had lobbied for the international copyright laws and the postal rate changes, emerged as the undisputed leaders of the industry, their publishing practices still slighted substantial segments of the reading public. Adventurous readers frustrated by the dearth of relevant texts often had to turn to expensive European editions for new, "modern" ideas.[2]

The family-as-corporation atmosphere of the Protestant publishing houses combined with an unembarrassed anti-Semitism to bar Jewish participation in American publishing. Excluded from the major houses and unable to learn the trade from the inside, most Jews interested in publishing moved to affiliated fields such as printing or newspaper publishing. Not until 1912 did a major publishing company employ a Jew, when Doubleday, Page and Company hired Alfred Knopf as a clerk.[3]

The century's first Jewish publisher, Ben W. Huebsch, considered himself a printer who dabbled in books. "Publishing was sort of an afterthought in a way," he later said, "because I had never thought of doing it before.... I had no plans. I had no training as a publisher at all—didn't know the game at all."[4] In 1905, Huebsch began to issue European titles rejected or ignored by other publishers because of their intellectual and literary experimentation. Starting with an obscure German philosophical work by Otto Pfleiderer, he followed during the first decades of the century with books by Maxim Gorki, James Oppenheim, James Joyce, and D. H. Lawrence. He published early works by Sherwood Anderson and Van Wyck Brooks and issued a volume explicating Karl Marx's writings.[5] Huebsch's "after thought" paved the way for others: in 1915 Alfred Knopf and his future wife Blanche Wolf opened shop, followed in 1917 by Boni & Liveright.

The new Jewish firms made modern European literature their mainstay. The time was ripe for these publishers: their books found an immediate though modest national audience among Americans frustrated by Victorian mores. They appealed especially to a group of young, vocal radicals coalescing in Greenwich Village. Deeply attracted to modernism and bent on tearing down what they perceived as a hopelessly old-fashioned, stuffy, and bankrupt genteel culture, the Greenwich Village radicals looked to literature as a weapon to forge a new egalitarian society based on an integration of art and life. The Jewish publishers made available to these New York bohemians—and their confederates in the hinterlands—Europe's delightfully shocking new literature by authors such as Émile Zola, D. H. Lawrence, and Anatole France, social commentary and philosophy from Nietzsche and Schopenhauer, and Freud's psychoanalytical theory.[6]

Conservative in nature, most older houses worked to marginalize the new Jewish ones. They denied them entry into the Publishers Lunch Club and used anti-Semitism to lure away their authors.[7] Liveright, said Cerf, "was deeply resented by the established publishers. They hated him; they even hated Alfred Knopf and B. W. Huebsch, who had started at about the same time. There had never been a Jew before in American publishing, which was a closed corporation to the rising tide of young people described in *Our Crowd*. Suddenly there had burst forth on the scene some bright young Jews who were upsetting all the old tenets of the publishing business—and the flashiest of all was certainly Liveright."[8]

Even some of their own authors resented being published by Jewish firms. T. S. Eliot, published first by Huebsch and then by Liveright, longed to establish himself with "a decent Christian publisher in New York," because, as he put it, "I am sick of doing business with Jew publishers who will not carry out their part of a contract unless they are forced to."⁹ Although Huebsch claimed he only once faced blatant anti-Semitism (he withdrew his name from consideration at the Century Club when he learned he would be blackballed) and Knopf remained publicly mute on the subject, Liveright battled anti-Semitism throughout his publishing career.[10]

Ironically, because young intellectuals saw established publishers as "pillars of a whole moral and cultural order" they were trying to overthrow, the purposeful marginalization made the young Jewish publishers appear, in the intellectual historian Henry May's words, "part of the world of Rebellion, committed to it, necessarily interested in all parts of it."[11] In addition, Freud's centrality and the celebrated Dreyfus affair that inspired Proust and led to Zola's brief exile from France created a powerful link between European modernism and the Jewish community. Many champions of modernism respected Liveright, Huebsch, and Knopf for their commitment to modern literature, but also because their Jewish heritage created a cultural alienation that made them appear especially modern to idealistic young radicals.

ALBERT BONI IN GREENWICH VILLAGE

The Modern Library's beginnings are intimately tied to the coming together of bohemianism and cultural–political radicalism in Greenwich Village. The narrow, crooked streets of the Village offered a small community haven in the heart of Manhattan. It had an established tradition as a site of intellectual ferment—Thomas Paine, Edgar Allan Poe, Washington Irving, and Herman Melville had all lived there, and Mark Twain and Willa Cather made it their home—but it was primarily a colony of Italian immigrants and Jewish shopkeepers. In the early 1910s the low rents in the Village attracted "long-haired men and short-haired women" eager to experience a bohemian lifestyle.[12] Although the Village housed many middle-class and wealthy dilettantes, it also sheltered a group of art-minded social and political radicals. Among them were seasoned radicals Emma Goldman and Lincoln Steffens, but also a younger crowd of intellectuals such as Floyd Dell, Susan Glaspell, Max Eastman, John Reed, and Randolph Bourne.

These "Young Intellectuals," as they were later labeled, were daring social experimenters, and the Village became the nation's hotbed for revolutionary politics.[13] The radicals embraced Freud's theories (Susan Glaspell remarked that "you could not go out to buy a bun" south of 14th Street "without hearing of someone's complex")[14] and explored feminist ideas and open sexual partnerships. Politically, they favored socialism. They perceived America as philistine and materialistic, and many dreamed of a socialist revolution that would reverse modern capitalism's alienating effects and integrate art and life. Three key institutional voices of artistic and political radicalism in America emerged from the Village: the *Masses,* the *New Republic,* and the *Seven Arts.* To these was added the *Dial,* which shed its conservative flavor and relocated from Chicago to Greenwich Village in 1916.

In 1911, Albert and Charles Boni purposefully cast themselves into the heart of Greenwich Village when they invested Albert's Harvard Law School tuition in the Washington Square Book Shop on MacDougal Street. To the Bonis' deep satisfaction, their bookstore quickly became a hub of Village activities. Its location next to Polly Holladay's restaurant and the Liberal Club helped. The club, "A Meeting Place for Those Interested in New Ideas," consisted of a loose consortium of Village radicals including John Reed, Emma Goldman, Max Eastman, Edna St. Vincent Millay, Lincoln Steffens, Theodore Dreiser, Sinclair Lewis, Louise Bryant, Mabel Dodge, Floyd Dell, and Alfred Kreymborg. The Bonis' shop became the club's unofficial reading room, and a door was cut into their common wall to facilitate that function.[15]

The bookstore was founded on "the theory that books should not be sold in the same manner as shoes or other commodities, but should be displayed under the most inviting conditions and disposed of by literate clerks who should be lovers of literature rather than salesmen," an attitude that promoted a welcoming intellectual enclave but did little to stimulate sales. According to Lawrence Langner (one of the bookstore's financial backers), even though the shop was always crowded with readers enjoying its comfortable couches, chairs, and warm fire, it progressively lost money: few readers ever actually purchased the books. Compounding the problem, chief among the "literate clerks" was Cuthbert Wright, a regular contributor to the *New Republic,* who could only with difficulty be stirred from his own studious labors to advise customers or tend to a sale.¹⁶

Albert Boni further ensconced himself in the Greenwich Village community when in 1913 he helped found the Washington Square Players, an experimental theater group that later evolved into the Theatre Guild. The Players' manifesto rejected the then-current American theater devoted to safe entertainment for safe profits; instead, it emphasized the sanctity of art over commerce: "The Washington Square Players believe that a higher standard can be reached only as the outcome of experiment and initiative.... We believe that hard work and perseverance, coupled with ability and the absence of purely commercial considerations, may result in the birth and healthy growth of an artistic theatre in this country." The stress on "experiment" illustrated the Villagers' desire to shed the conventions of the past to create and nurture a new art. Their idealism was evident as well: "artistic merit" was the only criterion for choosing to stage a script, and because the troupe was funded by subscription, art and ideas could trump profit. To one Villager participant, the group's statement "indicated our serious purpose in bringing intelligence, an interest in social matters, and a serious critique of life into the theatre."¹⁷

The Washington Square Players' ambition to invest the theater with social criticism drew on the new conception of culture being worked out among intellectuals in Greenwich Village. In 1915, Huebsch published Van Wyck Brooks's *America's Coming-of-Age,* a key document of the emerging sensibility. Its first essay outlined Brooks's view of the degraded state of American culture and mapped out a vision of what that culture might potentially become. The national culture, for Brooks, was paralyzed by the vicious dichotomy of "highbrow" and "lowbrow" without a "middle ground." For Brooks, both terms had pejorative connotations: the highbrow, quietly contemplating "a quite unclouded, quite unhypocritical assumption of transcendent theory," failed to understand everyday reality, while the lowbrow could not see beyond "catchpenny realities." He outlined a history of American thought that barred communication between highbrows and lowbrows, then asked, "But where is all that is real, where is personality and all its works, if it is not essentially somewhere, somehow, in some not very vague way, between?"¹⁸

Four years later Brooks's friend and fellow *Seven Arts* associate, Randolph Bourne, gave greater specificity to Brooks's ideas in his autobiographical intellectual history of "Miro," a young man from the country seeking his way into the urbane world of culture. In reading the "literary odds-and-ends" he collected, Miro confronted a terrible cultural split. Steered by his teachers toward the "canonized saints of culture," he found:

> There was nothing between them and that popular literature of the day that all good men bemoaned. Classic or popular, "highbrow" or "lowbrow," this was the choice, and Miro unquestioningly took the orthodox heaven. In 1912 the most popular of Miro's English professors had never heard of Galsworthy, and another was creating a flurry of scandal in the department by recommending Chesterton to his classes. It would scarcely have been in college that Miro would have learned of an escape from the closed dichotomy of culture.

Miro confronted the same pernicious division between high and low in American culture that Brooks had described. But rather than search for a genial middle ground, Miro, "the literary radical," craved a more revolutionary alternative. A lecture delivered by William Lyon Phelps introduced him to literary modernism, and "a new world opened to Miro that was neither 'classic' nor 'popular.'" From his encounter with a new culture (represented by Tolstoy, Hardy, Turgenev, and George Meredith) transcending the high–low axis, Miro developed the theory that art and literature must have social purpose. He dreamed of a community of like-minded individuals: "They would be men who had not been content to live on their cultural inheritance, but had gone out into the modern world and amassed a fresh fortune of their own. They would be men who were not squeamish, who did not feel the delicate differences between 'animal' and 'human' conduct, who were enthusiastic about Mark Twain and Gorki as well as Romain Rolland, and at the same time were thrilled by Copeau's theatre." He found such a community in Greenwich Village that believed in "culture as a living effort." Culture gained significance because it shaped experience and was in turn renewed through daily activities. Only after Miro fell in with the "cultural 'Modernists'" could he sort through the American tradition to find ideas "not tainted with sweetness and light and burdened with the terrible patronage of bourgeois society" to invent what Van Wyck Brooks had called "a usable past."[19] Bourne searched for and found an escape from the high–low axis in a new form of instrumental culture released from the tyranny of outdated, Arnoldian concepts and capable of critiquing modern life.

In his essay Bourne acknowledged the powerful impact of a new group of publishers. The idyllic Greenwich Village colony of intellectuals Bourne discovered was created in part "through the enterprise of publishers" such as Knopf and Huebsch, both of whom had established offices in the Village.[20] It consisted of open-minded individuals, and its publishers offered access to new ideas through their active importation of European modernism and promotion of new American literary talent. More than a geographical region, the Village was a site where various institutions came together in support of emergent American modernism. The "little" magazines, Polly's restaurant, the Liberal Club, the Washington Square Players, and the Washington Square Book Shop all shared membership–patrons while the new publishers were feeding the group with texts for discussion and performance.

Following the mood of the Village, Albert and Charles Boni hoped to overcome "the philistine attitude of the American public toward the arts."[21] Their struggle led them to publishing. According to Harry Scherman, another Village habitué, the Boni brothers "were bitten by the idea of being publishers of *avant garde* things."[22] To this end, and with Scherman's substantial financial and marketing support, they founded the Little Leather Library in 1915. The Whitman Candy Company immediately ordered fifteen thousand copies of the short classics and abridgments bound in limp "leatherette" covers to distribute as premiums with each Whitman Sampler.[23] Boni's initial quest to topple philistine tastes became a bit of throwaway reading to accompany a box of chocolates. Bookstores shunned the low markup and small profit margin on the books, but the Woolworth stores sold thousands of copies at twenty-five cents, and, later, as thirty-title sets at only $2.98. The Little Leather Library was hardly avant garde: Shakespeare figured prominently, as did the English Romantic poets, although the Bonis also included Shaw, Tolstoy, and Ibsen. Money problems—mostly of the Washington Square Book Shop—forced the brothers to sell the series in 1916 to Scherman and Maxwell Sackheim, who proceeded to exploit mail-order distribution methods and push sales to more than a million copies per year. The Little Leather Library collapsed in 1926 after having reached nearly all its limited audience. Still, the series inspired two of the twentieth century's most important publishing ideas: Scherman and Sackheim discovered that mail order could be used effectively to distribute books, which they subsequently did in founding the Book-of-the-

Month Club; and Albert Boni parlayed his initial idea of an inexpensive series of quality titles into the Modern Library.

BONI & LIVERIGHT

In 1915 financial exigency forced Albert Boni to sell his share of the Washington Square Book Shop. His capital was nearly exhausted, but he was still attracted to publishing. It is ironical that both the Little Leather Library and the Washington Square Book Shop achieved financial success *after* Boni's departure, perhaps because, unlike him, his successors were more interested in profit than art. Boni's ideas were good, but he lacked business acumen.

Horace Liveright had fled school when he was just fifteen with the idea of finding fame and fortune writing Broadway musicals. His first musical never made it out of rehearsal, and his career shifted to the bond market. After losing one brokerage job for his avowed socialist sympathies, he found success at another. But bond selling bored Liveright: he wanted a profession demanding creativity and one that would allow him to hobnob with the bohemian crowd his brother Otto had discovered in Greenwich Village. At thirty he quit his brokerage job and embarked unsuccessfully on a series of inauspicious manufacturing adventures.[24]

Boni and Liveright met in 1916 when they fortuitously shared an office lent them by a mutual friend. Boni showed him sample copies of the Little Leather Library, and Liveright found his calling. Together he and Boni conceived of the Modern Library — modern titles, unabridged and in a larger format than the Little Leather Library, designed to sell to a wide audience at sixty cents a copy. The series, as they conceived of it, was a perfect match for each man's desires. Liveright could adapt his marketing and selling experience to a product associated with the kind of cultural glamour he always wanted. For Boni, the partnership offered needed capital to satisfy his longing to be a publisher of "avant-garde things." In addition, both men were avowed socialists (Liveright called Boni & Liveright "socialism in action"), and the series had a socialist feel right from the start: it offered titles previously sold for up to ten dollars (though most sold for around two) for the democratic price of sixty cents.[25] According to Lawrence Langner, both Liveright and Boni approached him for advice on the feasibility of their forming a partnership.

Langner gave both identical advice, correctly predicting that neither was capable of sustaining such an enterprise. Nonetheless, the next day they made their move, with the necessary capital from Liveright's father-in-law, and founded Boni & Liveright.[26]

Publishers' Weekly duly reported the new venture: "An excellent new series of popular reprints has appeared this spring under the imprint of a new publishing house, Boni & Liveright." It inadvertently pointed to culture's "genial middle ground" that Brooks longed for: "The aim of the publishers is to build up a standard series of unquestionably worth while reprints that lie between the classics in *Everyman's Library* and the new fiction of the Grosset & Dunlap and A. L. Burt reprints."[27] The Modern Library began with twelve titles, all but one unprotected by U.S. copyright and thus requiring a minimal capital outlay: Wilde's *The Picture of Dorian Gray*, Strindberg's *Married*, H. G. Wells's *War in the Air*, Ibsen's *A Doll's House, Ghosts,* and *An Enemy of the People* in one volume, Anatole France's *The Red Lily*, de Maupassant's *Mademoiselle Fifi and Twelve Other Stories*, Nietzsche's *Thus Spake Zarathustra*, Dostoyevsky's *Poor People*, Maeterlinck's *A Miracle of St. Antony*, Schopenhauer's *Studies in Pessimism*, Kipling's *Soldiers Three*, and Stevenson's *Treasure Island*.

Although Liveright's biographer Tom Dardis believed the charismatic neophyte must have helped choose the early titles, probably most of the selections were made by Albert Boni.[28] Liveright had little experience in the book trade, and Boni's tenure as a bookseller and manager of the Little Leather Library had taught him something about the market. He shrewdly selected important titles that appealed to a modern sensibility and were still in demand, but either out of print or available only in expensive editions. Of its first titles, the Modern Library claimed that neither *Married* nor *A Miracle of St. Antony* had ever been issued in the United States (even though *Married* had been published in Chicago by J. W. Luce only four years earlier), so, while the series consisted only of reprints, for a few early titles the Modern Library edition was the first U.S. edition.[29] For other out-of-print titles, it was the only available edition. Despite Boni's past privileging of art over profit, and perhaps because of Liveright's more determined commercialism, the partners built their list with twentieth-century business sense. They eschewed direct competition with other "libraries" and chose titles to capture a specific niche in the reprint market. In short, the Modern Library catered to the tastes of Boni's former Washington Square Book Shop patrons.[30]

Most of their authors exuded a scandalous air that was attractive to these social experimenters. Wilde was still considered a deviant by most Americans aware of the flamboyant aesthete; Strindberg and Ibsen scorned middle-class values with their dark realism; France and de Maupassant wrote openly of sexual matters; Nietzsche's and Schopenhauer's ideas were antipathetic to the democratic ideals professed by many Americans, a fact especially apparent with the U.S. entrance into World War I; Maeterlinck (a favorite of the Washington Square Players) and Dostoyevsky emphasized society's irrational absurdity; even the popular Wells trumpeted socialist ideas. Only Kipling and Stevenson obviously appealed to a "wide audience."

Initial orders surpassed the partners' expectations and they immediately added six more titles, all equally "modern." Four of them, Samuel Butler's *The Way of All Flesh,* George Meredith's *Diana of the Crossways,* Hardy's *The Mayor of Casterbridge,* and George Moore's *Confessions of a Young Man,* delved into the contradictions in Victorian sexual mores; Shaw's *The Unsocial Socialist* was politically iconoclastic; and *The Best Russian Short Stories,* edited by Boni's uncle Thomas Seltzer, satisfied a growing curiosity about Russian culture as the Revolution unfolded. As with the Little Leather Library a few years earlier, demand outstripped production, and Boni & Liveright ran an advertisement in *Publishers' Weekly* to apologize to booksellers for delivery delays but also to inform them of the tremendous demand the series inspired.[31]

In the flush of their early success Boni & Liveright placed advertisements in a wide array of magazines that catered to book readers. They approached their core market through the pages of the *New Republic, Dial,* and the *Bellman.* They sought converts in those bastions of genteel culture, the *Atlantic Monthly* and the *Nation* (still under the conservative editorial control of Oswald Garrison Villard); and they used more popular bookish magazines such as *Review of Reviews,* the *Independent,* the *Outlook,* and even the nationalistic, prowar *Life* to reach "the general reader."[32] Their scope of advertising was noticeably ambitious. The series was built on the tastes of the Greenwich Village intellectuals, but the partners believed a national audience of interested readers awaited the books.

Boni & Liveright's strategy was to spread the word about the Modern Library and foster brand-name recognition, while also locating the series firmly within Brooks's and Bourne's vision of a new, modern culture. A discursive *New Republic* advertisement titled "Trench Affinities" (Figure 1)

TRENCH AFFINITIES

WAR makes strange bed fellows, but it would keep a Grand Rapids furniture factory working overtime to make beds for the unmatched palships this war has developed.

Booky was a mild-voiced, diminutive little runt—no one could ever understand how he got by with his physique—with a thoughtful face, going fifty-fifty on everything with his pal, Hank, a strapping whale of a man with a baseball vocabulary that would have made George Ade turn green with envy.

Certainly the mud of the trenches has grown some queer affinities but to all outward appearances the iron cross for queerness goes to Booky and Hank. So far as an outsider could discover, in every particular they were as far apart as the poles. Booky's constant lament was the absence of a Carnegie Library back of the trenches; he loved books and he actually suffered for the the want of them. Except as missiles, Hank had no use for them—sporting papers, yes. They had the real stuff in them and he understood and appreciated every word he read in them. He did his best to get Booky enthusiastic over the World Series' articles and the lives of famous pugilists; but to put it his way, "there was nothing doing."

Things had been going on this way for some time when one day there arrived in the trenches a number of magazines that the home folks had sent to the boys after they finished reading them. In an idle moment, Hank took up one which happened to be a copy of the NEW REPUBLIC, and believing it was a story about the mix-up in Russia, Hank started in to give it the once-over. Before he quite realized what he had tackled, his eye rested on an advertisement of "The Modern Library of the World's Best Books," hand-bound in limp croftleather at 60c a volume.

Little did Hank dream how Booky's mouth would water at the titles this library offered. The fact that it included some of the best modern books by English, Irish, French, Russian, German and American authors, their stories, their plays, and their poems, meant nothing to Hank's baseball soul. The introductions by Lafcadio Hearn, Padraic Colum, H. L. Mencken, Alexander Harvey, Joyce Kilmer were of no importance whatsoever to him, but 60c a volume bound in limp croftleather, even to his untutored soul meant a bargain. So he took the ad to Booky and in a truly characteristic way said, "Say, Booky, here is something that might interest you a bit—I do not know anything about the innards, but the description of the outside at 60c per, would send a bargain-hunting woman out in the rain with her new Easter bonnet."

Booky took the ad and in an instant his eyes began to sparkle with interest. Here was a list of his favorite authors in a convenient-to-get, and a convenient-to-read edition. Life began to mean something to him, and Hank observing his pal's mood also began to enthuse. "Some ad, ain't it?" he said to Booky. "Kind of makes you forget you are back-stopping for the Busy Berthas. I suppose you'll order the whole bunch sent in one shipment, and cross your fingers on the submarines until they arrive."

"Hank, my boy," said Booky, "for once in your young literary life you are right. They've got here the books I've always wanted to read. There's Nietzsche's 'Thus Spake Zarathustra,' the philosophy that put the pep into 'Schrecklichkeit.' Every time a Boche throws a hand grenade over the trenches his inspiration can be traced to that book. Of course you don't know that one of the greatest living English authors has called Samuel Butler's "The Way of All Flesh" the greatest novel of the 20th Century. But there's a book here that will get even you. H. G. Wells' "War in the Air" is the most thrilling imaginative story of war in modern times, and is full of prophetic suggestions of things that are actually happening on the battlefield today. Then there's a collection of the best Russian short stories all in one volume. Don't the events now taking place in Russia make you feel that you ought to know more about this wonderful people? This list has surely got me. If there was any question in my mind this quotation from Clifford Smyth, literary editor of the New York *Times*, would settle all doubts. He says, ' If real merit in typography, binding, convenience, and best of all, subject matter, counts for anything these books are certainly deserving of a fine measure of success. They fill a need that is not quite covered, so far as I have observed, by any other publication in the field just now.' Here goes my order for the whole shebang and if the submarines get in the way, I'll show some Germans what real *Schrecklichkeit* means."

This is the list that Booky ordered:

PREVIOUSLY PUBLISHED

Oscar Wilde..........................Dorian Gray
Strindberg................................Married
Kipling........................Soldiers Three
Stevenson....................Treasure Island
H. G. Wells..................The War in the Air
Henrik Ibsen........Plays: *A Doll's House, Ghosts, An Enemy of the People*
Anatole France.....................The Red Lily
De Maupassant................Mademoiselle Fifi
Nietzsche...............Thus Spake Zarathustra
Dostoyevsky......................Poor People
Maeterlinck..........A Miracle of St. Antony
Schopenhauer.............Studies in Pessimism
Samuel Butler..........The Way of All Flesh
George Meredith.......Diana of the Crossways
G. B. Shaw..................An Unsocial Socialist
Geo. Moore........Confessions of a Young Man
Thomas Hardy........The Mayor of Casterbridge
Thos. Seltzer............Best Russian Short Stories

JUST PUBLISHED

Oscar Wilde................................Poems
Nietzsche...............Beyond Good and Evil
Turgenev.........................Fathers and Sons
Anatole France......The Crime of Sylvestre Bonnard
Swinburne ....Poems
Wm. Dean Howells........A Hazard of New Fortunes
W. S. Gilbert.........The Mikado and Other Plays
H. G. Wells..........................Ann Veronica
Gustave Flaubert..................Madame Bovary
James Stephens.......................Mary, Mary
Anton Chekhov............Rothschild's Fiddle, etc.
Arthur Schnitzler..........Anatol and Other Plays
Sudermann............................Dame Care
Lord Dunsany..................A Dreamer's Tales
G. K. Chesterton......The Man Who Was Thursday
Henrik Ibsen..Plays: *Hedda Gabler, Pillars of Society, The Master Builder*
Haeckel, Thompson, Weismann, etc.,
Evolution in Modern Thought

Hand bound limp croftleather, 60c per vol., at all stores, 6c extra by mail
Published by BONI & LIVERIGHT, 107 West 40th St., New York.

FIGURE 1. The Modern Library seals a highbrow–lowbrow trench affinity. From *New Republic,* 17 November 1917. Cochrane-Woods Library, Nebraska Wesleyan University.

featured two unlikely friends fighting the war in France: Hank, "a strapping whale of a man with a baseball vocabulary that would have made George Ade turn green with envy," and Booky, "a mild-voiced, diminutive little runt—no one could ever understand how he got by with his physique—with a thoughtful face." Hank read mostly the sports pages, while Booky "loved books and he actually suffered for the want of them." Perplexed by the "mix-up in Russia," Hank picked up a copy of the *New Republic* and ran across a notice for the Modern Library. Smitten by the bargain the books represented at sixty cents apiece, he enthused to Booky, "I do not know anything about the innards, but the description of the outside at 60c per, would send a bargain-hunting woman out in the rain with her new Easter bonnet." Booky's equally enthusiastic rejoinder had a different basis: "They've got here the books I've always wanted to read." His preferences ran to Nietzsche and Samuel Butler, but he assured Hank, "There's a book here that will get even you," Wells's *War in the Air* is "the most thrilling imaginative story of war in modern times." Booky decided to order the whole series to share with Hank.[33] The Modern Library attracted the practical man by its economy, while its stimulating "innards" drew the bookish man of ideas. Thus, the series offered a form of culture that combined highbrow ideals with lowbrow commercial sense. With its appeals to the intellect (Booky) and the pocketbook (Hank), the Modern Library purveyed a common culture to seal a symbolic trench affinity. The Modern Library presented itself as a truly democratic manifestation of Brooks's ideal American character, for it offered a form of culture financially available and intellectually palatable to highbrows and lowbrows.

The press greeted the Modern Library with guarded admiration. Early assessments reflected the attitudes of Booky and Hank: some reviewers were attracted by the titles, others by the price. The cautious *Independent* warned that the series ran "now and again into needlessly unhealthful regions," but applauded it for giving "in pleasant and cheap form books still of moment, that are not readily come at save in the regular editions."[34] *Life*'s J. B. Kerfoot assured readers he usually paid "more attention to whether you are getting your mind's worth than your money's worth," but coined a gastronomic metaphor to celebrate the marriage of intellectual stimulation and value. The Modern Library, he said, provides "a full mental meal for sixty cents."[35] Antagonistic to modernism, the *Nation* also resorted to a gastronomic trope. "The initial score of volumes rather slights the Victorians and all their predecessors in favor of the highly condimented meat that younger stomachs are supposed to affect," but nevertheless, it found the series "a commendable achievement" for the economy it offered.[36] An evenhanded reviewer in the *New York Times* noted that the Modern Library fills "a need that is not quite covered, so far as I have observed, by any other publication in the field just now."[37] The *New York Evening Mail* "heartily supported" the series and urged readers to "gallop to the nearest book store and inspect the volumes"; the *Springfield Republican* admired the books' format; and the *New York Evening Post* called them "delightful volumes."[38] The *Bellman,* a socialist Minneapolis magazine, applauded the titles' "notable catholicity and excellence of taste."[39] The reviewers' occasionally mixed signals about the Modern Library reflected an ambivalence toward modernist cultural enterprises. The fact that the books could be had for so little accorded with a long-held democratic notion that all citizens should have equal access to culture, but the scandalous nature of some of the titles was particularly worrisome to magazines representing the guardians of traditional culture. Access to culture was generally applauded as a fundamental good, but the kind of culture being offered tempered some critics' enthusiasm.

The attention the Modern Library garnered from the press and the public marked a significant change in how Americans perceived reprints. Shortly after the Civil War, new technologies in papermaking, printing, and typesetting combined with increased literacy to create a tremendous explosion of cheap "libraries." Book-grade paper prices fell after the Civil War, from sixteen cents per pound in 1871 to only six and a half cents in 1889.[40] Low postal rates made distribution cheap, and the absence of an international copyright law offered a wealth of royalty-free material. But the majority of "cheap books," as they came to be called, represented some of the worst examples of bookmaking in the history of printing. Most were ungainly quartos printed on low-grade, woodpulp paper in densely packed columns of type (much like a newspaper) with only flimsy paper covers. Priced between ten and fifty cents, competing editions of the same titles flooded the market and drove down production quality as profit margins were squeezed thin. Even before the 1891 copyright law and 1901 postal rate hike, cheap reprints were in serious economic jeopardy, undone by overproduction (October 1877 alone saw the printing of over 2.5 million books) and price slashing that eliminated any advantages obtained through an economy of scale.[41] Most of the "libraries" not bankrupted by the copyright bill of 1891 were finished off by Congress ten years later.

Harper's entered the field with its own Franklin Square Library in 1878, but most established publishers reacted with chagrin to the economic chaos the cheap books of the 1870s and 1880s had caused, and the general book trade worked to dissociate legitimate books from cheap reprints by establishing them as aesthetically inferior products. Labeling them "broadsheets," many established booksellers, offended more by low markups than their lack of craftsmanship, refused to carry the cheap books. Shoddy production standards and the disconcerting paper covers made the cheap books different in feel and appearance from traditional books. Their promiscuity increased their poor reputation. Reprint publisher George Munro churned out 449 titles in one year in his various "libraries" with almost no regard for editorial integrity.[42] Even worse, as demand dropped and markets dried up in the late 1880s, reprint publishers dumped millions of these books on the market. Anticipating the Little Leather Library's initial treatment as a Whitman Sampler candy premium, publishers gave away cheap books with boxes of soap and even offered them at discount with bottles of patent medicines.[43] Established publishers recoiled from their industry's close association with soap and patent medicine. Traditional publishers considered themselves involved in gentlemanly pursuits rather than base marketing ploys, and many in the trade, as well as many book buyers, thought classic reprints published side by side with sensational fiction cheapened the industry and degraded the prestige so long associated with books and reading. According to John Tebbel, "It was claimed that whatever benefits the mass public might gain from the introduction of the classics into its consciousness at prices it could afford was more than offset by what the conservatives and moralists generally saw as a lowering of 'tone,' a blow to good taste and high literary standards inherent in the flood of low-quality novels."[44] As late as 1907, *Publishers' Weekly* still worried that, "while these books undoubtedly represent a large value to the occasional bookbuyer for his fifty cents they do not attract the still goodly number of booklovers who demand, and are willing to pay for, a well-made and substantial book, fearing that a cheap book makes a cheap man."[45]

Almost all these series featured "library" in their titles. Richard D. Altick pointed out that publishers used the word "library" to create an aristocratic aura and attract repeat buyers.[46] The public library was an anomaly in the nineteenth century, and the private library was still seen as the rightful property of the wealthy, so such a collection of books was firmly associated with the leisured classes. Cheap reprints tried to open new markets, and their publishers hoped that liberal use of the gentlemanly term "library" would lend status to their middle- and working-class audiences. "Library" connoted purposeful collecting and connoisseurship, and publishers hoped it would elevate their wares above the feminized world of fiction casually arranged in the parlor. The library was a man's retreat, inherently more serious than the parlor, but ironically, the cheap libraries were marketed as premiums with consumer goods purchased by women. "Library" intimated "class," but it also brought brand-name marketing to the publishing business and connoted a certain unity publishers hoped to capitalize on. They reasoned, perhaps correctly, that a consumer who sampled one or two books from a series might seek to complete "the library."

By 1900, booksellers and publishers strongly associated cheap books with piracy, poor workmanship, and detrimental competition.[47] Booksellers in the larger cities (where most books were sold) believed reprints unsettled the market, luring buyers away from more profitable trade books and confusing them about the legitimate price of books. Worse, several publishers experimented with finding new markets by issuing reprints shortly after the initial publication, which ended up killing the original editions' sales and leaving booksellers and publishers with overstocks.[48] Still, a new market of readers had been discovered, those who were unwilling to pay full price for a trade book but would buy popular books if the prices were right—a fact not lost on Grosset & Dunlap and A. L. Burt, who started reproducing popular novels in solid, hardbound editions for thirty-five to fifty cents a copy.

When the Modern Library began in 1917, a concerted effort to rehabilitate (and rejuvenate) inexpensive books was well under way. The leaders of the reprint industry used quality production to distance their books from their inferior predecessors. J. M. Dent's set of classic reprints, Everyman's Library, distributed in the United States by Dutton and Sons beginning in 1906, received widespread critical acclaim for its elevated titles and close attention to the craft of bookmaking. One reviewer called attention to the series' canonical nature, referring to it as "the memory of the race," while another evoked scripture to assert, "A cosmic convulsion might utterly destroy all other printed works in the world, and still if a complete set of Everyman's Library floated upon the waters enough would be preserved to carry on the unbroken tradition of literature."[49] Title selection was conservative: classics were not presented beside popular fiction as they were in George Munro's day. As a result, the "mass public" that *Publishers' Weekly* worried about was not subject to a lowering of "tone" by "low-quality fiction."

The Arts and Crafts movement had instilled a deep sense of craftsmanship in Dent, and each Everyman's Library title page was an act of typographical homage to the design principles of William Morris. Printed on quality paper (a blend of rag and wood pulp) with clearly set type, each literary category represented in the series sported flexible cloth covers in its own distinct color. Everyman's Library offered readers their own classified home library, a subtlety carefully pointed out by critic Percy Bicknell: "Fiction glows in a warm crimson; history clothes itself scarlet, perhaps thus symbolizing the bloody battle-fields that inevitably stain its pages; poetry and drama appear in olive green; the oriental classics in dark blue; biography in lavender; and reference books in maroon."[50] By maintaining high production and editorial standards, choosing canonical titles long in the public domain, and establishing a serious purpose through classification, Everyman's publishers avoided the unfavorable reputation of and response to the earlier reprint libraries. Rather than a "cheap library," Everyman's was a library appropriate for a scholar's shelves yet priced for "everyman."

In the early part of the twentieth century, while Everyman's Library was proving that inexpensive reprints need not be "cheap," the idea of single-author libraries was also enjoying a return to prominence. Established publishers drew on their backlists to issue "authoritative," uniformly bound sets of authors' complete works. The most famous example is Scribner's twenty-six volume "New York Edition" of the *Novels and Tales of Henry James,* but nearly every established nineteenth-century author was honored with at least one "library." Sets of Twain, Cooper, or Dickens could command solid sales with almost no financial risk. Some critics charged that uniform editions catered to nonreaders eager to acquire the trappings of culture without submitting to the arduous task of becoming cultured. Advertisements that stressed the handsome gold-stamped bindings marketed the sets as luxury goods that would indicate refined taste and add distinction to the home. These "libraries" were lampooned in the press, and Sinclair Lewis used their faux-culture reputation to roast Main Street's lack of cultural urbanity.[51] Hopelessly bourgeois or not, the sets reinvigorated the idea of a "library" as an index of cultural respectability, while Everyman's Library maintained a positive image of an inexpensive series for all readers. When Boni & Liveright initiated the Modern Library, "libraries" had shed their bad odor, but they still lacked the cultural prestige monopolized by other forms of trade publishing.

Today a publisher's decision to acquire a literary property often rests on the value of its reprint rights, but that was not so eighty years ago. Most titles were never reprinted, and if they were, most publishers saw them only as a way to eke a few more dollars out of a title. Just as commonly, publishers, booksellers, and even authors shunned reprints, fearing that a cheaper edition would simply replace high-profit sales with low ones. Most people in the industry reasoned that reprinters skimmed the cream off the lists laboriously and expensively assembled by *real* publishers. Only on the rare occasions, as when a reprint would stimulate a revival of a title or author, did the mainstream publishers consider the reprinters more than parasitic.

The Modern Library represented a change in the nature of American book reprinting. More than a collection of titles, the Modern Library imitated the British Everyman's Library and sought to become a cultural entity in and of itself. While a Grosset & Dunlap reprint was simply an inexpensive version of the original title, Boni & Liveright designed a Modern Library reprint to be something more, an entity beyond the original work, as an integral part of a recognizable series with its own established reputation for excellence. The publishers encouraged the public to see the series as a *coherent* whole: uniform leatherette bindings with identical gold-stamped spines made the books similar in appearance (because they were printed from publishers' original plates, they sometimes varied slightly in size), and advertising featured the entire list (rather than individual titles) under the Modern Library brand name. Cooperative bookstores displayed all the Modern Library books together, as a collection, rather than breaking up the series and mixing it with other editions.

More than uniform bindings and decoration unified the series. The Modern Library sought to reformulate, institutionalize, and propagate the specific "advanced" literary tastes of the Greenwich Village intelligentsia. Individual titles together comprised a larger entity intended to represent modern thought accurately, if not entirely comprehensively. Albert Boni hoped the Modern Library would disseminate radical literary and social thought.[52] For the years in which it was edited by him and briefly by his uncle Thomas Seltzer, and then by T. R. Smith (former editor of the *Century Magazine*), the series self-consciously reflected the literary tastes of the American avant garde. While these editors occasionally saved money by using already published short essays by writers such as William Dean Howells as introductions, they increasingly solicited prominent figures known and admired by the Greenwich Village intelligentsia to write original introductions to many of the volumes. Often these literati were friends of the editors; they included Floyd Dell and John Reed of the *Masses,* symbolist critic and poet Arthur Symons, Nietzsche scholar and *Evening Mail* reviewer Willard Huntington Wright, and H. L. Mencken of *American Mercury,* all of whom contributed introductions in the first four years of the series.

Floyd Dell's preface to Moore's *Confessions of a Young Man* exemplifies the dual purpose introductions served. To establish Moore as a truly modern writer, Dell begins: "These 'Confessions of a Young Man' constitute one of the most significant documents of the passionate revolt of English literature against the Victorian tradition. It is significant because it reveals so clearly the sources of that revolt. It is in a sense the history of an epoch—an epoch that is just closing. It represents one of the great discoveries of English literature: a discovery that had been made from time to time before, and that is now being made anew in our own generation—the discovery of human nature." Dell then grounds Moore's revolt in a literary heritage that includes, among others, Théophile Gautier, Swinburne, and Tolstoy, three authors either already appearing in the Modern Library or soon to be added. He alludes to the second Nietzsche title in the series, *Beyond Good and Evil,* by claiming that Gautier, Baudelaire, and even Moore approached the "truly revolutionary conception of life which has begun to obtain acceptance in our day—a conception of life which traverses the old conceptions of 'good' and 'evil.'" The introduction embraces a literature that moves beyond the Victorian understanding that "lust, brutality and selfishness" could be embodied only in "'bad' people" to expose without compromise the depths of the human soul.[53] Moore's writing is important because it constitutes one of the first English attacks on the old order that Greenwich Village radicals found so abhorrent. The net effect of Dell's and other similar introductions was to create a mutually referential set of books doubly modern: first, by the actual titles selected, and second, by the introductions from young champions of modernism that illuminated each book's "modern" qualities.

Randolph Bourne believed genuine culture evolved out of a community of artists and critics brought together by common aims, and that the stagnation of genteel culture resulted partly from its blind devotion to the dead. The Modern Library actively engaged a living artistic community. Although it included many dead authors, it chose only their writings that still animated heated admiration among many young intellectuals. For its efforts, Boni & Liveright was recognized by one influential voice of prewar Greenwich Village, the *Seven Arts,* as a partner in a shared cultural mission. Less than four months after the first Modern Library volume appeared, the *Seven Arts* (with its predominantly New York audience) could assert that the Modern Library, "by far the happiest enterprise in recent publishing," is "already too well known to need any praise of ours." Proclaiming Boni & Liveright "the most interesting of all" young American publishers, the magazine held the firm up as a model of cultural relevance:

> But now Messrs. Boni & Liveright announce that they are to conduct a general publishing business, and their statement is so interesting that we feel we ought to mention it: "Our aim," they say, "is to publish only new books with permanent value—books which will be as vital in twenty-five years as they are today. Our standard of accepting a manuscript will be based wholly on its enduring merit, and we will issue no transient or merely popular work. In short, we have set for ourselves a definite literary ideal; and intend to make our imprint stand for something genuinely worth while to the discriminating booklover. We know we will never get rich—but that is not primarily our ambition. We believe that there is a sufficient number of the better-class readers in America who will co-operate with us to such an extent that we will not altogether fail." There are few, but certainly very few, publishers who take this position, which we like to think is characteristic of the younger generation. Publishers who take it are so much friends of everything THE SEVEN ARTS stands for that we think it only just to make this statement.[54]

The editorial was occasioned by Boni & Liveright's plans to begin original publishing, but the opening acknowledgment of the Modern Library indicated that the series itself justified the confidence *Seven Arts* had in the firm's commitment to cultural renewal. The enthusiastic endorsement positioned the firm as a confederate with a wider, spirited "younger generation" ready to cast off old, impotent ideas to release the promise of America. That the article appeared literally as the final words of the *Seven Arts* (on the last page of the final number) gave it a certain poignancy, as if the editors believed that even though their attempt to give voice to the new radicalism was to be censored due to the entry of the United States into World War I, others, like Boni & Liveright, were taking up the good fight.

The series catered to young intellectuals' needs: familiarity with its texts and authors would assure an appropriate level of cultural literacy in bohemian and other intellectually adventurous circles. While the *Seven Arts* warmly recognized Boni & Liveright as "friends," Louis Kronenberger saw the firm as a comrade-in-arms. "For young people hungry for what was sophisticated, subversive, avant-garde in literature, the Modern Library signified to the early twenties, one can almost say, what the whole world of quality paperbacks does today," he later remembered; Boni & Liveright, "was something of a clarion, rousing the young to what stirred and streamed forth in the arts."[55]

Bitter arguments between the quiet bohemian Boni and the flamboyant Liveright (who was affecting a dandyish cane) dissolved their partnership in less than a year. In a coin flip, Liveright won the right to buy out his partner. The firm retained the name Boni & Liveright, and, under Horace Liveright's command, it quickly emerged as one of the most influential American publishers of the twenties' renaissance. Liveright, always a glutton for intensity, loved the excitement and glamour associated with publishing and relished his role as the "Gambler in Publishing." Besides enormously popular titles such as Anita Loos's *Gentlemen Prefer Blondes* and Gertrude Atherton's *Black Oxen,* the Boni & Liveright list featured acknowledged and rising "literary" authors such as Gertrude Stein, Alfred Kreymborg, T. S. Eliot, Eugene O'Neill, Theodore Dreiser, Sinclair Lewis, Ernest Hemingway, William Faulkner, and e. e. cummings. Liveright also published some of the era's most powerful social criticism by John Reed, Waldo Frank, and Lewis Mumford, and the firm helped to popularize Sigmund Freud in the United States.

Certainly a large measure of Liveright's success was due to the impressive staff he assembled. Walker Gilmer writes of the appointment of T. R. Smith as editor-in-chief: "The arrival of the forty-year-old Smith at Liveright's not only provided the firm with an erudite and discriminating reader, but widened its already valuable contacts with writers in the Village, editors of little magazines, and budding theatrical groups to include such well-known critics and editors as H. L. Mencken, George Jean Nathan, Burton Rascoe, and Ernest Boyd, all of whom were good friends of Smith."[56] The other editors (Lillian Hellman, Beatrice Bakrow Kaufman, Thomas Seltzer, and later Saxe Commins) also attracted lively and prestigious new talent. Julian Messner and his assistant Edward Weeks (later editor of the *Atlantic Monthly*) managed the sales force that included young executives Donald Friede, Bennett Cerf, and Richard Simon who enthusiastically pushed the list to booksellers. Aaron Sussman created innovative advertising, and production was handled by budding novelist Manuel Komroff.

Although he kept a hand in all Boni & Liveright activities, Liveright's forte was marketing. He believed that books could and should be promoted as aggressively as automobiles. It was Liveright who first conceived of the now ubiquitous book-launching party. He promoted Christopher Morley's lament about Prohibition, *In the Sweet Dry and Dry*, by reopening the bar at the Majestic Hotel with a "bartender" who served Boni & Liveright books to a gathering of authors and the press.[57] To stir up talk about Hutchins Hapgood's *The Story of a Lover,* Liveright solicited testimonials from Hollywood stars Mary Pickford and the Gish sisters as advertising copy. In the 1920s he spent the then-enormous sum of more than a million dollars on advertising. All of this ballyhoo shocked the staid established publishers, but its results would soon change the way all of them did business.

Along with Knopf and Huebsch, Boni & Liveright profoundly enlivened the postwar American intellectual climate. Much of the "modernist literature" the three firms published sought to lay bare the human psyche's complex workings and to criticize what it believed to be an outmoded standard of personal, social, and political morality. Its frank discussions of human desire and sexual repression (often in Freudian terms) and exposure of contradictions in Victorian morality especially appalled John Sumner's Society for the Suppression of Vice and other guardians of public morality. In 1923, Liveright marshalled his authors and friends

Theodore Dreiser, Waldo Frank, Gertrude Atherton, and, most important, New York Mayor Jimmy Walker (who had said for the ages, "No woman was ever ruined by a book") to fight a Clean Books League–sponsored bill in the New York legislature. The bill would have vastly expanded the definition of indecent materials. Liveright's efforts, which included significant gambling losses to key state legislators in a three-day poker binge, helped defeat the bill, and the defeat was heralded in New York literary circles as a major victory for intellectual freedom.[58] Not surprisingly, Liveright appeared in court on obscenity charges more often than any other publisher, and he risked financial instability and even jail to defend intellectual freedom. It was the notoriety of the obscenity charges that scared off the old family-run publishing houses that worried about preserving public morality, but Liveright recognized that fighting censorship was good business: court battles sold books to a public intrigued by sexual scandal, while they also made friends in the avant-garde literary community.

Despite very different publishing and personal styles, Liveright, Knopf, and Huebsch are consistently linked in publishing histories.[59] Alas, they rarely had amicable relations. Knopf's disdain for Liveright became apparent to Bennett Cerf after he and Klopfer purchased the Modern Library. Knopf introduced himself and then said, "I've heard about you two boys, and I just wanted to find out if you're going to be as bad crooks as the man you bought The Modern Library from." Knopf strongly disapproved of Liveright, according to Cerf, and even though he was slightly younger than Liveright and of the same German-Jewish heritage, he was at pains to dissociate himself from "that class of 'fresh young Jews.'"[60] "That class" cared little for Knopf's management style: junior editor Edith Stern lamented that she had to spend "nine months' servitude" in "bleak orderliness" at Knopf before the Boni & Liveright office burst on her "like a disturbing new world."[61] Huebsch avoided the limelight that Liveright so actively chased and had far less concern for the prestige or profit Knopf sought and found.[62] But because all three ventures were run by Jews, and because of the modernism they promoted, authors, booksellers, and the trade press tended to lump them together. This puzzled Cerf. To him they were distinct, similar only in having a shared openness to new ideas that the older houses lacked.[63] The Knopfs, while intellectually adventuresome, operated according to a finely calibrated calculus of prestige and profit. Huebsch's small operation reflected his personal interest in European literature and politics. What started as a sideline blossomed into a modest but respected publishing enterprise, which merged with the new Viking Press in 1924. Boni & Liveright focused its original publishing on fostering home-grown literary talent and used the Modern Library to reprint European writers. The firm often selected titles whimsically and pursued sexy big-sellers so that it could also publish young authors whose sales would be limited. At times Liveright regarded his firm as a cash cow to finance his extravagant personal tastes, but he also courted prestige and was willing to spend lavishly for it, as in the case of Dreiser, whom he lured with large advances and high royalty percentages incommensurate with Dreiser's sales.

Liveright's association with Knopf and Huebsch lent the Modern Library an added measure of legitimacy. Liveright was a champion of intellectual freedom and supporter of modernism, but his personal style more often elicited the term "charlatan" than the phrase "distinguished publisher." Boni & Liveright's implicit connection with the dignified Knopf and the intellectual Huebsch tempered Liveright's excesses. The Modern Library may have been published by a capricious fop, but in most people's eyes it emerged from a segment of the publishing world clearly linked with sophisticated intellectual rebellion.

Nearly all accounts of life at Boni & Liveright bustle with excitement. Edith Stern described the office as "the Jazz Age in microcosm, with all its extremes of hysteria and of cynicism," then soberly continued:

> Yet though the madness, the extravagances, the orgies, the empty bottles that occasionally littered the stairs in the morning and the parties that cut into office hours are the truth, they are by no means the whole truth. So much did they fascinate contemporaries for whom Horace loved to put on a show, so much have they been publicized in print, on the screen, and by word of mouth, since his death, by both the tenderly nostalgic and the jealous, that they have tended to obscure the profound emotional and intellectual ferment whose end products were literature—and people."[64]

For Walker Gilmer the office became an enclave to which Liberal Club members could repair for intellectual stimulation, financial support, and bootleg liquor.[65] Bennett Cerf also looked back at Boni & Liveright with a kind of blissful nostalgia, though he was always scandalized by the level of excess—so much so that he earned the nickname "Jesus Junior."[66]

Although the Modern Library nearly always comes up in any recounting of Boni & Liveright's salad days, it is usually an afterthought (Stern casually adds "and always the classics in the Modern Library" to her description of life at Boni & Liveright), reflecting the limited prominence it occupied in the firm after its initial success.[67] Reprints, although they paid the bills, were safe and boring, so Liveright left primary control of the series in the hands of its able editor T. R. Smith. By 1923, management of the series was communal; any Boni & Liveright employee could offer suggestions and there was no organized method for selection. Titles were added, the occasional advertisement was placed, and the series slowly grew. But even though the Modern Library was never the most risqué or flashy bit of news emerging from the brownstone at 61 West 48th Street and it suffered periodic neglect, sales continued to increase.

THE SALE OF THE CENTURY

At the height of his publishing career Liveright's lust for excitement sent him back to his first love: the theater. Although he had had a few Broadway successes (including the first production of *Dracula* with Bela Lugosi in the title role), his more frequent flops drained the assets of Boni & Liveright. His gambling (both in speakeasies and on the stock market) and his free-wheeling advances on sketchy book outlines exacerbated his theater losses. To maintain Boni & Liveright's capital base, Liveright took on "a parade of vice-presidents," wealthy young men wanting to invest in the literary life.[68] Among the paraders was the young Bennett Cerf, who came to Boni & Liveright in 1923 with a cash investment of twenty-five thousand dollars (which he doubled two years later).

Born near 125th Street and Seventh Avenue in Manhattan, Bennett Cerf grew up in a predominantly Jewish neighborhood of Harlem. At Columbia University, where he took a degree in journalism in 1921, he edited the comic magazine, the *Jester*. After a humiliatingly brief episode as a *New York Tribune* financial reporter, he went to work on Wall Street. When a close friend, Richard Simon, told him he was leaving Boni & Liveright to start his own firm, Cerf jumped at the chance to get out of the bond business and invest himself and his maternal inheritance in publishing.

Liveright's strategy for raising capital by selling vice presidencies allowed Cerf to start near the top. As a vice president, Cerf's duties included selling to bookstores along the east coast and writing copy for book jackets and catalogs. He entered his job with youthful exuberance (a quality he retained throughout his life) and eagerness to learn the trade. Not only was Boni & Liveright the nation's most innovative publisher, but their offices were a hive of social activity, where famous authors and the rising stars of the literary world met for cocktails. It was a perfect setup for someone of Cerf's genial temperament, permitting him to establish a network of key connections to draw on later. But most important he learned the trade—from both positive and negative examples.

Liveright's self-interested vice-presidency system proved to be excellent training ground for the second generation of Jewish publishers. While Liveright, Boni, and Huebsch had to master the publishing business through trial and error, Cerf (Random House, Modern Library), Richard Simon (Simon & Schuster, Pocket Books), and Donald Friede (Covici-Friede) learned from their apprenticeships. The once-closed doors of publishing had been thrown open to a group of innovative young publishers. Cerf regarded his vice presidency as an active internship in a venturesome and successful publishing company. He invested his capital without much expectation of a return in kind, reasoning that his experience would provide a foundation for the firm he hoped one day to establish.

Cerf romantically characterized himself as a kind of Boswell to Liveright—he followed him around, meeting "his Greenwich Village characters and the literary and theatrical people." Although Cerf admired aspects of Liveright's personality and considered him a good friend, he was always bothered by Liveright's lack of "class." In Cerf's eyes, Liveright's "sham and pretense" made him a pathetic, comic character, a generous poseur unable to achieve the dignity of his rival, Alfred Knopf.[69] Nonetheless, Cerf imbibed a certain flamboyance from Liveright that he could apply to the promotion of books, but he also learned from Liveright's excesses that he needed to practice a level of restraint.

On May 20, 1925, Bennett Cerf excitedly phoned his close friend, Donald Klopfer, with the news that Liveright wanted to sell the Modern Library. Desperately attempting to raise cash (perhaps to buy out his father-in-law's interest in the firm, but more likely to cover gambling debts), Liveright offered to sell his only reliable source of income for two hundred thousand dollars.[70] Cerf could apply the fifty thousand dollars he had already invested and was confident he could raise an additional fifty thousand from relatives. He told Klopfer, then an unhappy partner in his stepfather's diamond wholesaling business, that the opportunity to go into business together, as they had always planned, lay "on a gold platter."[71] Apparently, Klopfer's enthusiasm matched Cerf's and he sold his share of United Diamond Works at 80 percent of its book value to raise the matching one hundred thousand dollars.[72] Cerf set sail that night on his first journey to Europe with a signed contract guaranteeing their purchase of the Modern Library.

Liveright's staff tried unsuccessfully to persuade him to renege on the deal while Cerf toured Europe. Bookkeeper Arthur Pell, sales manager Julian Messner, and lawyer Arthur Garfield Hays knew that the Modern Library was "the chief asset and glory" of Boni & Liveright and "one of the great properties in the whole publishing business."[73] But, despite Liveright's many ethical and moral lapses, he considered his word sacred and would not back down. Under pressure, he asked for an advising fee of five thousand dollars a year for five years, which Cerf and Klopfer agreed to pay to keep the deal from stalling.

The Modern Library sale is famous in the annals of twentieth-century publishing: not only was it the highest price ever paid for something so insignificant as a reprint series, it also turned out to be a steal for Cerf and Klopfer. Liveright may have believed he was pulling off a shrewd business deal.[74] After all, seven years earlier the Modern Library was simply an idea—not even his own—and now he was selling it for (in Cerf's words) "a whacking big price."[75] Macmillan, with its powerful financial assets and backlist built up over generations of publishing, was rumored to be contemplating a rival series, but neither Liveright's advisers nor Cerf took the threat seriously.[76] In addition, Liveright was watching Albert Boni's first attempt at publishing, the Little Leather Library, collapse under its own weight; and the Modern Library was returning less than ten thousand dollars annual profit. Cashing in his chips for twenty times net may have seemed like a very good idea to an experienced gambler.

Just what opportunity was delivered to Cerf and Klopfer on that golden platter? The series came with 109 titles, all bound in "Croft" imitation leather, treated with "deodorized" castor oil that smelled of a fish market on hot days. It had a skeletal, but established distribution system and, despite Boni & Liveright's lackadaisical attitude, it was selling around 275,000 copies per year by 1925. Cerf and Klopfer had poured their fortunes into a specialized—and still stigmatized—segment of publishing, but on the other hand with indifferent attention the series had produced a steady if modest profit. More important for two energetic young businessmen, the Modern Library came with an established reputation among young intellectuals, members of the book trade, and important critics. It was up to Cerf and Klopfer, with a more aggressive sales effort, to achieve greater visibility and move into new markets.

Many have second-guessed Liveright's decision to sell the Modern Library. Six years later he was thrown out of a nearly bankrupt Boni & Liveright by his bookkeeper and financial nemesis Arthur Pell. His descent was rapid and final: he was broke when he died of alcoholism at forty-nine in 1933. By then, Cerf and Klopfer had quadrupled Modern Library sales and were using its handsome profits to develop their rapidly growing Random House imprint. But Donald Klopfer, never one to make rash judgments or exaggerate, believed that the Modern Library could not have saved Liveright. Even if he had pushed the series as hard as Cerf and Klopfer did, "He couldn't have weathered it, because he would just have thrown away more money. He had the seeds of his own destruction planted I guess at birth...."[77]

CHAPTER TWO

Advertising the World's Best Books

Bennett Cerf contended that before he and Donald Klopfer took over "nobody had ever bothered *selling* The Modern Library."[1] When the young partners purchased the Modern Library, it constituted their entire business, and they initially had no intention of publishing new titles. They were both avid salesmen, hungry for financial success, and the opportunity to turn Boni & Liveright's modest achievement into a booming publishing program energized their marketing imaginations. Recognizing that the Modern Library needed a more aggressive sales strategy, Cerf and Klopfer initiated a large-scale advertising campaign specifically directed at America's largest class of book buyers, urban, middle-class professionals. They also maintained close contact with Liveright's original core audience through a lesser advertising effort in the pages of political and literary magazines directed at the nation's self-defined intellectuals. The campaigns sought to build on the reputation of the series as genuine culture expressive of an American spirit, but winning multiple audiences demanded formulating specialized appeals. With a constant eye on audience, Klopfer and Cerf *sold* the Modern Library.

BOOKS AREN'T SOAP

The publishing trade repeatedly debated the merits of advertising books. Although everyone in the trade agreed advertising was necessary to keep fickle authors from abandoning a publishing house, most thought it did little or nothing to sell books. The development of national brand-name advertising met with little enthusiasm among publishers. They argued books were not soap and could not be marketed with the same techniques. In his 1931 economic report on the publishing industry, O. H. Cheney's litany of commonly heard complaints summarized publishers' dubiety about advertising: "Advertising doesn't sell books. Nobody knows what sells books. Only word-of-mouth publicity sells books. We advertise only to impress the bookseller and because the author would howl if we didn't. It's a waste of money to advertise heavily before a book shows signs of catching on."[2] Cheney was nonplussed to find that nearly all publishers advertised, and despite their doubts devoted an average of twelve cents of every retail dollar to promotion, a considerably higher percentage than in most other industries. Such large outlays suggested that most publishers hoped advertising would be effective, but each notable failure led to resentful carping about authors' unreasonable demands for more promotion.

Even when publishers reluctantly regarded books as commodities, each title's singularity restricted the effectiveness of modern advertising methods. Most publishers believed book advertising was fundamentally ineffective because each title had to be sold as a separate entity. Such an argument forms the core of "An Advertising Catechism," by an anonymous author who *Publishers' Weekly* guaranteed to be "one of the shrewdest and most experienced of the publishers' advertising managers."[3] It outlined publishers' past advertising failures and argued that limited advertising budgets must be systematically used to maximize their effect. Advertising simply "to get authors and keep them" squandered valuable resources and put publishers in the absurd position of advertising "not to sell their products but to get them!"[4] "Anonymous" believed advertising could sell books, but not without a strategy that identified and pursued a clearly defined audience. The article's stress on careful planning, effective strategies, and attention to placement surely was meant to drive publishers into the arms of expert advertising agents, but its suggestion that each publisher rethink its marketing philosophy was sound advice during a time of rapid change in the industry. It recommended that publishing houses select a few promising titles from their bloated lists and apply all their promotional resources to "make a real dent" in the public consciousness.

C. B. Larrabee, managing editor of the advertising trade journal *Printers' Ink,* read the catechism and wrote, "I have no comment to make because long ago I threw up my hands and vowed that I would never make any didactic statements about book advertising."[5] Recanting only slightly, four years later *Printers' Ink* reiterated in "They Aren't Toothpaste" that advertising books with potential sales of only a few thousand copies proved "in fact books are different." The magazine searched for ways advertising could help publishers, but without success. A book retailing for two dollars and fifty cents with potential sales of five thousand copies had an advertising budget of only seven hundred dollars. Such a paltry sum could not "provide much sales pressure." Toothpaste and soap advertisements depended on creating buyer loyalty and stimulating repeat buyers. An advertising campaign was not designed to sell one bar of soap, but to persuade the consumer to become a steady customer. Although these methods worked well for disposable products usually replaced by identical merchandise, any given individual is likely to buy only one copy of a book—if a reader really enjoys it he or she may buy additional copies as gifts, but repeat book buying is rare. As a result, both the advertising and publishing industries theorized that advertising techniques successfully employed to sell soap or toothpaste would fail with books. The ordinarily ebullient *Printers' Ink* hesitantly concluded that the advertising industry might be able to help publishers plan more effective campaigns in terms of timing and placement, but little else. Although the article praised a handful of publishers, including Bennett Cerf, Richard Simon, and Alfred Harcourt for exhibiting "the finest qualities of literary critic, artist and publicist" and taking their "marketing function seriously and thoughtfully," no specifics amplified these gassy abstractions. On a more concrete level, the article concluded that the Book-of-the-Month Club was the only publishing venture able to crack "the tough nut of repeat sales" because it "has a story to tell about itself."[6] Book-of-the-Month Club advertisements worked because they sold the *idea* of the Club rather than individual titles.

A few aspiring young publishing houses, however, thought advertising could work when energetically backed by a well-designed marketing plan. Horace Liveright used advertising in conjunction with parties and other promotions to pioneer the idea that a book's release could be an orchestrated media event.[7] Alfred Knopf maintained a high profile for his Borzoi books through advertising, and he consistently linked each title to his trademark to associate all his books with quality literature. Haldeman-Julius of Girard, Kansas, depended on advertising to fuel a booming mail-order firm that featured a phenomenal range of "Little-Blue-Books" for a nickel apiece. The Book-of-the-Month Club and Dr. Eliot's Five-Foot-Shelf of Harvard Classics sold their brand names through regular advertising and even ventured into mass-circulation magazines such as the *Ladies' Home Journal* and the *Saturday Evening Post,* which required substantial advertising budgets.[8] Experimenting with maximizing profit potential, Simon & Schuster kept their list as short as practicable and pushed each title with a gusto rarely seen before or since. Each successful advertiser would have agreed with the Modern Library's advertising agency's pronouncement that book advertising needed spirit, intelligence, enthusiasm, and "some editorial *raison d'être*" to be effective.[9] The adman's cliché call for more pep indicates most publishers' grasping efforts—no one really knew what kind of advertising would sell books, so most resorted to boisterous ballyhoo—but the editorial motivation rang true for modern publishers trying to link their products with quality.

The forerunner to the Modern Library's advertising campaigns was that of Everyman's Library, which piqued the publishing industry's attention in 1910 when it proved that books could indeed be sold like soap. E. P. Dutton (its American distributor) adopted "one of the biggest general periodical advertising campaigns ever attempted for retail books" to promote the series of classic reprints.[10] Although the campaign listed individual titles, it sought even more to produce a general awareness of the quality and coherence of the series. The advertisements focused on the brand name "Everyman's Library" and emphasized its slogan: "Books that fit the hand, the mood, the mind and the purse of every man." Its highly successful campaign established Everyman's Library as the premier literary reprint series in the United States until the Modern Library surpassed it in the 1920s. Everyman's advertising campaign presented the series as a replenishable line of goods—when one volume was consumed a nearly identical one waited on booksellers' shelves—at the same time it heralded its "editorial *raison d'être*": taken together, the books in the series constituted a dependable, affordable, well-rounded home library.

REACHING THE "CIVILIZED MINORITY"

Aware of Everyman's success in establishing a brand identity, but still conscious of the limitations of book promotion, Cerf (who was in charge of Modern Library advertising) placed advertisements in a host of national magazines catering to a specific market. Beginning in the midtwenties and continuing through the Great Depression, he actively pursued the nation's "civilized minority": a group the partners defined in three prospectuses written for a Modern Library magazine scheduled to appear in the spring of 1930 but aborted due to the Depression. Bearing the Modern Library imprint and sister to the book series, the magazine (variously named *Future, American Chronicle,* and *Horizon*) aspired to reach a fast-growing class of professionals. It was to be "radical" in that it hoped "to become a social force in itself."[11] But radical did not mean it was to be another *New Masses;* in fact, it was to be addressed to:

> the civilized minority, but in its view the "civilized minority" does not consist, certainly does not necessarily consist, of connoisseurs of the right proportions in the latest cocktail, or of the devotees to the various cults of serious-mindedness or to "art for art's sake," or to our highly conventionalized "radicals" of various schools or of no schools. The civilized minority is the minority in each enterprise, profession, and avocation of American life. It consists of people vitally interested in their own field who know what they are talking about, and want to know what people of their own kind are thinking in other fields.

The prospectuses further defined the "civilized minority" by its interests: it did not include "Babbitt," but businessmen seeking an understanding of "business structure and its social influence"; workers "vitally interested in labor and the industrial democratic movement"; and physicians, lawyers, and educators who would not swallow the vulgarities of their fields.[12]

Distinguishing itself from spurious, nonproductive forms of culture, the final draft of the prospectus promised the magazine "will not be highbrow, because it will be realistic and sincere, not smart and superficial.... Unashamedly intellectual, *Future* will cater to the tastes and the interests of the intelligent minorities that exist in every business, trade, occupation, profession, and in every social, economic and political group. In numbers, these minorities form a far from inconsequential aggregate. But their real importance lies not in their numbers but in their qualities of leadership in their respective fields."[13] Elmer Adler was to execute the cover design and typography, with the proposed editorial board including such luminaries as Sinclair Lewis, Stuart Chase, and Mark Van Doren.

The magazine's "radical" agenda differed from that championed by Albert Boni on founding the Modern Library twelve years earlier and from left-wing certitudes as well. Its projected audience had a firm commitment to Enlightenment individualism and the industrial–capitalist state. It consisted of the ambitious, educated Americans driving the nation's twentieth-century progress. Most from this "minority" fitted into a social–economic group Barbara and John Ehrenreich later labeled "the professional–managerial class."[14] These active individuals were not the passive pawns of the system Edward Sapir had worried about: they were concerned about the course of civilization and eager to hear from other "people of their own kind" in other specialized segments of society. Despite its rhetoric, for the Modern Library the "civilized minority" was liberal rather than radical, capable of critiquing the industrial state even while remaining a part of it. They were educated professionals whose independence, cosmopolitanism, and intelligence embodied America's cultural promise. For Cerf and Klopfer, if a genuine American culture was possible, it was the "civilized minority" in every field including the intelligentsia who would create the social and intellectual climate to produce it.

The "civilized minority" was a segmented audience and, despite the partners' hope that one magazine could attract all its members, several publications combined to serve it. Cerf and Klopfer recognized the diversity within their target audience and acted to reach each segment with specialized appeals. As a result, promotional efforts in such "intellectual" magazines as the *Nation* and the *New Republic* differed from campaigns in "sophisticated" weeklies like the *New Yorker*. Calling the *Nation* "an ideal medium for Modern Library books," Cerf pointed out to his friend Max Schuster of Simon & Schuster: "It is an interesting fact that we get a rather good response on the new titles that are announced in The Nation, but not very much when we list some of the books that have been in the series for some time." He went on to explain the phenomenon: "I believe we are correct in our assumption that the reason for this is that the type of person who reads The Nation is quite familiar with the Modern Library books, and has already secured the older volumes that he wants to own."[15] Advertisements placed in the *Nation* therefore highlighted new titles. The same was true for the equally intellectual, though politically more progressive, *New Republic*. The Modern Library often ran identical advertisements in both magazines: one listed "six important books just issued in the Modern Library." These six were featured in boldface type above a secondary list of seven additional recent releases.[16] The only copy was the list of titles, the price, and the series' trademark — no gimmicky art, no hyperbole, no implied narrative. These inexpensive, minimalist advertisements did not extol the merits of the series but kept an informed audience abreast of new developments within an already well-known series. They were directed to a small but important audience that required only the advertising equivalent of a press release to keep its appetite whetted.

The publishers approached an even more elite intellectual group similarly. In homage to the bohemian origins of the series, Cerf placed a prominent advertisement opposite the table of contents in the final issue of Margaret Anderson and Jane Heap's famous *Little Review*. It is doubtful the series had many Parisian customers, but the influential magazine reached America's literati and reminded them of the Modern Library's avant-garde heritage. The advertisement was disarmingly simple: it featured the Modern Library's publications of *Little Review* readers' "favorite authors," including Joyce, O'Neill, Proust, and Dreiser.[17] The low price of the books was dutifully noted, but no claims, fantastic or modest, were made. Cerf assumed the illustrious list of modern writers was ample incentive for *Little Review* readers.

The Modern Library showed an entirely different face when approaching workers "vitally interested" in social change. A campaign in the *New Masses* kicked off with "a contest exclusively for New Masses readers." It set forth the following questions: "Should New Masses readers read only new books? Only proletarian literature?—Or are there certain books, classics or outstanding titles of recent years, which should be read by every intelligent person? Which are they? Out of the 214 titles published by The Modern Library, famous books of the past and present, which 20 would you include in making up a 'required reading' list for New Masses Readers?"[18] Proletariat novels were conspicuously absent from the Modern Library, so the advertisement featured possible left-wing favorites, *God's Little Acre, Best Russian Short Stories,* and *The Theory of the Leisure Class,* as well as the class-conscious *Sons and Lovers*. The contest was timed to welcome into the series John Reed's classic reportage of the Bolshevik Revolution, *Ten Days That Shook the World*. Two more contest announcements appeared, each prominently displaying Reed's book. One week before the closing date of the contest, poised above a promotion for a winter vacation offering "proletarian camaraderie" at the inappropriately named Hotel Royale, a one-column, three-inch advertisement reminded readers that *Ten Days That Shook the World* featured a foreword by Lenin and a new introduction by Granville Hicks. Two months later the Modern Library editorial department published a letter in the *New Masses* to announce the contest winners and applaud their "clear grasp of literary history" and "awareness of contemporary problems."[19]

The Modern Library resisted use of the winning list for over four months, but then an advertisement using artwork to evoke a workers' rally appeared. A man in overalls stood at a simple table grasping a book and calling out: "The question before the meeting is the Modern Library."[20] The advertisement asked what the Modern Library could offer workers, and if it included Reed's *Ten Days That Shook the World*. The answers emphasized the series' leftist writings and low price and concluded with the previous spring contest's "must read" list. The advertisement evoked key left-wing values and implicitly linked the series to a revolutionary sensibility. The artwork focused on a political leader clutching a powerful symbol of culture, a book, in front of a poster for an upcoming "ball." The political–social movement (the ball and the meeting) was driven in part by the cultural message contained in the Modern Library. Furthermore, the gathering supported a grassroots democratic ideal emphasized by the incessant repetition of "worker." But curiously, other than the writings of Veblen, Dostoyevsky, Marx, and Dickens, the "must read" list showed little connection to leftist political philosophy, but it included *The Scarlet Letter, The Philosophy of Plato, The Divine Comedy,* and *Six Plays by Corneille and Racine*. Perhaps the list's conservatism reflected the paucity of workers' literature the contestants had to choose from, but because the winner was chosen by the Modern Library editorial staff, it more likely reflected the firm's conception of an American leftist literary taste concerned with social injustice and its historic roots. The advertisement presented the Modern Library as an ideal reading list for leftists. It supplied important new texts (*Ten Days That Shook the World*) and a cultural history of social conflict to support their leftist radical political opinions.

On the opposite end of the civilized minority spectrum, Cerf also courted its more economically advantaged and socially sophisticated members. Addressing such an audience that knew itself to be worldly and successful, Cerf traded earnestness for flattery disguised as urbane wit. Thus, a promotion in the *New Yorker* was headlined "The Worst Sellers in The Modern Library" and employed a narrative voice not unlike the one used in "The Talk of the Town":

> The writer of this advertisement takes it for granted that every reader of the New Yorker knows the Modern Library series . . . he furthermore presupposes that every reader of the New Yorker knows that this Modern Library list includes Douglas' SOUTH WIND, Anderson's POOR WHITE, Butler's WAY OF ALL FLESH, Hudson's GREEN MANSIONS, Cabell's BEYOND LIFE, Dreiser's FREE—and other outstanding titles listed on this page. But there are four titles in the Modern Library that people evidently do *not* know about, for they do not sell any better than rule books on mah jongg. Less than a thousand copies each last year, to be exact. Four bad sellers in a list of 115 titles is not a record to be ashamed of—but the publishers are worried that it is their fault.[21]

All the top-selling titles were cleverly sheltered under the cloak of the "Worst Sellers," while the commercial appeal was disguised by *New Yorker*–style humor. The shameless flattery of "every reader of the New Yorker knows the Modern Library series" assured the magazine's audience of their cultural preeminence, and the reference to mah jongg sent up passing fads that sophisticated *New Yorker* readers might or might not have been immune to. Stressing *unpopular* titles archly reversed the usual strategy of featuring best-sellers to lure readers who need to feel up-to-date. The advertisement potently combined self-mockery, gentle teasing, and flattery to position the series and its readers as the self-assured superiors to Book-of-the-Month Club members laboring to appear "cultured."

"THE NEW YORK TIMES BOOK REVIEW"

The *Nation,* the *New Yorker,* the *New Masses,* and the *New Republic* had a combined circulation of only around two hundred and fifty thousand, but they served select segments of the civilized minority. The *New York Times Book Review* reached the homes of three times as many readers each week and it was the nation's, and most of the civilized minority's, chief source of information on books.[22] Although its advertising space was too costly for Cerf and Klopfer to maintain a week-in-and-week-out campaign, throughout the 1920s and 1930s they concentrated their advertising on this venue and made certain to maintain their visibility in it with periodic advertisements.[23] These promoted the series as offering high-quality books at extraordinary values, but they also elevated the series and flattered potential buyers by suggesting it appealed to intelligent, modern individuals entirely capable of making independent aesthetic choices in a democratic world.

Readers skimming their *New York Times Book Review* on a lazy November Sunday in 1928 met with an advertisement that stood out from those of other publishers (figure 2). Dominated by an elongated, shaded triangle that flared diagonally up across the page with its apex in the lower right-hand corner like a spotlight, the unconventional design highlighted a surrealistically hovering edition of Proust's *Swann's Way*. Its dynamic tension caught the readers' wandering eyes and directed them to the boldly emblazoned words "The Modern Library." The arresting layout based on the asymmetries of modern art introduced *Swann's Way* and four other new titles and reminded readers of yet thirteen more "modern books" the Modern Library had made available. "It is a pity there is no room to list all the Modern Library books," the copy lamented, "but a glance at the titles below will show you what treasures you can own for 95 cents a copy." The advertisement's visual novelty, its insistent repetition of "modern" (eight times), and its promise that the "the world's best literature" was democratically available to all conspired to assure readers that as an entity the series was both up-to-the-minute and sanctified by time. If this paradox was too esoteric, the claim that the Modern Library was composed of "the best sellers of yesterday and today" added a more flagrantly commercial enticement.[24]

The advertisement is typical of the Modern Library's broader campaign in the *New York Times Book Review*. It was commercial yet based on the assumption that Modern Library readers were daring, intelligent individuals. Cerf and Klopfer thought highly of their civilized minority and treated its members with respect. Their attitude was made manifest by the cool reception given to an unsolicited set of advertising recommendations sent by an aspiring young adman. The Modern Library's advertising agent Aaron Sussman of Spier & Sussman believed the proposals were "insulting to the prospective buyer," and cited the patronizing slogan "If you ever read books (if you don't, you ought to)" as evidence. The green adman's attempt to shame potential buyers may have been a "classic in its field," but it was all wrong for the Modern Library: "The

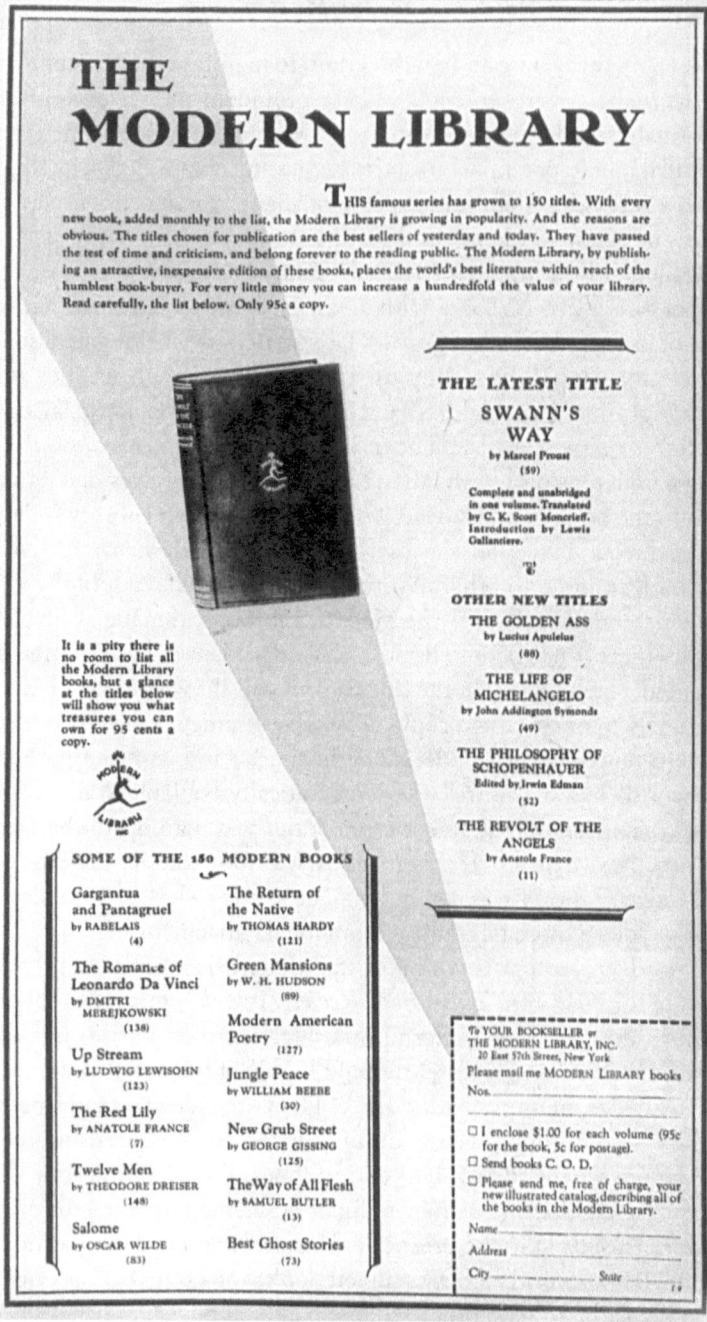

FIGURE 2. Advertisement textually and graphically asserts the Modern Library's modernity. From *New York Times Book Review,* 18 November 1928. Joseph Regenstein Library, University of Chicago.

people who buy the Modern Library books are certainly as intelligent as they come and I don't think it's necessary to be so snooty in appealing to them. Actually, the Modern Library public is a smarter public than any other book public and must be treated as such." Rather than browbeating potential buyers, Sussman—who had got his start at Boni & Liveright—thought Modern Library publicity ought to employ rational arguments that focused on the series' chief selling points: "It is my impression, borne out by the things people have said to me about it over many years (in fact ever since the Liveright days) that the value of the Modern Library book was that it was easy to carry, comfortable to hold, took up very small space in the home and took very little out of the pocketbook."[25] To Sussman, the format and price of the books deserved top billing in all advertisements. For the most part, Cerf agreed. As a result the Modern Library advertisements refused to shame the "civilized minority"—a group Cerf and Sussman felt would be offended by such appeals—with promotions that belittled their intelligence. Such methods might work with deodorants, soaps, or even Dr. Eliot's Five-Foot Shelf, but the Modern Library's assumed audience demanded a more "rational" approach. At the same time its advertisements were up-front in their commercialism. They treated the books as products by stressing their physical quality, repeating the distinctive colophon trademark, and always mentioning price. The civilized minority readers of the *New York Times Book Review*, it was assumed, were educated consumers who knew how to read advertisements and recognize a good deal.

Most book advertisements of the 1930s ignored price. Publishers and booksellers theorized that advertisements ought to pique potential buyers' interest and entice them into a bookstore where the sales staff would complete the sale. They reasoned that publicizing a book's price would only discourage buyers.[26] But Modern Library advertisements flaunt price: "95¢" is often the dominant typographic feature, and every Modern Library advertisement highlighted it. Price was a key selling feature rather than a liability. Books were (and continue to be) regarded by most people as luxury items, with, say, the three dollars for a copy of *Gone with the Wind* in 1935 a major entertainment expense six times the cost of a movie.[27] The typical trade novel of the 1930s cost between two and three dollars, while the Modern Library held its price at ninety-five cents from 1922 until after World War II.

Eager to keep a safe distance from nineteenth-century "cheap books," the Modern Library refused to equate inexpensive with cheap. The advertisements compared Modern Library edition prices with those of the original editions, but just as frequently they linked price to quality production. The designs of Rockwell Kent and Elmer Adler, the books' "attractive limp binding," and later, the "colorful balloon cloth," and the printing "from clear, new type on good paper," all were underscored by advertising to assure readers they would get fine examples of the bookmaker's art for just under a dollar: "Even if these books were printed on the cheapest paper, and bound in inexpensive cardboard, the value would be great. But each Modern Library volume is printed on high grade antique book paper, hand bound in limp Croft [imitation leather].... Never, in the history of publishing, has there been such an opportunity to secure works which have made their place in literature, in so beautiful a format, at so low a price."[28] Cerf and Klopfer clearly associated their product with the finely printed book, an object with a rich history imbued with wealth and aesthetic sophistication. In this way they could push price while distinguishing both their readers' tastes and their books' quality.

Furthermore, price could be used to ally the Modern Library with an egalitarian ideal central to most visions of an organic culture. In its advertisements the Modern Library became a democratic institution committed to dismantling economic barriers in the important arena of reading.[29] As early as 1926 an advertisement stressed the Modern Library's capacity to transcend class barriers and create a true literate democracy: "The finest works of the world's greatest modern writers have been gathered in this one series—fiction, biography, drama, poetry, belles-lettres—and designed to sell to those thousands and thousands of people who, either because they could not or would not pay more than a dollar for a book, never had the opportunity of adding them to their library before." In this view, financial constraint alone barred a literate, intelligent public with an already developed personal taste from enjoying the great modern writers. By making prior cultural disenfranchisement a purely economic function, the advertisement tacitly confirmed that, given a chance, Americans could nurture a genuine culture and that the Modern Library had opened the doors to "those thousands and thousands." Not without guile, the advertisement even proposed a modern, convenient monthly buying plan: "Begin building your own Modern Library shelf now. A few titles added each month—ninety-five cents a copy is such a trifling cost!—and in short order you'll have a row of fine books that will be a distinct addition to your library table or shelves."[30] Mentioning the library table and shelves, traditionally associated with wealth, provided a dose of flattery to soothe over any suspicions about the propriety of building a home library on the installment plan and reiterated the Modern Library's fine physical attributes.

Other advertisements encouraged potential buyers to regard the series as an equalizing force in culture rather than as a series of cheap reprints: it could make any interested reader the bibliophile's equal. The assertion, "The books that sell in the Modern Library series for 95¢ each cost from $2 to $10 a copy in other editions—and the contents are exactly the same," was a mainstay of its publicity. "Four of the latest Modern Library titles were never before obtainable except in *expensive limited editions*," trumpeted one advertisement, and another featured the entire list under the bold, cursive banner, "Out of the Luxury Class for the First Time."[31] Ten years later the class appeal was even more pronounced: a cartoon juxtaposed a grand manor with a mobile home and was captioned, "Whether you live in a castle . . . or in a trailer . . . the Modern Library provides you with 215 of the greatest books ever written . . . for only 95¢ each."[32] Despite the obvious economic disparity between the dwellings, each could house the same quality library. Books, home libraries, even the act of reading all have a long association with those to the manor born; although the Modern Library could not erase economic differences, it could help create a genuine "republic of letters" by collapsing class differences in reading. Through the series everyone had equal access to "the best," at least in one realm.

In the depths of the Depression, an advertisement suggested taking a few Modern Library books along on vacation: "There is no depression deep enough to spoil the pleasure of really good books."[33] This advertisement's uncharacteristic hard-heartedness, appearing as it did in the summer of 1932 when one-fourth of the nation's workforce was unemployed, suggests the limits of the Modern Library's attempt to enlarge the republic of letters. Summer vacations, at least of the paid variety, still belonged only to the professional and business classes, and for all its declarations of a reading democracy, it was among these consumers that the Modern Library sought its audience.

Although some advertisements claimed, "The Modern Library is a reading habit many people, rich and poor, young and old, are proud to have acquired," and others appealed to the thrifty, their egalitarian claims were somewhat disingenuous.[34] The advertisements nearly always depicted typical readers as economically comfortable. In the early 1930s, Cerf himself appraised his audience: "A good half of the people who now buy *Modern Library* books regularly, the new titles each month as they are issued, can well afford to spend more than 95¢ a copy for their books. Many of them have extensive and expensive libraries and buy the *Modern Library* mainly on account of the high standard of titles issued and the convenient format. The price, although pleasant, is to them incidental."[35] Relatively insulated from the worst effects of the Depression, most Modern Library buyers could still afford such discretionary purchases as books. In addition to enjoying vacations, advertised readers often possessed a home library, played golf and bridge, and occasionally boarded airplanes, all suggesting the "luxury" class from which the books purportedly had been liberated. A 1936 advertisement illustrated a well-dressed man packing his suitcase with four Modern Library volumes. Above and off to the side, an idealized "thought bubble" depicted a sailboat underway with a crew of three vacationers. "Take along Modern Library Books! convenient to carry, inexpensive to own," the text enjoined.[36] Part of the appeal is associational—buy Modern Library books and become like the wealthy people portrayed—but it was also a frank appeal to the theorized base market for the Modern Library.

The constant repetition of price was a two-edged sword pointed at the minds and hearts of professional–managerial *New York Times Book Review* subscribers. Buying quality books in a good format at the lowest cost appealed directly to the thinking person's thrift—the series was a smart buy—but the egalitarian angle also dovetailed with the political views of many members of that class, which, sandwiched between the true bourgeois capitalists who owned the means of production and the working class, felt a deep ambivalence about advanced capitalism. As a class, it was an agent of capitalist coercion, but its members resented their own ultimate lack of control over the means of production; they saw their labors producing profits and power for a more elite class. Educated and concerned about social progress, it is not surprising that many of its members were deeply attracted to socialist and reform movements, especially those that sought to empower trained experts.[37] Modern Library advertisements not only made the series a liberal means to achieve social equality—its low price erased class inequity in the all-important arena of culture—but their glorification of the civilized minority established a social arena ordered around intelligence.

Members of the professional–managerial class fancied themselves distinctly "modern" in outlook, and they exercised personal taste to display their status. They bought the latest streamlined automobiles, chose the fashions displayed in *Vogue* or *Harper's Bazaar,* and looked on modern art and architecture with approval.[38] They were not, as Cerf and Klopfer conceived them, money-grubbing Babbitts, but civilized, literate, and self-consciously forward-looking. Although the Book-of-the-Month Club offered a refuge from the pressures of modernity, and the Harvard Classics drew on the genteel notion that "background" could come from reading the correct texts, both shied away from the complexities of modernism. The Modern Library, true to its name, embraced modernity, both as an up-to-date lifestyle and as an aesthetic. Its advertisements pointedly alluded to "the modern mind" or "the modern age" and constantly stressed the freshness of the series. Each title in the Modern Library "has something that *stimulates* and *profits* the modern mind," read one advertisement.[39] Another boasted that each book in the series "can justly be called a 'modern classic,'" and "each is a miracle of modern publishing."[40] The reiteration of "modern" was complemented by depictions of Modern Library readers being conspicuously modern: boarding planes, playing golf or bridge (both popularized in the 1920s), and climbing into jaunty roadsters.

These emblems of modernity connoted leisure time—a precious asset that became increasingly available in the twentieth century. The Modern Library purposefully equated reading with "modern" leisure activities at a time when critics were concerned that reading habits might diminish as moviegoing, card playing, and automobile touring sapped free time.[41] Cerf and Klopfer saw no conflict between modern recreation and reading, and they pointed to the portability of their books as evidence that reading still fitted into modern recreational patterns. Taken together, the images and texts present the series as a thoroughly modern set of books appealing to men and women with modern lifestyles and minds, while positioning reading as a relaxing leisure activity.

American modernity of the 1920s contained "an extended tradition of questioning and contesting dominant gender norms" especially in intellectual circles: the modern mind embraced the Nineteenth Amendment, flappers defied traditional roles, women made modest economic and legal gains, and Greenwich Village radicals explored ways to create gender equality.[42] With a modern sensibility, Modern Library advertisements courted both men and women. In an era in which the masculine pronoun was routinely used to identify unspecified individuals, 1920s and 1930s Modern Library advertisements often used inclusive language or the personal "you." Women appeared in illustrations as often as men in their advertisements and more frequently as actual readers. One advertisement made the traditionally masculine library unisex when it averred that the Modern Library contained "books which belong in the library of every well-read man or woman."[43] Such inclusiveness was practical and not altogether unprecedented in trade book advertising. Publishers knew women constituted the majority of fiction readers, and they certainly read more than men in the 1920s and 1930s.[44] Curiously, the Book-of-the-Month Club tried to explain away its 60 percent female membership by suggesting that women subscribed for their husbands. Likewise, the Harvard Classic promotions were always directed toward men. Critics often linked these and other "middlebrow" ventures with a moribund and decidedly feminine genteel culture.[45] The self-consciously "modern" Modern Library could invite women readers without fear of being marginalized or dismissed as genteel, even as the Book-of-the-Month Club and Harvard Classics felt a constant need to shed their genteel–feminine associations. The Modern Library had much to gain by employing the trappings of sexual equality. Gender-neutral advertising not only welcomed all book buyers, but it also presented the series as socially progressive enough to appeal to the political views of most professional–managerial readers.

Throughout the 1930s a tension emerged from the insistent stress on newness and modernity as the Modern Library embraced older literary classics. A 1928 advertisement had confidently, if illogically, declared that its wares had "passed the test of time and criticism, and belong forever to the reading public," despite the predominance of such recent titles as James Joyce's *Portrait of the Artist as a Young Man,* Virginia Woolf's *Mrs. Dalloway,* and Theodore Dreiser's *Twelve Men.*[46] Nearly a decade later, after the addition of such authors as Confucius and Horace, advertising described the books as "the classics which are still modern: the modern works which have become classics."[47]

Cerf recognized the potential in this tension and saw a list that embraced the moderns and the classics as a powerful selling point.[48] Its heterogeneity indicated that the series was neither sectarian nor prescriptive: it permitted wide latitude to the intelligent reader who, advertisements consistently stressed, could exercise his or her personal taste. "Which of these 109 Outstanding Books Do You Want," asked one; another introduced new titles with "Now... Your Choice of these 201 World Famous Books"; a third assured the reader, "You, too, can have your choice of these great Modern Library books."[49] Occluding the suggestion that any institutional force directed the Modern Library, one advertisement misleadingly credited the readers themselves with selecting new titles in the series by claiming, "More than a million American book-lovers aided in the selection of these books as outstanding, all-time favorites."[50]

In a logical sense, such praise of its audience's discriminating taste contradicted another claim the Modern Library advertised almost as frequently, that its books were so carefully culled from literature that an errant choice was impossible. One advertisement claimed the series had "an unswerving policy of publishing nothing but established successes—thus eliminating all costly experiments"; another, quoting a *Chicago Daily News* critic, claimed, "'You could stand before a stack of these books, shut your eyes and pick out the right one every time.'"[51] Personal choice perhaps, but the Modern Library's publicity assured insecure consumers that no choice could be a *faux pas* because each title was a sure thing. The Modern Library applied virtually the same strategy used to sell luxury goods: an honored trademark guaranteed unimpeachable quality, and the purchase of such a commodity demonstrated the buyer's discriminating personal taste. Seen in this light, the Modern Library, not individual titles, was the wise choice.

Highlighting the notion of choice did more than simply flatter the audience's presumed intelligence, however; it further emphasized the Modern Library as a force for literary democracy. Not long after Cerf and Klopfer acquired the series, an anonymous writer in the *Bookman* asked, "Has America a Literary Dictatorship?" The writer worried about the Book-of-the-Month Club's potentially chilling effect on American literary production because its vast membership virtually assured that the five-member editorial board's selection would be a bestseller. The club, with its automated distribution system, spoon-fed books to members "too feeble-minded, too lazy, or too busy to make their own choice of a book in a bookshop."[52] The board and the distribution system supporting it constituted an anti-American restriction of freedom. Janice Radway sees the *Bookman*'s contrast of "the independent, rational, democratic subject against a vision of authority as centralized, organized, interested, and despotic" as a rhetorical attempt to rescue disinterested culture from the clutches of monopoly capitalism and restore culture's democratic quality.[53] The Modern Library's heightened attention to reader choice and discrimination established the series as the antithesis of the Book-of-the-Month Club. In reality, the Book-of-the-Month Club and the Modern Library were not so dissimilar in one important aspect: both offered readers preapproved goods, while maintaining a fiction of unfettered choice. Club promotions always reminded members that they could reject the editorial board's choice and select from the fairly extensive list of sanctified alternative selections, or choose nothing at all so long as they purchased at least four books per year. The Modern Library also offered an extensive list of prechosen titles each with its trademark stamp of approval. The two services were by no means identical, but they both presented readers with a limited range of books culled from the world's literature. A key difference for critics such as *Bookman*'s "Anonymous" who were wary of "standardization" lies in distribution. Modern Library advertisements placed capable readers in bookstores where they could choose any book from any publisher in good democratic fashion. Book-of-the-Month Club promotions restricted the consumer to the home where an authoritative organization delivered a book for selection or rejection. The club's "negative option" system depended on consumer inertia and ensured steady sales, but its aggressive demands erased the notion of disinterested choice that the Modern Library cultivated.

Rarely, the individual autonomy so many of the advertisements proclaimed was subverted by appeals to mere popularity. On these occasions the Modern Library violated its own maxim: rather than treat its readers as members of a select group of discriminating individuals, the advertisements made them part of a mass audience. After yearly sales passed one million, figures were deployed to proclaim its importance: "1,160,306 readers a year can't be wrong."[54] Other advertisements boasted bestseller status for many titles (which in the current sense of the word they were not, although they were among the most-purchased Modern Library titles). Cheney had been disgusted by the whole notion of "bestsellerism," and thought it was an "unhealthy" method of promotion and "a tribute to the theory that book buyers are sheep."⁵⁵ "Best-sellerism" defied disinterested reason to make a book's virtue rest purely on its sales record rather than its literary merit.

Although some advertisements may have claimed popularity to attract readers wanting to fit in with the larger group, they avoided the naked exploitation of potential buyers' personal insecurities. Many types of producers, particularly of soap and mouthwash, but also purveyors of cultural goods, used this tactic—the attack-mode strategy Sussman had rejected when he ridiculed the "If you ever read books (and if you don't you ought to)" ploy. Most trade publishers shied away from such demeaning promotions for new titles, but they reveled in them when issuing standard sets or promoting various book clubs. The Book-of-the-Month Club and Dr. Eliot's Five-Foot Shelf of Harvard Classics shamelessly played on consumer insecurities and promised to act as cultural advisers. The Harvard Classics penetrated "the cold stone front of a public library" to answer the mysterious and intimidating question, "What are the really great books?" A typical Five-Foot-Shelf advertisement virtually shouted: "How to get rid of an INFERIORITY COMPLEX," and continued with, "A true story of a man who found that self-confidence is not a matter of education or luck." This unfortunate young businessman lacked "the mysterious thing called 'background,'" which, it turns out, was simply "an understanding of world culture." Not surprisingly, the advertisement narrates a transformative success story: the man purchased his Harvard Classics, obtained "culture," and then, "instead of envying his once better informed associates" became "their equal." The advertisement sketched out an educational deficiency and a cultural naïveté that created a social failing, and then offered a cure as the motivating force for purchasing the Harvard Classics.⁵⁶

The Modern Library tapped into readers' guilt, too, but did so without demeaning their intelligence. One advertisement began in the first person, "Here are the books I have always wanted to read," and then switched to a pluralized conversational completion of the wish:

> But you've never gotten around to it? That is the way with all of us and the books we really want. We haven't time! They're too expensive! We can find excuses forever. It is a pity, for the books we look forward to reading are invariably the most worthwhile. And all the treasures you have promised to yourself some day, can be yours now for

very little money.... It's for you and me and all of us who enjoy good literature that the Modern Library publishes invaluable books, knowing we will want them some day. Read the list of titles below and turn that SOME DAY into NOW.[57]

Although there is a gentle chiding in the advertisement ("We can find excuses forever."), its overall tone is one of empathetic commiseration. The reader is neither grossly inadequate nor deficient in "background." The appeal is a positive one: the reader is motivated by pleasure and a genuine desire to read for enlightenment. Moreover, he or she is made equal to the conversational partner by the use of collective pronouns. The potential consumer's failure is explicable, no disgrace—only a pity. Neither did the artwork in this advertisement pander to a notion that this reading would be effortless. Two of the three books depicted were *Swann's Way* and *The Brothers Karamazov,* among the most demanding works of modern fiction in both time and mental effort, although the third, *The Comprehensive Anthology of American Poetry,* perhaps represented the more recreational side of reading. The advertisements assumed consumers whose taste did not require expert guidance because they already had ideas about which books were most worthwhile, those they had "always" meant to read. In assuming this stance, then stressing availability and low cost, the Modern Library masked the fact that they had already selected "the best" and were acting as a guide to good reading.

The Book-of-the-Month Club advertisements often addressed potential subscribers with some of the same pitches the Modern Library employed, but always with an element absent from Modern Library promotions, one that evoked consumers' anxieties. One advertisement resembled a Modern Library promotion by asking readers, "How often have outstanding books appeared, widely discussed and widely recommended, books you were really anxious to read and fully intended to read when you 'got around to it,' but which nevertheless you *missed*!" But rather than "turn[ing] that some day into now," as the Modern Library brightly urged, the Book-of-the-Month Club attempted to evoke self-loathing and shame: "Why is it you disappoint yourself?" Negative feelings could be overcome by showing resolve and accepting the expert advice of the Book-of-the-Month Club. It would sift through the dross and identify the cultural gold for busy would-be readers. Joan Shelley Rubin has denominated this the "symptom and cure" approach. The club assured efficient and modern expertise to provide intellectual and cultural security in a confusing world. It targeted educated consumers and offered to help them join "the intellectual elite of the country"; the Modern Library sought out the same group but treated them as though they were already members of that elite by avoiding allusions to their inadequacies.[58]

The Modern Library was not immune to the 1930s advertising obsession with guilt, but when it did subtly try to activate potential consumers' guilt, it did so in a way that also invoked their "inherent" good taste. Such appeals to purchase the Modern Library cleverly combined a gentle reprimand with flattery. One advertisement asked rhetorically, "Are you sick of reading Trash?" and another, "Sick of Sappy Stories?" Formulated so, these questions could only evoke a positive, and slightly shamefaced, response. Disgusted with their light reading indulgences, purchasers of the Modern Library would discover "the best literature of every age," books "worth while and entertaining." The advertisements also assured readers they were up to the task: "Out of the 190 titles there will be many to interest you," and they are "the books you know you will enjoy."[59]

The idea that the Modern Library contained "the best literature of every age" could easily be transformed into claims for the instructive qualities of the series, and, in this way, establish it as a cultural guide without demeaning its readers' intelligence. The Harvard Classics always centered its appeal on the idea that it offered a complete liberal arts education. The Modern Library at times expressed the same idea, but less brazenly. "There is no better guide to good reading than the list of Modern Library titles," which "has grown to a national institution" proclaimed one advertisement.[60] Another stated, "There is no better proof of good taste in reading, than a thorough knowledge of the titles included in this enduring series."[61] And a third parenthetically stated, "(Some say this famous list can show quite accurately how well-read one really is.)"[62] The Modern Library could easily have turned its reputation as a guide to good reading into high-pressure sales pitches—and on occasion it did so. One advertisement, for example, asserted: "The Modern Library includes books by the great authors of the past and today—titles that inevitably enter any intelligent discussion of literature."[63] The threat of social embarrassment is invoked, but in a more subdued way than by the Harvard Classics.

By compiling important writings from different traditions, eras, and genres, Cerf and Klopfer positioned the Modern Library as a well-rounded introduction to literature and culture. In their first catalog they began to extol the series as an educational institution: "Purposeful reading is taking the place of miscellaneous dabbling in literature, and The Modern Library is being daily recommended by notable educators as a representative library of modern thought."[64] The catalog stressed the potential service of the series to individuals seeking self-culture by presenting it as an educational alternative to aimless reading; the series provided a map for anyone eager to navigate the complexities of modern thought.

Autodidactic reading such as that proposed by Modern Library promotions received a significant institutional boost from Columbia University. At the same time that Albert Boni was selecting the first Modern Library titles and young Bennett Cerf was attending Columbia University, John Erskine was laying out plans for a two-year course to familiarize undergraduates with Western Civilization's "great books." Like many of his colleagues, Erskine worried that too many of his students perceived an impenetrable barrier between themselves and the classics. He reasoned that all classics were originally written for popular audiences, but their haughty reputations, exacerbated by scholars' often obtuse interventions, made them daunting to students. For Erskine, "A great book is one that has meaning, and continues to have meaning, for a variety of people over a long period of time," and a true classic ought to speak to the modern mind as effectively as it spoke to its original audience. He wanted his students to both delight and profit from the confidence and intellectual stimulation inspired by direct encounters with the great books.[65]

The war allowed Erskine to test his plan on soldiers overseas, and in 1920 he began to teach his reading list at Columbia, where it soon entered the regular curriculum. The American Library Association reproduced and widely distributed Erskine's list in *Classics of the Western World* to facilitate library-sponsored great-book reading groups. True to Erskine's vision, the list was presented with a minimum of scholarly apparatus. Capitalizing on its public library success, the program of self-culture through purposeful reading reached a kind of popular apogee in 1940 with the release of *How to Read a Book: The Art of Getting a Liberal Education* by Erskine's former student Mortimer J. Adler. Adler also believed a direct relationship with the great books would enable people "to lead the distinctively human life of reason," although he felt it necessary to accompany his list with nearly four hundred pages of instructions.[66]

As their first catalog suggested, Cerf and Klopfer recognized that America's tradition of democratic self-culture offered enormous sales potential. Fifteen years later they snatched at the advertising possibilities afforded by Adler's popular guide. A full-page advertisement boasted that fifty-one of the titles listed in *How to Read a Book* were included in the Modern Library (figure 3). With a bit of Adler's pomposity, the advertisement claimed: "Here are the books on which our civilization rests. They are the basic works of all literatures (here presented, of course, in the English tongue) which intelligent people today as always turn to for inspiration, guidance, enrichment." But then it echoed Erskine's original ideas and eased readers' insecurities that might bar access to the classics: "And lest that sound too austere, let us remind you that here, too, are *the most popular* of all books: the great novels, the fascinating stories and plays and poems that have thrilled, literally, millions. They provide the best kind of relaxation."[67] The advertisement featured *Tom Jones, The Wisdom of Confucius,* and *The Prince,* sandwiched between *Six Plays by Clifford Odets* and Vincent Sheean's *Personal History* and *Of Human Bondage,* to modernize the classics and give the stamp of authority on the contemporary authors in the series.

Self-culture was originally touted as an honorable path toward a cultivation of character. A deep, internalized understanding of culture gained through careful study of "the best which has been thought and said" could lead to moral goodness. This concept of character development was blended with the twentieth-century emphasis on an outward display of refinement (personality) by such institutions as the Book-of-the-Month Club and the Harvard Classics.[68] The Modern Library, proudly in alliance with a movement dedicated to breaking down genteel notions of culture, self-denial, and refinement, seemed unafraid of linking itself with the tradition of self-culture—a stance overtly displayed in the series slogan, "The World's Best Books." Modern Library advertisements promised a thorough knowledge of its books would promote "good taste" and "intelligent discussion," but, tellingly, the *How to Read a Book* tie-in subordinated the educational qualities of the series to the "thrilling stories" and "relaxing reading" the series provided. The Modern Library always mixed appeals to self-culture with professions that, above all else, the series was fun. The genteel notion of serious,

FIGURE 3. Tie-in to Mortimer Adler's *How to Read a Book*. From *New York Times Book Review,* 19 May 1940. Joseph Regenstein Library, University of Chicago.

disinterested study collapses beneath the idea of personal enjoyment that comes from reading "a few really good books." In this way Cerf and Klopfer told readers they could have their cake and eat it, too. As intelligent, autonomous beings they could follow their aesthetic sense to select a really good book for personal pleasure. The self-culture was a fringe benefit that came naturally through the exercise of good taste and the rejection of "trash" or "sappy stories."

The advertisements Cerf targeted at the largest potential market through the pages of the *New York Times Book Review* presented the series as particularly expressive of key American ideals: it offered a popular choice of titles independent of a "literary dictatorship," while its price overcame class inequity to foster a truly democratic republic of letters. Equally important here, the progressive series absorbed the relevant ideas of the past. Erskine thought a "true culture" would involve the past but "circle through the moment in which we breathe," and his radical counterpart, Randolph Bourne, sought a genuine culture reflective of the modern mind. The Modern Library advertising satisfied both versions of authentic culture: it embraced the past while remaining modern in spirit.

Cerf never overexpanded his advertising. A 1938 study by Harcourt, Brace and Company found that many book readers regularly bought the *Saturday Evening Post* and the *Ladies' Home Journal,* and their combined six million readers must have seemed attractive to a publisher seeking larger markets. But Harcourt's study also showed that the percentage of book buyers who read mass-market magazines was astoundingly low compared to the percentages who read more "bookish" magazines such as the *Nation, Atlantic Monthly,* and the *Saturday Review of Literature.*[69] As a result, advertising in bookish magazines with smaller circulations was a far more efficient use of the advertising dollar. An advertisement in *Life* might reach five times as many book buyers as one in the *Atlantic Monthly,* but it cost roughly twenty times as much. Cerf believed he could expand his market by focusing his limited resources on media appealing to book buyers. Inexpensive, closely targeted advertisements reflected the kind of strategic planning recommended in "An Advertising Catechism" and "They Aren't Toothpaste."

Despite the admission of *Printers' Ink* that "books are different," Cerf succeeded in using brand-name strategies to sell the series as a whole. But *Printers' Ink* had also warned that, even if book advertising could successfully generate consumer desire, the nation's primitive book distribution system would limit advertising's effectiveness. As *Printers' Ink* put it, "You can't force a river through a six-inch pipe."[70] To make the Modern Library's advertising an effective part of a broader marketing strategy, the partners' next step was to find a way around an outdated, inefficient national book distribution system.

CHAPTER THREE

Booming the World's Best Books

Surveying the expanded reprint market in 1939, *Publishers' Weekly* editor Frederic G. Melcher observed: "The pocket library idea of the Bonis and their *Modern Library* flowered into a vast distribution program when Bennett Cerf and Donald Klopfer took it over."[1] The blossoming occurred in part because the young partners gladly treated their books as basic consumer goods amenable to the strenuous marketing that befitted soap, beer, or any other manufactured commodity. At times their "booming" pushed the limits of respectability: they explored mass-distribution strategies such as mail-order plans, pyramid schemes, "traps" in vacation resorts, and their own "Book-A-Month Plan."[2] Although such inventive distribution plans produced modest sales, traditional outlets including bookstores, college stores, and department stores proved to be the Modern Library's key to success. With wit and ingenuity Cerf and Klopfer persuaded these outlets to adopt modern marketing techniques such as attractive point-of-sale displays, promotional contests, and high-visibility product placement. Sales skyrocketed during the Depression, but all the while the partners obscured their overt commercialism from potential critics' limited fields of vision to preserve the Modern Library's reputation as America's finest reprint series.

EXPANDING THE SIX-INCH PIPE

In 1931 a baffled Malcolm Cowley decided Americans had abandoned the book-buying habit. *Ben Hur* had sold over one million copies in the 1880s and, Cowley reasoned, with the 1920s population more numerous and more affluent, the best-selling *Main Street* ought to have sold in the millions.[3] Although the actual sales figure of six hundred thousand copies left him grasping for a clue to a possible "book strike," many people in the publishing industry merely shook their heads in resignation. According to the conventional wisdom of the industry, the country could claim only two hundred thousand regular book buyers.[4] In America, "serious literature" sold to the discriminating thousands, never the millions. Firmly believing most Americans were anti-intellectual and only semiliterate, contemptuous critics such as H. L. Mencken dismissed the public as incapable of supporting a healthy book industry.[5] Even Lewis Mumford, who held fast to his faith in America's promise, thought, "The real difficulty with increasing the circulation of good books—and this is the only kind that need seriously concern us—is the fact that we have not a sufficiently large audience of intelligent and cultured people ready to absorb them."[6]

Defenders of the public taste such as J. George Frederick, president of the New York Business Bourse, on the other hand, thought the country's book-buying woes resulted from the "bookish snobs" dominating literary production. Members of the literati were "haters of the public at large," he said, who antidemocratically wrote for their own exclusive cult of the "Seven Smart Sophisticates." He believed that, when authors stopped "sneering at the pit," book buyers would number "not in the thousands, but in the millions."[7] While publishers, writers, and most critics damned the public taste, and Frederick scorned a cliquish system, all parties agreed on one thing: in the current climate, literature and the American middle class were at serious odds.

Despite paltry book sales, the United States had a large reading public, but only mass-market magazines and a few exceptional novels could reach the coveted millions. In 1929, two dollars and fifty cents was spent on magazines and newspapers for every dollar on books.[8] Taking into account the tremendous cost differential between a book and a magazine or newspaper, it is not surprising that critic Robert Duffus thought periodicals carved "heavy lines in our cultural pattern," while books were "but faint traceries." Drawing on public and rental library circulation figures, book sales statistics, and personal experience, Duffus generously estimated that the typical American read seven books per year (two purchased, two rented, two borrowed from a library, and one borrowed from a friend).[9] But public library surveys supported book-industry claims of a small book-buying public by showing that a small minority of Americans read well above Duffus's seven-book average and the "vast majority" rarely, if ever, opened a book.[10]

Buoyed by the Little Leather Library's fleeting but spectacular mail-order sales in the early 1920s, aggressive marketers such as Harry Scherman were convinced that lack of availability, rather than insufficient interest, inferior taste, or poor reading ability, frustrated millions of potential book buyers.[11] In the late 1920s, over 26 percent of U.S. counties lacked a bookseller of any kind, and in rural areas the figures were even more dismal. Thirty-two million Americans, slightly more than one-fourth the population, did not have ready access to a retail bookseller.[12] Compounding the problem was the fact that most book outlets were not bookstores, but drugstores or stationery shops carrying only a small stock of popular books. Most of the 5,662 book outlets listed in 1929 carried a limited line of Grosset & Dunlap books as an inconsequential "side line."[13]

Cerf and Klopfer cautiously expanded their new business by scouring the Eastern seaboard to secure new outlets. They were excellent face-to-face salesmen who enjoyed selling. "We just had a ball," Klopfer remembered of those early days. "We split the selling. One trip I would go north from New York with a bag of books, to Stamford, New Haven, New London, Providence, Boston, up as far as Portland, Maine, into Worcester and Northampton to get the Smith College trade, Springfield. . . . Then he would go South. Next time I would go South and he would go North. We went as far as Richmond. From Richmond to Portland."[14] And Cerf recalled the benefits of ownership: "When we went into a store to sell our books, the bookseller knew he was meeting the actual publishers. They liked that. We'd also take the time to check to see what titles were missing. We weren't just salesmen now, we were in it for ourselves. And we were beginning to be heard about. We got The Modern Library into many stores that Liveright had never bothered with."[15]

Face-to-face expansion into regional bookstore outlets could never keep up with the Modern Library's production capabilities, and as early as 1930 the series' supply outstripped its distribution network. The partners knew how to produce an attractive product at an attractive price, and their advertising was stimulating demand, but economies of scale in mass production could only be implemented if the products were to be delivered to a mass audience. In 1930, Cerf told advertisers in *Printers' Ink*, "Today the reprint publishers are just getting into the question of mass distribution. That, probably, is the next big problem to be solved."[16]

The college market was a natural site for expansion. Like many other Modern Library devotees, Cerf and Klopfer had first encountered the series as college students; and as modern literature crept into the syllabi of English departments in the late 1920s, many Modern Library titles became required reading.[17] Their portability and price were well suited to student needs. Granville Hicks used the series extensively because his courses at Smith involved "a great deal of reading" and, "Inasmuch as we cannot ask the girls to buy many expensive books, we are trying to select for assigned reading works which are available in reasonably priced editions."[18] In 1928 he assigned his class the Modern Library editions of Wells's *Ann Veronica,* Joyce's *Dubliners,* Anderson's *Winesburg, Ohio,* and Lawrence's *Sons and Lovers* and recommended Butler's *The Way of All Flesh,* Hudson's *Green Mansions,* and Douglas's *South Wind* as supplementary reading.[19]

Initially Cerf and Klopfer contracted textbook publisher F. S. Crofts to push the series in the college market, but when Crofts failed to achieve satisfactory results, Cerf took over college promotions.[20] He addressed mailings to philosophy, contemporary literature, and English department heads touting the series as a teaching tool.[21] He then followed up with letters to college bookstores that focused on the series as profitable staple stock.[22] All college bookstores supplied textbooks, but only a few maintained general book departments.[23] Although several titles were routinely assigned in classes, including Dewey's *Human Nature and Conduct,* Darwin's *Origin of Species,* and Hardy's *The Return of the Native,* Cerf reasoned that the series was a convenient, cost-effective way to establish a book department and stimulate noncourse-related book sales.[24] He backed his mailing campaigns with editorial copy secured in the *College Store* (the National Association of College Stores' trade magazine) as a quid pro quo for advertising.[25] In "A Modern Interview," the magazine asked rhetorically, "How many booksellers have studied how to utilize this excellent low-priced series to the best advantage in building a real book department that meets the special needs of students?" The magazine article drew on prepared copy to expand on the Modern Library's benefits: "For these little books are 'feeders' for a whole book-merchandising program. Students who come in to look over the Modern Library titles are potentially the most permanent book buyers. They are habitual readers and can become buyers of other—and more expensive—kinds of books."[26] An advertisement in the same issue declared synergistically, "Here's your complete, self-contained book department," and promised "generous discounts, displays, catalogs for distribution, and other helps" to interested college bookstores.[27] The college market offered immediate sales but, more important, it reached fledgling members of the professional–managerial market Cerf and Klopfer coveted. The partners knew that, if they could hook these "habitual readers" young, they might well keep them for life.

College bookstores produced new Modern Library sales and cemented the series' educational association implied in its advertising campaigns, but these stores served a severely limited market. The postal system appeared to hold much greater promise: the Little Leather Library had thrived on mail distribution, and the Book-of-the-Month Club was still undergoing rapid expansion. But the mail-order coupons Cerf and Klopfer routinely featured in Modern Library advertisements attracted few buyers, even from rural areas without book outlets.[28] Little Leather Library sales only exploded after Harry Scherman and Maxwell Sackheim teased prospective buyers with sample covers enclosed in direct mailings that presented the books as elegant markers of cultural distinction.[29] Similarly, the Book-of-the Month Club advertisements offered readers compelling reasons to subscribe. Merely providing the coupon mechanism for mail-order sales was not enough: the Modern Library would have to present an appeal beyond convenient delivery.

Modern Library sales agent J. J. Hatcher thought more commercial hype might stimulate greater mail-order sales and he designed a direct-mail campaign to attract new buyers with the promise of self-improvement: "It seems to me that the most effective note, is the cultural note, in other words the idea that 'here is the thing that you have been waiting for' and [that] 'if you wish to be informed and if you wish your intellect to help you in business etc.'"[30] Hatcher's shorthand description of the "cultural note" without elaboration and ending in "etc." illustrates just how conventional the sentiment had become. For two decades the Harvard Classics had been filling magazine pages with just such a "cultural note," and the Book-of-the-Month Club employed the same stratagem.[31] It insinuated that the purchase of recognized "culture" would translate into personal fulfillment, social confidence, and financial success; and it was just such an approach that Modern Library newspaper and magazine advertisements had avoided. Hatcher's admission, "It is a cheap note but it sells the books and more than that it can be done not only adroitly but with a pseudo dignity," substantiated the fears critics such as Robert Duffus had about false "culture."[32] Advertisers' cynical manipulations and snobbish posturing stripped legitimate culture of its disinterested air and transformed it into a mundane commodity. The "pseudo dignity" ruthlessly cheapened organic culture so it became spurious "culture" passed off for profit on a gullible public.

Cerf and Klopfer resisted Hatcher's "cultural note" until 1931, when they wedded it to reader guilt in their new "Book-A-Month Plan." A direct-mailing boldly emblazoned "Entertainment," "Instruction," and "Self-Culture" chided readers: "many MODERN LIBRARY buyers say to themselves: 'Now, I am going to buy at least one book every month.' But other matters intervene and the 'vow' is forgotten."[33] The subscription service plan could alleviate the guilt of forgotten vows (an especially unsettling suggestion considering the flyer promoted the plan as "the perfect gift for bride and bridegroom") by conveniently and automatically delivering the "world's great masterpieces." The "cultural note" introduced the specious claim that the books would be the reader's "choice." New Modern Library titles were released on a monthly basis until 1936, and the Book-A-Month Plan would simply deliver the latest release. The consumer "chose" the Modern Library, not individual titles. The Book-A-Month Plan's utilization of a disingenuous "choice" and hard-sell "cultural note" is a rare instance of conscious misrepresentation by the Modern Library, and it marked the partners' notable early attempts to find a more commercial alternative to traditional book-selling methods. The next year the Modern Library quietly unveiled an elaborate chain-selling system to create a second alternative to traditional distribution. According to the plan, again promoted through direct mail, an individual who bought two Modern Library volumes at regular price would then be issued a serial number and become a commissioned selling agent. After selling four titles, the individual would earn a fifty-cent commission, but as a 1932 flyer promised, the profits were just beginning:

Step 2   People that you sold to sell 4 books—you earn $1.50
Step 3   They sell 4 more—you earn $4.50
Step 4   They sell 4 more—you earn $13.50
Step 5   They sell 4 more—you earn $40.50[34]

The Book-of-the-Month Club caused a furor in the 1920s and 1930s in part because its organizers successfully bypassed traditional book distribution systems. Although the loudest and most durable charges emanated from magazines such as the *Bookman,* the *New Republic,* and the *Atlantic Monthly,* which feared the club was bent on standardizing literature, the initial attacks came from inside the publishing industry.[35] The Book-of-the-Month Club threatened to change the very nature of American book publishing by usurping the bookseller's role. Comparing the club to "an octopus which had fastened its tentacles about the throats of the publishers and is sucking away at the vitals of the book business itself," Dutton chief John Macrae feared it would bankrupt bookstores already operating on a narrow margin and come to dominate American book distribution.[36] If the club controlled distribution, it would become the nation's lone literary gatekeeper and dictate the terms of literary production.

Significantly, Cerf and Klopfer carefully orchestrated both the Book-A-Month Plan and the chain-selling pyramid scheme so they could be tested without drawing unwanted attention. No Modern Library advertisements ever mentioned the new selling plans, and they were promoted only through direct mailings. Executed thus, they targeted select groups using specialized mailing lists and, in this surreptitious way, got past concerned critics, booksellers, and other publishers.[37] Neither nonretail scheme had a significant impact on sales primarily because the partners never committed the resources necessary to make them work. Initiating an unorthodox selling system called for more than direct mailings, it demanded extensive magazine promotion. The Book-of-the-Month Club and the Little Leather Library frequently used direct mailings, but backed them with enormous magazine advertising budgets to attract subscribers.[38] Cerf and Klopfer were unwilling to disseminate information on their potentially risky ventures outside tightly controlled channels. The cultural cost of a full-fledged campaign was too high a price to pay for two businessmen proud of their place in a respected profession. They were just beginning to explore the potential of Random House—a firm they envisioned could become "a publisher of trade books of excellence"—and a well-publicized failure might have destroyed their product's reputation and crushed their hopes of becoming known as distinguished publishers.[39]

SMALL OUTLET RETAIL TRADE

Grosset & Dunlap offered another model for extending distribution beyond bookstores' limited reach: it expanded into the nation's drugstores and newsstands in the 1920s to make its reprints of popular novels the most widely distributed books in America. This option, too, was fraught with peril. O. H. Cheney noticed "the feeling" shared by many authors and most booksellers that "a 'drugstore book' is degrading whereas a 'bookstore book' is uplifting, even though it may be the same title."[40] Theodore Dreiser dogmatically declared, "I don't want my books sold in drugstores," and conservative booksellers wondered how ignorant soda jerks and prescription clerks could possibly proffer bookstore service.[41] That Dreiser, with his legendary disregard of established tradition, agreed with old-guard bookstore owners on this cultural issue illustrates the strange affiliations created by changes in the book distribution system. Hysterical reactions to drugstore marketing justified J. George Frederick's charge that booksellers and most "serious" writers rarely deigned to consider the public at large; instead they satisfied America's "bookish snobs." The iconoclastic Gilbert Seldes saw the drugstore debate as emblematic of an insidious classism among the literati. He scolded writers who considered themselves "friends of the masses" but hated to see their books sold in drugstores where they might fall into the hands of lowly "drugstore customers."[42] Drugstore distribution could reach more readers and sustain mass production, but it risked the character of a series like the Modern Library. Grosset & Dunlap's methods were a highly visible form of commercialism that would threaten to transform the Modern Library from an honored cultural entity into a degraded bit of merchandise.

Cerf and Klopfer shied away from drugstore distribution, probably because it was a highly visible snub to bookstores.[43] Still, they saw potential in newsstands and other small "miscellaneous outfits" that did not threaten booksellers' livelihood. By 1930 the American News Company, which supplied newsstands throughout the country and acted as a jobber for many stationery stores, had placed Modern Library books in railway station newsstand racks.[44] Cerf surmised newsstands and other small outlets reached "the casual buyer, the man who is buying 'something to read' rather than 'a book.'"[45] His analysis suggests the man seeking "something to read" at a newsstand is implicitly less serious than the man buying "a book," presumably at a bookstore. Newsstands, already devoted to reading material, were convenient distribution points serving commuters and other rail travelers looking for distraction, and booksellers reasoned their sales were "water over the dam"[46]—that is, impulse sales to buyers who would not have gone to a bookstore. On the other hand, a government survey showed drugstores attracted Cerf's man looking for a book and might very well pull trade from bookstores.[47] Newsstand distribution might still cheapen the Modern Library in Dreiser's stern eyes, but the general trade saw little potential harm in such methods. Books sales through newsstands never would have occurred without a well-placed bookrack, they reasoned, but drugstore sales kept buyers out of traditional outlets and sapped bookstore profits.

In the early 1930s, Cerf and Klopfer hired Sarah Ball, their most creative and energetic sales agent, to expand intensively into small outlets on the East Coast. She reasoned vacationers wanted good reading, yet often forgot to pack books, so she placed Modern Library racks stocked with forty-five top-selling Modern Library books in tearooms, taverns, inns, and exclusive resort hotel lobbies throughout New England. In *Publishers' Weekly* she blithely explained how books, when chosen rightly, "can hold their own" with beer, ham, and fishing tackle. Like Cerf and Klopfer, Ball thought of the Modern Library as merchandise, but more ambitiously, for she considered every individual a potential buyer: "A trap, when skillfully baited with the kind of food which experience tells us a mouse finds irresistible, and carefully placed where we feel sure he will pass, will not only catch one mouse but may be depended upon to succeed again and again. In much in the same way human beings may be tempted to part with money and buy even books if exposed to traps skillfully baited with easy sellers and so placed that the contagions of touch and sight are allowed to have free play." Thus she baited areas untouched by book outlets but teeming with casual readers. Ball saw consumers as gullible, unwary creatures, and as Cerf suggested, she knew the books had to find readers, not the other way around. Skilled product placement teased the senses to capture the attention of those buying "something to read."[48]

Cerf himself had already tried to market the series to summer camps. In 1929, he mailed flyers that urged camps to stock twenty-five Modern Library titles "suitable for readers under twenty years of age" for inevitable "moments of enforced idleness."[49] Well aware that idleness led to boredom and confident that face-to-face selling would succeed where Cerf had failed, Sarah Ball established a traveling caravan to follow the migrations of New York's elite and fill its reading needs. She visited New England resorts in the summer months, on to Florida in the winter, selling Modern Library books to vacationers from her trailer. She also initiated a sales program through private schools. One student was named "librarian," and he or she would maintain the "station." *Publishers' Weekly,* fascinated by Sarah Ball's flouting of book-selling tradition (on four separate occasions in 1933 and 1934 the magazine ran a picture of Ball with her Modern Library caravan), gushed that "a score of famous private schools in New England have been enrolled in the plan." This distribution strategy proved to be "a great stimulus to the students to buy books," and it reinforced the Modern Library's desirable association with education.⁵⁰

Ball claimed all people were potential buyers, but she must have believed the series was fundamentally elite in its appeal. She directed her distribution efforts toward the economically advantaged at a time of serious economic depression. Her "stations" catered to those privileged few who could still afford private schools, New England vacation resorts, and winters in Florida. The aristocratic locales Ball chose deflected her commercial zeal: she was not pandering books to the common man but carefully targeting the nation's civilized minority.

Other than Sarah Ball's services for exiled urbanites, Cerf and Klopfer did little to reach outside urban markets. In 1929 they thought their series did not sell in all parts of the country because it was "high-brow and big-city."⁵¹ For Cerf and Klopfer, two native New Yorkers who had spent nearly all their lives on Manhattan Island, "high-brow" coupled naturally with "big-city," and they subscribed to the general antirural bias then common among urban intellectuals. Edgar Lee Masters's *Spoon River Anthology* portrayed stifling small-town narrowness, and Sherwood Anderson catalogued Winesburg, Ohio's grotesques, but it was Sinclair Lewis who coined the phrase "the Village Virus" to describe provincial attitudes that elevated the "worship of 'a good deal, ten plunks more per acre,'" over any ambitious intellectual pursuit. His *Main Street* protagonist, Carol Kennicott, hoped by establishing a little theater in Gopher Prairie that she might "yet escape the coma of the Village Virus," but the town's scholarly lawyer called the malady "more dangerous" than cancer and likened it to a hookworm infecting those "who stay too long in the provinces."⁵² The only possible cure was to leave for the city when still young and never turn back. Lewis's biographer points out that *Main Street* (originally titled "The Village Virus") was so successful because Lewis satirized small-town life "at a propitious historical moment." Hutchisson explains, "By the end of World War I the village was no longer an important element in a capitalist economy, and the social and moral attitudes that it represented were regarded as outdated."⁵³ For Cerf and Klopfer, the Modern Library's sophisticated literature representing modernism's "advanced" moral and social ideas appeared unsuited to rural Americans stricken with "the Village Virus."

Not all publishers shared this disdain for country life and several "dollar lines" emerged in the late 1920s and early 1930s to serve rural book buyers. Blue Ribbon Books, the Star Dollar series, and the Sun Dial Library all distributed popular novels and unprotected classics in America's small towns. Robert de Graff (who would later reconfigure American book distribution when he founded Pocket Books) reveled in his success in selling Star Dollar books in rural areas. In 1933 he offered Cerf the services of one of his sales agents to push the Modern Library in rural districts for thirty dollars a week. Cerf was skeptical and genially refused the offer: "Frankly, I don't believe that the Modern Library is geared to small town trade, and while Mr. Fisk might be able to pick up a little business here and there on a straight commission basis, he could no more earn $30.00 a week for himself on our books on the towns that you have listed than I could beat you at golf."⁵⁴ Chiding his friend with mimicry, de Graff replied, "Frankly, I do not see why the Modern Library books do not sell in smaller towns as well as large, chiefly I think because you have never tried to get the business."⁵⁵

Cerf's reluctance to risk thirty dollars a week even when his business was booming was based partly on the judgment of James L. Crowder, who handled the Modern Library's midwest distribution. Crowder had told Cerf: "My own observation in the past has shown me quite conclusively that the Modern Library is very essentially a big town series. In this respect it differs very materially from the Star Library and the Blue Ribbon Books which, for two reasons, their subject matter and their bulk, make a much readier appeal to the average reader."⁵⁶ Crowder's reasoning illustrates his dim assessment of provincial America. Rural intellectual capacities were only up to undertaking popular novels such as those found in the Star Dollar series and Blue Ribbon Books, and country folk were fooled by bulky paper and wide margins into believing they were getting more for their money. The Modern Library, according to Crowder, was too heavy in content and too light in physical bulk.

Klopfer was somewhat less convinced of the hinterland's dullness and by 1930 he had come to believe that rural states might have untapped sales potential. He told Carl Smalley, the Modern Library's western field agent, "I definitely want you to cover thoroughly as many of the smaller cities not mentioned in your itinerary as possible. We feel very strongly that there is an untouched market in these places."[57] Still, the smaller cities Klopfer referred to (Boulder, Greeley, Reno, and Logan) were among the largest cities in these rural states: Winnamucca, Sterling, and Cedar City would not have been considered worth the seller's time.[58]

The partners' ambivalence about cultivating a rural trade highlights their own struggle over the Modern Library's nature. They wanted big sales and they knew the publishing industry underserved a potentially significant market. The Modern Library was a mass-produced commodity demanding a mass-distribution system to expand markets, but the partners' own assumptions—conceiving of the Modern Library as "high-brow" and rural audiences as unsophisticated—kept them from advancing into rural markets. Their antirural stance forced them into the circular logic de Graff believed was holding back the publishing industry: never marketed outside the cities, serious literature's low rural sales supported publishers' beliefs that it appealed only to discriminating urbanites, hence aggressive rural marketing was futile and a waste of money. Cerf's refusal to commit even modest resources to rural marketing indicates his confusion. He postulated the series as high culture inappropriate for "average readers" or drugstores even though he hoped his merchandise would reach the "casual reader" at newsstands and other small outlets.

MODERN COMMERCIALISM IN TRADITIONAL OUTLETS

While the partners cautiously sought new distribution networks, they still targeted an inordinate amount of publicity and marketing attention at traditional booksellers. Ironically, Cerf and Klopfer, who thought the Modern Library was too sophisticated for many markets, had to persuade traditional booksellers of its legitimacy. The nation's few full-service bookstores catered to, in Robert Duffus's words, "an aristocracy of taste," and, consequently, many bookstores were generally antagonistic toward "cheap books" in the 1920s.[59] Still drawing on the old axiom, "A cheap book makes a cheap man," bookstores sustained their feud with inexpensive books started in the 1880s. Not only were "cheap books" looked down on for aesthetic and moralistic reasons, but booksellers argued that it was as difficult to sell a copy of a ninety-five-cent book as a three-dollar book, for a profit only one-third as much.[60]

On two separate occasions (once in 1929 and again in 1935), *Publishers' Weekly* ran special issues to warn booksellers of the phenomenal sales potential they were wasting by neglecting their "dollar lines." Apparently dollar books were *much* easier to sell than three-dollar volumes especially if booksellers employed modern marketing strategies. Duffus believed the "air of dignity" surrounding most bookstores served "in this modern age" as a significant economic disadvantage because it created a forbidding environment and resulted in low-volume sales.[61] Booksellers accustomed to purveying fine goods were not particularly enthusiastic about vending products Ruth Leigh of *Publishers' Weekly* labeled "the Fords of the book business." Acknowledging that, "this may be heretic," she tried to convince "booksellers who still regard[ed] bookselling as a 'literary' profession" to see reprint series as *"merchandise—not as literature."* She implored booksellers to get "in tune with the trends of modern merchandising" and "actively sell these books." By "selling prices first—then books," a dollar line like the Modern Library could be used "as a leader to bring people into the store, to accustom them to book buying," especially if the bookseller put his "snappiest saleswoman" in charge.[62] Dollar lines with big window displays attracted a new clientele by moderating the forbidding environment of bookstores, and they were easy-selling. A companion article claimed that the bookseller "with very little pressure" might make "a sale of from $10 to $60," and continued, "If a complete stock of all the dollar books is at hand, it is likely that the innocent person who comes into the store at the call of a single title will find himself (perhaps more often herself) trundling home with a package that breeds longing glances at taxis which couldn't possibly be afforded now!"[63]

Weighing in with "pointers on making the appeal of The Modern Library deadly," Cerf in the same piece urged booksellers to act on their opportunities: "It is possible for a poor man to gather unto himself a library as extensive and correct as any bibliophile if he will make use of the Modern Library and kindred inexpensive series of older classics. New customers can be coaxed into buying one book a week, at a cost scarcely noticeable. Show him the range of titles from which he *can choose for himself,* at one dollar a copy, and ask him to compare the service offered with that of any book club in existence."[64] Cerf's rhetoric reveals how he tried to persuade culturally minded booksellers to see the Modern Library as both a sacred object *and* a commodity. The elevated language of the King James Bible—"gather unto himself"—was folded into the notion of a bibliophile's "correct" library to justify the cultural standing of the series. Furthermore, Cerf reminded booksellers worried about book-club meddling that, with the Modern Library, the customer may "choose for himself." His elevated tone was countered by his advice to seduce new customers. If the bookseller took an active role in *selling* the series, Cerf promised a bevy of new and regular book buyers devoted to retail booksellers rather than book clubs. *Publishers' Weekly* adopted Cerf's conflation of culture and commerce and presented booksellers with a novel selling tool: a list compiled by the Wisconsin Library Association of a fine home library comprised only of dollar books.[65]

Just three years later, Cerf (then in charge of all publicity matters) dropped his cultural pretense and urged booksellers to see the series as profitable merchandise. In 1932 he placed an extraordinary advertisement in *Publishers' Weekly* (figure 4), featuring a full-page cartoonish drawing of a woman in a bathtub. While the soap remained securely in its holder, the Modern Library editions of *The Magic Mountain, Droll Stories, Of Human Bondage, Swann's Way,* and *Sanctuary* floated among the frothy suds. The text read "They Float! The Modern Library 200 Famous Books at 95 Cents a Copy."[66] With the fillip of a little sex, the advertisement cleverly alluded to Ivory Soap's well-known slogan to send up the old book-industry adage "Books aren't soap," at the same time assuring retailers that the Modern Library was a proven high-turnover product. The floating volumes grouped individual titles to emphasize the brand name and the potential of its standardized format for creating repeat sales; the titles themselves were less important than their trademark. Cerf's playful attack on tradition came at a time when many titles with feeble sales were ruthlessly dropped from the series, thus elaborately tying into Ivory's other famous tagline, "99 $^{44}/_{100}$ % pure." The Modern Library was purged of any commercial flops, and it could boast of being pure gold for booksellers.

FIGURE 4. The Modern Library playfully sends up the old publishing adage that "books aren't soap." From *Publishers' Weekly*, 14 May 1932. Joseph Regenstein Library, University of Chicago.

Once booksellers were persuaded to stock the Modern Library, Cerf used its reputation for high turnover to cement their loyalty. He was stuck with booksellers as his main distribution agents, and he cultivated a close relationship to coax them into using his modern marketing strategies. The firm's stated policy of weeding from the series "anything that could possibly be construed as deadwood" promised booksellers they could count on steady sales from every title.[67] In a 1933 flyer, Cerf came on more like a grocers' wholesaler than a publisher: "By keeping your stock fresh and up to the minute, you will help us in our endeavor to maintain the Modern Library's reputation as one of the most profitable items in your stock."[68] Cerf's injunctions to booksellers presented the Modern Library as a proactive corporation vigilantly bent on increasing its product's marketability, and he set the firm up as their partner in selling.

Cerf's whimsical, slightly daring attitude led him to strike a partnership with the renowned Old Corner Bookstore in Boston. As one of the country's largest and oldest bookstores, once frequented by Oliver Wendell Holmes, John Greenleaf Whittier, Henry Ward Beecher, Harriet Beecher Stowe, and Ralph Waldo Emerson, it was a revered site in Boston's literary landscape. But this bookstore was not adverse to modern marketing techniques and it deployed them to amass a full one percent of U.S. retail book sales.[69] Cerf and store manager Richard Fuller developed a promotion based on the best-selling Modern Library titles. A poster tempted customers with thirty free volumes of the Modern Library for the "three persons making the most accurate guess at the ten best selling titles in The Modern Library at our store during the present month." The Modern Library supplied promotional materials, entry blanks, cooperative local advertising, and the thirty prize books; the bookstore was responsible for tallying sales and determining the winners. Entry blanks listed the twenty-five best-selling Modern Library titles from the past year, but the bookstore "warned" contestants they "must take into consideration new titles which always have a considerable sale on their addition to the series."[70]

The hallowed birthplace of this contest gave it legitimacy among less commercially minded booksellers, and it was subsequently repeated in other stores across the country. Cerf knew it was a boon to Modern Library's promotional efforts: "The cost to us is the 30 Modern Library titles that go as prizes, and the inconsiderable cost of the posters and entry blanks. The benefits are big window displays and renewed interest of all the customers on the entire Modern Library list."[71] At modest expense, bookstore customers were cajoled into a careful study of the complete series (then numbering over two hundred titles) with a special emphasis on the new titles, *and* a return visit to the bookstore to see if they won. Cerf's *Publishers' Weekly* announcement of the contest's success featured the Old Corner Bookstore to persuade stodgy book dealers to adopt the program. Although bookstore attention was heightened, the taint of commercialism that may have tinctured the contests was partially covered by the "air of dignity" surrounding the sponsoring cultural institution.

The Modern Library spent lavishly on bookstore publicity. The firm expended over $14,000 in 1929 and increased spending by a third in 1930 on bookstore-related "circularization expenses." Cerf supplied bookstores with Modern Library flyers bearing their name, posters featuring either new titles or the entire series, and even matchbooks inscribed with the Modern Library trademark over the slogan "Keep a good book in your pocket."[72] Book racks offered at cost (free with large orders) displayed the series in eye-catching ways and assured prominent product placement. The display racks impressed William B. Liebmann, a longtime New York bookseller, who recalled that they were a "new approach in book publishing" and a feature of the "modern and innovative merchandising methods" pioneered by Cerf and Klopfer.[73]

Special display racks, posters, and contests drew attention to the series, but the books themselves needed to do more than idly wait for buyers — they had to create desire. To make their volumes more eye-catching in crowded bookstores Cerf and Klopfer replaced Liveright's brown, typographic dust covers with brightly colored pictorial book jackets. The jackets extended their advertising into distribution sites and encouraged what Ball called the "contagions of sight and touch." Here the partners were following an industrywide trend. In the 1910s publishers had realized that the plain jackets used to protect bindings during shipment could be printed with testimonials as a form of inexpensive advertising; by the late 1920s book jackets had metamorphosed from drab, typographic wrappers into colorful marketing tools.

Alluring book jackets bespangled with "multi-colored pictures that go with the worst blurbs" stirred critics to charge publishers with using "ballyhoo" to promote their books.[74] A decidedly unflattering term, "ballyhoo" originally referred to the outrageous gestures and claims of carnival barkers at their "bally stands," but by the 1920s the term was leveled against advertising hyperbole.[75] The *Outlook* thought the very sound of "blurb" suggested "the exuberance of the side-show ballyhooer," and it charged that book jacket "blurbers" had a V complex, because "if the story isn't virile, it is vital or vigorous or vivid."[76] While critics accused each other of writing reviews based on book jackets, articles appeared in the *New Republic* and the *Bookman* titled "Sublurbia" and "Confessions of a Blurb Writer" to condemn the way book jackets cheapened literature by wrapping it in modern commercialism's worst hype.[77] To these critics, book jackets affirmed that publishers thought of books as nothing more than commodities to be hustled in the marketplace. The *New Republic* apocalyptically likened blurbs to insidious pests, a mass of gnawing caterpillars able to devour the truth and eventually the human soul. Although the editorial's own hysteria perhaps nibbled at the truth, in a more sober moment it found: "The blurb wouldn't be so pathetic, or so funny either, if it didn't represent a high degree of genuine belief as well as the mere desire to sell a book. It is written in the fundamental principles of salesmanship that those who have something to sell to the world usually sell it to themselves first of all." The key phrase is "sell to the world." Blurbs were unnecessary as long as literate publishers directed books to a well-informed elite, but once publishers turned into profit-driven promoters seeking greater markets among philistine suburbanites and rural dwellers, commercialism began its perfidious assault. According to the *New Republic,* "sublurbian" commercialism would one day invade society's every crevice, and a man might propose to his beloved: "Emmy, I am masterly in my romanticism. My humor is infectious. I am breezy, swiftly-moving, compelling. Marry me: I will charm you to the end."[78] Nothing was safe from the gnawing of commercialism, not truth, not love, and especially not culture.

Under Boni & Liveright's management, long quotations from critics or descriptions of the contents left jackets dense with type. Cerf and Klopfer followed a *Publishers' Weekly* injunction that jacket design ought to be "the science of marshalling an immediate and aggressive attack upon the eye," so they exiled such large blocks of type to the front flap to make room for catchy blurbs and bright illustrations on the jacket front.[79] Every Modern Library jacket back emblazoned a *New York Times* endorsement, "The greatest book bargain in America today," and the back flap enumerated the series' merits as a set of inexpensive, well-made volumes of the world's best books.

Soon after they took control of the series, the partners filled the jacket's reverse side with a complete list of Modern Library titles, ordering information, and a mail-order coupon.[80] Today most book buyers keep book jackets and they are considered an integral part of a hardbound book, but until World War II dust jackets, even those featuring illustrations, were merely protection from the hazards of shipping and a selling tool for the real product within. Not even book collectors thought jackets worth saving until the late 1930s.[81] Belle Rosenbaum, assistant editor of the *New York Herald Tribune Books,* displayed her books with original jackets, but she knew herself to be an anomaly, for "in the best homes jackets are removed from books before they are placed on the shelf." Even though she acknowledged they were only advertising, she specifically admired the Modern Library's jacket checklists: "How else could I find out, quickly, without leaving my room, whether a certain book I wanted could be obtained in that edition?"[82] Once removed, as nearly all Modern Library jackets were, each became a coupon advertisement for the entire series. Asking the provocative question, "Which of these [200] outstanding books do you want to read," the jackets offered a tease many readers found irresistible.

At the point of sale the jackets attracted the attention of would-be buyers, and by 1937, when coated stock began to be used, they provided a high-gloss finish to the partners' promotional efforts. The jackets offered books as packaged merchandise and emphasized their commodified nature as the "greatest book bargain," but Cerf and Klopfer framed their promotion so as not to offend more cultivated tastes. Unlike most publishers who hired hack artists, Cerf and Klopfer secured well-known book illustrators such as Lynd Ward, Paul Galdone, Valenti Angelo, Joseph Blumenthal, and Rockwell Kent to design the jackets.[83] If pictorial jackets seemed too garish, the work of respected artists might meliorate the ballyhoo and reserve an "air of dignity" for those suspicious of too much commercial flash.

Once attracted to the book, a prospective buyer was treated to an additional motivation to select the Modern Library over a competing reprint. Original introductions to most titles made a Modern Library edition a unique text. Three to five pages of new material distinguished

Modern Library editions from competing imprints shelved nearby. The early Boni & Liveright editions featured introductions by prominent New York critics, as did many later volumes, but whenever possible Cerf and Klopfer commissioned original author introductions. From 1925 to 1941, forty well-known authors accepted such a commission.[84] These introducers included a fair representation of the leading contemporary American and British novelists (Anderson, Dos Passos, Faulkner, Fitzgerald, and Woolf), a number of popular, but critically acclaimed ones (Buck, Caldwell, Saroyan, and Steinbeck), as well as popular philosophers (Bertrand Russell, John Dewey, and Havelock Ellis). A self-deprecating Steinbeck sent in his introduction for *Tortilla Flat* with the terse disclaimer: "Enclosed is the introduction. It is the only thing I want to say. If it won't do—toss it out and have some one else do it. This is not a clever introduction. I mean it."[85] A few months later a Modern Library title page ignored Steinbeck's reservations and promised bookstore browsers that its edition had something special, "A Foreword by the Author."

For older titles Cerf and Klopfer turned to established academics to solidify the series' pedagogical function and distinguish the particular edition. They recruited dozens of Ivy League professors, and Cerf believed the series "should contain at least one introduction apiece by every prominent member of the Columbia English department."[86] He flatteringly told Yale's popular lecturer William Lyon Phelps, "I would rather have an introduction by you to the SCARLET LETTER than by any other man in the country today," adding, "I feel that it is a pity indeed that there is no introduction by you to at least one of the volumes in our Modern Library series."[87] Basking in such flattery, Phelps enthusiastically signed on and told Cerf he knew the series well and was "proud to be included."[88]

Well-known educators such as Phelps reassured book buyers anxious for expert guidance, and other introductions reprinted by the Modern Library flaunted academic titles for the same purpose: *The Philosophy of Santayana* featured "An introductory essay, by Irwin Edman, Professor of Philosophy at Columbia University," while "Edward Mead Earle, Professor of History, Institute for Advanced Studies, Princeton, N.J." introduced *The Federalist*.[89] The impressive academic credentials probably attracted a few anxious students hoping to find clues to a work's significance; they also proffered a certified professional endorsement of the text's intellectual importance.

Cerf clearly recognized the distinctive qualities the introductions gave Modern Library editions and he protected them jealously. When Max Eastman requested permission to reprint his preface to a Karl Marx volume he had edited, Cerf replied: "I think it would be extremely bad business to use your introduction for the Marx volume in the set of the World's Great Thinkers. That introduction is the exclusive feature of the Modern Library edition of the book, and we wouldn't want to see it appear in any other format."[90] Cerf knew the bookseller's shelf held several Marx collections, but only the Modern Library edition could attract book buyers with Eastman's comments made controversial by his well-publicized split with the Stalinist Communist Party faithful.

Even with all the Modern Library's attractions, keeping booksellers' attention was a continuing battle. Random House distribution manager Lewis Miller once opened his sales speech to a conference for the Modern Library traveling sales force, "Talk windows, windows, windows. You are being provided with a half dozen pictures of successful windows in all sections of the country, together with the testimonials. Remember please the whole reprint business is a struggle for space. If the other reprint boys get quantities and we don't, we wind up in the back of the store, out of sight."[91] The next summer he urged the sales force to "shock dealers out of their lethargy," and charged that "the dealer who says 'They don't sell as they used to' is generally the fellow who has got Modern Library in the back of the store."[92]

The focused selling points directed at bookstores were far more strident than the gentle promptings of the previous generations. The Modern Library adopted modern business practices to conceive of the product as merchandise demanding dealer attention. Cerf's booming defied the long-standing attitude that good books sell themselves, and it would have enraged those who believed the arts must remain separate from twentieth-century capitalists' sordid market manipulations. "Talk windows, windows, windows" and references to "other reprint boys" and "quantities" probably would have sounded alarmingly commercial and philistine to most authors represented in the Modern Library had they been privy to the sales talks for the series.

The Modern Library's commercial din might have grated on the literati had they heard it, but it was refreshing music to Macy's book department manager, the single largest buyer of the series. The series had already been established in Macy's and Gimbels' book departments before Cerf and Klopfer took control. In their first months of ownership, Cerf and Klopfer would start each day by counting the new orders, and Cerf remembered, "When we'd get a big order from Macy's, we'd dance around with glee because it ran the total way up."[93] The series became an even more important feature for department stores after Cerf and Klopfer began extensive marketing directed at urban, professional-managerial–class readers. These consumers could be depended on to shop in other departments after making their book purchases, which was especially important because department store book departments often operated at a loss.[94] As a result Macy's and Gimbels regularly featured the Modern Library in advertisements and promoted it with large displays, while Bloomingdale's devoted twenty feet of prime mezzanine retail space to the series.[95]

Department stores pioneered most of the modern marketing techniques Cerf and Klopfer used, and it was their aggressive commercialism that the partners hoped to foster in booksellers. Bookstores may have found the Modern Library's methods "innovative" and a "new approach," but most were old-hat to experienced department store managers. Cerf's treatment of books as commodities and his posters and display-rack publicity fitted department store sales strategies that stressed attractive product display and attention-grabbing gimmicks.[96] The Modern Library's pervasive trumpeting of its ninety-five-cent price lent itself to department store loss-leader techniques. When the books were sold for fifty cents a copy or even, at times, a dime, customers *knew* they were getting a bargain. Department stores found in the Modern Library a firm that did business as they did. The admiration was mutual: these "palaces of consumption" catered to the nation's most voracious readers, middle-class women, and offered the Modern Library high-volume sales without the "snobbish" atmosphere of bookstores or the profane mercantile pragmatism of drugstores.[97] At Macy's, Gimbels, or Bloomingdale's, the books were featured as high-turnover merchandise, marketed to modern urban shoppers, in a dignified but highly commercial setting.

Cerf and Klopfer trod a fine line in the late 1920s and early 1930s. Earlier in their careers, they had thought unorthodox distribution plans might offer a solution to the problem of reaching a mass audience. Their cautious allocation of resources and their fear of imperiling the cultural cachet of the series doomed the new plans but upheld the reputation of the series as aloof from commercial ballyhoo. Their timid forays into radical distribution schemes are a striking contrast to the dynamic alliance the partners formed with traditional booksellers. Their energetic publicity and personal service persuaded conservative booksellers to adopt modern marketing techniques that secured consistently high sales *and* cultural success. Just as Cerf and Klopfer kept news of their attempts to circumvent the traditional book distribution network secure from booksellers' information channels, they also hid the onslaught of commercialism heaped on booksellers and other retailers from the literati. As a result Lewis Mumford, like other critics, thought the success of the series was cheerfully independent of "high-pressure salesmanship."[98]

CHAPTER FOUR

Packaging the World's Best Books

According to Bennett Cerf, after title selection, the Modern Library's chief selling points were its price and format. He and Klopfer believed that, within the limits imposed by the low price of the books, their physical format could be designed to increase their functionality as carriers of texts and to make them tempting to middle-class book buyers. Adhering to a form-follows-function modernist aesthetic that favored "authenticity" and "honest" design, the partners sought to imbue the series with "class," a term connoting an elegance of style and refined taste that both men greatly admired. Initially, they emulated Knopf's celebrated Borzoi imprint to spruce up the shabby physical appearance of the books. But their own typographic interests, manifest in Random House's establishment in 1927, brought about subsequent redesigns of the series to propel sales and heighten its reputation for quality.

A SERIES WITH "CLASS"

The Modern Library's inaugural volumes garnered praise for their clear type and attractive format, but attention to detail was lax at Boni & Liveright, and over time the appearance of the series suffered. The imitation-leather covers "smelled like the inside of a taxi-cab" and had the "unpleasant habit of sticking to each other."[1] Casual inattention to physical uniformity, a key element tying a disparate selection of titles into a unified series, led to a "bewildering variety and combination of printing and binding styles from 1917 to 1925." Surveying the Liveright period, bibliographers George Andes and Helen Kelly found: "No less than five major styles of title-page combine with two types of endpapers and three bindings in nine so-far-discovered combinations. Eight early titles have been found each showing four of these combinations by itself. Two more minor (one unique) title-page styles create two additional combinations."[2]

But by December 1928, book critic Frances Lamont Robbins could assure her *Outlook* readers of a new fastidiousness at the Modern Library:

> When these books first began to appear, they were pretty hard to read. The paper was marred by zeniths and nadirs of thickness; lines rambled off the bottoms of pages; the type faded out in spots like the Cheshire cat's grin; pages seventeen to fifty-two of "Thus Spake Zarathustra" repeated themselves throughout one whole volume to doubly confound confusion. But those things don't happen now. The books are now clearly printed, on decent paper and are bound in what is not, praise be, limp suede although they are flexible and "fit the pocket."[3]

Robbins was so enthusiastic about the books' beauty and low price that she suggested they could replace cards and calendars as simple yet thoughtful Christmas gifts (though she used a typically old-fashioned name to warn—and tantalize—readers that their "Aunt Clarissy Duffus" might not appreciate all the titles in the series, especially Havelock Ellis's *The New Spirit*).

Transforming the books from something reminiscent of the grubby interior of a New York taxi to Robbins's "sprig of holly tucked within the scarlet bow" took several years.[4] In 1925 Cerf and Klopfer hired typographer Elmer Adler and graphic designer Lucian Bernhard to revamp the Modern Library.[5] A Federal Trade Commission decision banning the use of the phrase "Limp Croftleather" for its tendency to "mislead and deceive the purchasing public" surely served as one exigency for seeking an alternative to the imitation leather covers, but the insincerity of cloth posing as cowhide offended the modernist creed that the plastic arts should be honest to their materials.[6] In the same sense, Liveright's colophon of gothic initials misrepresented his firm's character and the modern spirit of the Modern Library. So the partners began to experiment with suitable cloth bindings to displace the drab, foul-smelling "croft-leather," and Bernhard's leaping torchbearer replaced Liveright's anachronistic colophon.[7] Bernhard also designed graceful endpapers and Adler set typographically austere title pages to carry the reader into the text.

Adler faced a difficult task in creating a new title page. Because most Modern Library books were printed from rented plates with differing typefaces, consistent title-page design was especially important to maintain the series' typographic unity. Yet adhering to the dominant typographic theory, that a title page ought to display the same basic components (of typeface and decorative devices) used in the body of the text, would have demanded a host of title-page designs. Adler finessed this dilemma by stripping the title pages down to the bare essentials. He featured Bernhard's torchbearer framed by author and title above and the publisher's name below. The prominence of the Modern Library's trademark assured series unity, while the simplicity of presentation mitigated the typographic clashes made inevitable by borrowed plates.

Adler's simple title pages also sharply differentiated the Modern Library from its chief competitor, Everyman's Library. The William Morris–inspired extravagance of Everyman's title pages displayed some of the Arts and Crafts movement's gaudiest excesses. Cluttered with thick borders of interweaving floral designs and further cramped with long quotations, Everyman's title pages evoked nostalgic reminiscences of late Victorianism (figure 5). In contrast, the Modern Library's streamlined simplicity featured an aesthetic based on a straightforward, honest presentation and announced that the series was particularly modern and up-to-date (figure 6).

Such unembellished modernism was Lucian Bernhard's hallmark. In 1905 he achieved European fame when he won a poster contest sponsored by Berlin's Priester Match Company. Bernhard had defied convention by boldly filling the entire poster with two matches set against a black background beneath the single, hand-lettered word "Priester." The poster evolved from an earlier design of a spent match beside an ashtray holding a pluming cigar: the smoke cleverly scripted "Priester" in an Art Nouveau motif. In a minimalist exercise, young Bernhard subtracted elements (first the cigar smoke, then the cigar, then the ashtray) until he was left with only the word "Priester" and two matches.[8] His spare design inspired imitation throughout European poster advertising, and by 1915 Bernhard headed a successful poster agency while dabbling in other forms of design, most notably interior design and typography.[9] He applied a Bauhaus austerity to his typefaces and experimented with sans serif display types, which later became staples of the advertising world. Like his posters, his interior designs employed stark color contrasts, whose hard lines and spare furnishings defied Victorian clutter.

Fleeing the economic chaos of the Weimar Republic, Bernhard emigrated to the United States in 1922 and set out to establish himself anew. But as the art historian Steven Heller points out, Bernhard's designs were

FIGURE 5. William Morris inspired Everyman's Library title page, 1925. Joseph Regenstein Library, University of Chicago.

"too modern" for American manufacturers. His singular visual images with little or no text suited European markets but were ill adapted to the copy-driven advertising dominating American mass-market magazines.[10] Failing to impress manufacturers, Bernhard turned his attention to interior design.[11] Among his satisfied customers was Elmer Adler, who advised Cerf and Klopfer to hire Bernhard to design their colophon and endpapers at a time when he was virtually unknown in the United States (it was not until the 1930s when he created trademarks for Cat's Paw and Ex-Lax that his work became widely recognized), but Adler felt his aggressively modern designs fit the spirit of the series.[12]

Bernhard's colophon, a bounding "Promethean bringer of enlightenment," fitted into a long tradition of symbolic publishers' marks first popularized by the late-fifteenth–early-sixteenth-century Italian printer and typographer, Aldus Manutius.[13] Manutius, who published the earli-

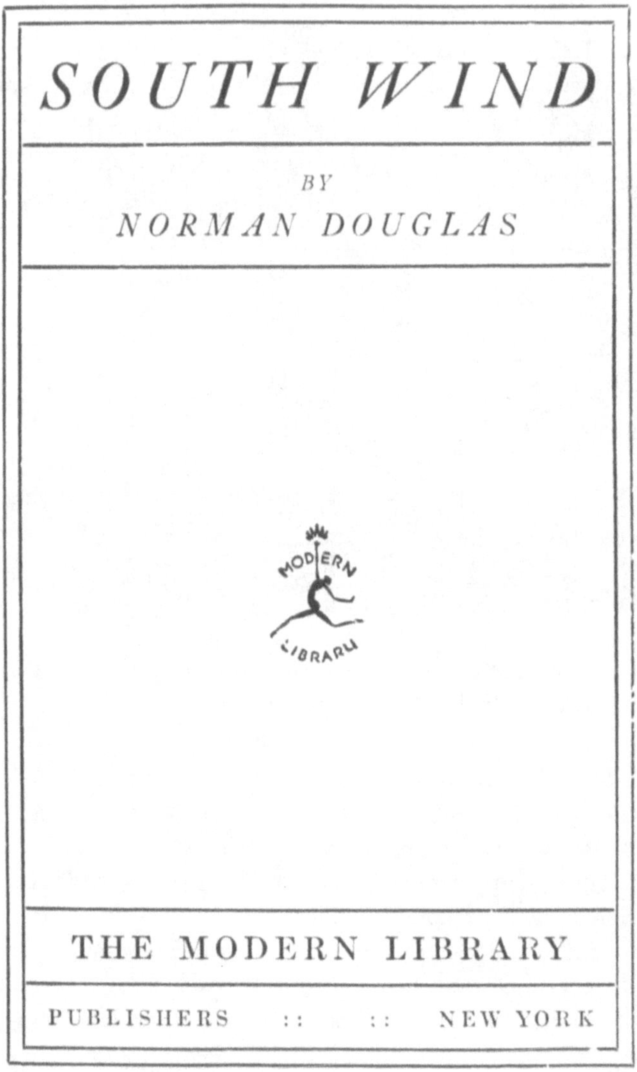

SOUTH WIND

BY

NORMAN DOUGLAS

THE MODERN LIBRARY

PUBLISHERS :: :: NEW YORK

FIGURE 6. Modern Library title page designed by Elmer Adler, 1925. Author's collection.

est small-format printed books, marked each title page with a dolphin entwining an anchor: the anchor symbolized "the period of deliberation before a work is begun, the dolphin the speed of its completion."[14] Other printer–publishers emulated Manutius for over a century, but the tradition slowly faded until it was reinvigorated by the English fine-press movement in the late-nineteenth century. In 1927, *Publishers' Weekly* reported that trade publishers had rediscovered the "Cult of the Colophon," and many were using the devices to bring modern, brand-name recognition to their wares.[15] The colophon's twentieth-century revitalization as a quality trademark was symptomatic of literature's commodification, although it drew on a tradition of fine printing consciously detached from commercial interests by its aesthete progenitors. Its adoption by trade publishers illuminates a modern melding of interests: publishing sought to maintain an air of disinterested dignity associated with art and literature, yet also yearned for the sales potential modern commercialization promised.

Bernhard's distinctive Promethean image, repeated on endpapers, title pages, in innumerable advertisements, and even on bookstore display racks, called attention to the series and served as a brand-name assurance of quality. Noticing the "man dancing" on the spine of a book she had enjoyed as an adolescent in the 1950s, Annie Dillard remembered, "Like so many children before and after me, I learned to seek out this logo, the Modern Library colophon."[16] Though she found the Modern Library was not quite so reliable as *Mad Magazine* (which she said "never failed to slay" her), to Dillard and others the colophon became a trusted beacon in libraries and bookstores teeming with otherwise undifferentiated books.

The era's most aggressively promoted colophon was Alfred Knopf's Borzoi. In 1917, Knopf proposed that "Borzoi stands for a new idea in publishing." Believing that "the best books can result only when author and publisher truly collaborate," Knopf felt his responsibility was to create books that reflected and illuminated his authors' texts.[17] For Knopf, publishers literally gave form to authors' words, and finely crafted texts deserved well-designed books.

Although not new in the history of publishing, Knopf's ideals about book design were unprecedented in American trade publishing. Until Knopf's arrival, trade book design received little attention—publishers reserved typographic excellence for expensive, "de-luxe editions." But seventeen years earlier, T. J. Cobden-Sanderson (founder of Doves Press, which sparked the English fine-press movement along with William Morris's Kelmscott Press) expressed the same ideals in a short treatise *The Ideal Book, or, Book Beautiful: A Tract on Calligraphy, Printing, and Illustration and on the Book Beautiful as a Whole*.[18] Cobden-Sanderson was one of the era's most revered book designers and a lifelong champion of typographic simplicity who influenced a generation of designers in both England and the United States. These acolytes were the artists Knopf employed to design his Borzoi books. His authors appreciated his efforts, and the trade took note of his success. A 1943 *New Yorker* profile enthused, "the pioneering Knopf did in the production of good-looking books made his early authors feel that they were in sympathetic hands and gave his list a certain cachet with the reading public."[19] His books frequently made the American Institute of Graphic Arts "Fifty Books" list, *Publishers' Weekly* praised his innovations, and nearly every history of American publishing credits Knopf for arousing a new interest in quality book manufacture.[20]

Knopf's epiphany that "a good-looking and well-made book will never do its author any harm anywhere at any time," and that such a book could escalate both sales and an author's reputation at little cost, led to his long, productive relationship with many of America's top typographers, including W. A. Dwiggins, Warren Chappell, and Elmer Adler.[21] Adler was a consummate perfectionist and one of the highest-priced designers in the country. His firm, the Pynson Printers, became eminent for its obsessive devotion to fine printing. Bibliophile–typographer Frederick B. Adams Jr. dubbed Adler an "Apostle of Good Taste," and the print historian Joseph Blumenthal (head of Spiral Press and onetime Modern Library designer) said of Adler: "His books and miscellaneous printing were neither tightly bound by the past nor affectedly modern. He displayed a natural and personal typographic versatility, ingenuity, wit, and daring. And, withal, his work remained within the province of readability in debt to literature."[22] The 1922 Pynson Printers' prospectus announced that the firm was prepared "for the planning and production of all printing in which quality is the first consideration," and that it would accept no work "in which quality must be sacrificed to exigencies of time or cost."[23] Adler's first job came when Knopf commissioned him to design Willa Cather's *April Twilights*. After seeing the final product,

Cather (who was exceptionally particular about manifestations of her works) wrote to Adler: "We have set a new standard of relations between writer and printer. The pains you have taken with this volume and the absolutely satisfying result you have achieved have quite revived my interest in the text."[24] The designer's labors illuminated and anticipated the text by giving it a physical form in harmony with the author's tone and mood—exactly what Cobden-Sanderson asked for when he intoned, "The whole duty of Typography, as of Calligraphy, is to communicate to the imagination, without loss by the way, the thought or image intended to be communicated by the Author."[25]

In his own words, Bennett Cerf "worshipped" Knopf, and, using his highest accolade, he testified, "Alfred Knopf had the one thing Liveright lacked: he had class."[26] His assertion located Knopf and Liveright on a social hierarchy based on a concept of good taste. In the 1890s the slang word "class" was coined to describe a superior athlete, but by the 1920s the term had been transformed to mean a superiority of personal style. That Knopf "had class" denoted that he possessed a certain elegance of sensibility. "Class" had become closely associated with the idea of good taste, at least as Emily Post defined it in 1928, as something "revealed in everything we are, do, or have.... Our speech, manners, dress, and household goods." She considered her lengthy rules of etiquette as "nothing more than sign-posts by which we are guided to the goal of good taste."[27] One's "class" referred to an ability to embody the whole range of good taste. Although it indicated a way of life reflecting good taste and superior manners, the term applied equally to material objects. The son of Sinclair Lewis's Babbitt thought a sedan had "a lot more class" than an open-air Model T because it had a more elegant style—but, for the materialistic elder Babbitt, the elegant style correlated exactly with its more prohibitive price.[28]

The term "class" acquired its meaning of social distinction based on style and taste at a time, ironically, when many Americans were becoming increasingly class-conscious in the Marxist sense. A heated discussion of class conflict and class warfare appeared in popular magazines throughout the 1920s and escalated during the Great Depression, bringing on a minor crisis in the people's vision of America as an egalitarian, democratic, and "classless" society. In 1927, contributing editor to *Outlook* Lawrence F. Abbott discussed the heightened interest in class division brought on by economic prosperity. In answer to a query concerning social stratification in the United States, Abbott asserted that the mere accumulation of wealth did not translate directly into the attainment of superior social class. Rejecting a purely economic measure of standing on the social hierarchy, he proposed a new anatomy of social distinction for "the man who believes that a democracy is a form of government based primarily on intelligence." The "intelligence classification" he proposed used the "recently invented . . . term 'middlebrow' to designate the decent, more or less conventional, fairly well educated, reasonably thoughtful body of men and women who really constitute the backbone of the United States." Calling the term "middlebrow" a "happy invention," Abbot asked: "Highbrows, middlebrows, and lowbrows—how better can the American democracy be divided into its component parts?"[29] Economic distinctions did not constitute the social hierarchy, but intelligence level manifest in personal taste did.

The redefinition of the term "class" to describe a general state of good taste, combined with the development of a tiered hierarchy of taste, offered Americans a way to make social distinctions without adhering to an economic determinism they saw as antidemocratic and antiegalitarian. "Much more than a study of transportation," the Babbitt family's discussion of cars belied "an aspiration for knightly rank. In the city of Zenith, in the barbarous twentieth century, a family's motor indicated its social rank as precisely as the grades of the peerage determined the rank of an English family—indeed, more precisely, considering the opinion of old country families upon newly created brewery barons and woolen-mill viscounts."[30] Babbitt may have thought a sedan classy because it was more expensive and a marker of economic class, but in the system of taste hierarchies devised by Abbott, anyone, regardless of economic standing, could still possess "class." Post echoed Abbott's sentiment in her definition of the "Best Society": "Thus, Best Society is not a fellowship of the wealthy, nor does it seek to exclude those who are not of exalted birth; but it *is* an association of gentle-folk, of which good form in speech, charm of manner, knowledge of social amenities, and instinctive consideration for the feelings of others, are the credentials by which society the world over recognizes its chosen members." Had she not disparaged slang expressions as the "little foxes that spoil the grapes of perfect diction," she might well have said the "Best Society" is made up of those who "have class."[31]

So when Cerf and Klopfer set out to endow the Modern Library with class, in essence to make themselves and the Modern Library a part of publishing's—and the culture's—"Best Society," they turned to one of Knopf's favorite typographers to set new title pages for the Modern Library. Next, the partners commissioned Adler to design their first catalog. In his memoirs Cerf related: "Instead of the old trashy-looking catalogue, we wanted to put out something with class. In those days publishers' catalogues didn't amount to anything; they were all unimaginative and routine. So Elmer Adler also redesigned our catalogue." By opposing "class" to "trashy-looking," "unimaginative," and "routine," Cerf implicitly connected it to good taste, creativity, and a certain daring style. But Cerf also understood "class" was closely connected to money: "His bill was fabulous. Bills and estimates didn't mean anything to Elmer—he'd tell you he'd do something for a thousand dollars, and when it was finished he'd charge three thousand, and when he was reminded that he was supposed to do it for a thousand, he'd say, not the least bit abashed, 'Well, I figured wrong.'"[32] Adler's ability to create work with "class" not only justified a "fabulous" bill, but it also absolved him from the business ethic Cerf demanded from others.

A Modern Library advertisement proposed that the catalog was "worth preserving on its own merits" and *Publishers' Weekly* thought it "tasteful" and a "model of what a straightforward book catalog can be."[33] Printed on laid paper, "The Modern Library Descriptive Catalogue" boasted, "This catalog was designed by the Pynson Printers and printed for the Modern Library, Inc. in November 1925." The catalog presented itself as fine-press craftsmanship.

The fine printing distinctively introduced the new ownership of the series:

> On August 1, 1925, The Modern Library became a separate unit in the publishing world. An experienced and strongly fortified organization, with no general publications over which to concern itself, is today devoting its entire energies to one project—the growth and development of The Modern Library. Its endeavor will be to bring to an even higher standard of excellence a series which is known and appreciated wherever English books are read.... Suggestions for new titles or improvements in the format of the Modern Library books will be gratefully received and should be addressed to Bennett A. Cerf,

President or to Donald S. Klopfer, Vice-President / 71 West 45th Street / New York.[34]

To some it must have seemed ironic—one of the country's most respected typographers designing title pages and a finely printed catalog for a set of inexpensive reprints—but Adler's work underscored the young partners' vision of the series as a distinctive product worthy of an aesthete's touch. In a sense, the Modern Library was an extension of their personalities. Drawn to publishing partially by the distinguished cultural milieu associated with the literary life, but also desirous of success as businessmen, they shaped the Modern Library to emulate Knopf's prestigious and profitable Borzoi Books. The work of Adler and Bernhard was designed to sell books, but it was also intended to convey connotations of "class" in a world of literary pursuits.

RANDOM HOUSE

Two years after buying the Modern Library, Cerf and Klopfer again teamed up with Elmer Adler to found Random House "for the purpose of creating and distributing in America books of typographic interest."[35] Though they shared an office, Random House and the Modern Library were separate corporate entities (necessitated in part by Adler's participation). Cerf and Klopfer planned to maintain the Modern Library as their principal business operation, but even with the attention they lavished on the series, its management left them plenty of time for bridge, golf, and backgammon during business hours.[36] Klopfer was a lifelong book collector and an avowed bibliophile before he entered publishing, and Cerf, too, had been infected by the "gentle madness" of bibliomania. Random House, conceived of as a distribution agent for fine-press editions, offered "a play toy and an opportunity to exercise another interest in books."[37] It also served as a second commercial outlet for two very ambitious young businessmen.

Flush economic times gave the American fine-press movement a boost in the 1920s. Partly inspired by the English Arts and Crafts movement of a previous generation, but even more by the typographic innovations in the United States from the active imaginations of Bruce Rogers and Daniel Berkeley Updike, small private presses were established throughout the country.[38] Decentralized, and often located in small towns, most private presses had haphazard distribution systems. With press runs usually of fewer than five hundred copies, most editions were sold by direct mail or through a handful of dealers. Random House proposed to step in and become the exclusive distribution agent for the top fine presses in America and England. It offered to buy entire press runs at a 60 to 65 percent discount, then use the Modern Library distribution system to deliver the books to market. Random House would net a small profit, save fine-press artisans from the hassles and risks associated with distributing their wares, and, in time, rationalize the chaotic limited editions market.

While in England discussing Modern Library acquisitions, Cerf paid an unannounced visit to the home of Francis Meynell, owner and chief operator of the prestigious Nonesuch Press. The producer of expensive limited editions and modestly priced, pocket-sized editions bound in soft vellum, Nonesuch was perhaps the most respected and admired private press of the time. Cerf laid out Random House's plan and asked to become Meynell's American distributor. Meynell, who had turned down dozens of similar offers in the past, was caught up in Cerf's enthusiasm and agreed to his proposal after being assured of his integrity by a mutual friend. Writing to his friend Manuel Komroff, an ecstatic Cerf explained how the deal would promote Random House's reputation: "As far as I can see, there will be little or no profit accruing to us from the sale of these books; what we have to look forward to is the prestige that we may gain through handling the line and the hope that one day we may be able to publish something in conjunction with them."[39] Cerf recalled that, as soon as Random House became the exclusive distributor of Nonesuch Press in the United States, well-known fine presses such as the Golden Cockerel Press, Spiral Press, and Shakespeare Head Press "came begging" to sign with Random House, "since they would then be basking in the reflected glory of the Nonesuch Press."[40]

Though only a fledgling enterprise, Random House provided Cerf and Klopfer with added clout in the marketplace. Because fine-press books were often oversubscribed in the 1920s, Random House could dole out limited editions as it saw fit. Although there is no evidence that Cerf or Klopfer ever used Random House to strong-arm a bookseller into stocking more Modern Library books, they did see their distribution rights as an opportunity to bestow personal favors on booksellers. Personal friendship networks can make or break a reprint series, and

Random House gave their already accomplished salesmen one more way to build up positive relations with booksellers.

The first three years of Random House were devoted almost entirely to limited editions. Most of the firm's activities involved distribution, but they also published special editions printed by fine presses associated with the firm. The first book to carry the Random House imprint was Rockwell Kent's lavishly illustrated 1928 edition of *Candide,* designed by Elmer Adler, set in a Bernhard typeface, and printed by Pynson Printers. Over Adler's objections, Random House published an inexpensive, trade edition of *Moby Dick,* also illustrated by Kent. R. R. Donnelley, a large commercial printer in Chicago, originally commissioned and distributed Kent's limited edition *Moby Dick* as advertising for its printing achievements. The Random House trade edition (which neglected to mention Melville's name on the title page) was Rockwell Kent's biggest financial success, and it became a Book-of-the-Month Club selection.

Random House's most ambitious project was a cooperative venture with the Grabhorn Press to publish a stunning, fully illustrated edition of Whitman's *Leaves of Grass* at one hundred dollars a copy. Calling it a "brute of a book," Cerf told Edwin Grabhorn "to figure out what it would cost to do this in as beautiful a format as you can possibly contrive for it."[41] In November 1929, shortly after the book's release and less then one month after the stock market crash, Cerf wrote optimistically: "The difficulty of collecting accounts is about the only fly in the ointment for Random House at the present time. I suppose that the business depression that everybody is predicting will cramp our style for a time, but we are perfectly willing to sit tight for a few months until the storm blows over. We have a most successful year [going], and the business is in a most flourishing condition."[42]

Those "few months" turned into years of waiting. By 1930, the deepening Depression had affected the sales of limited editions. Random House scaled back its fine-edition program, and Klopfer and Cerf begged contracted presses to cut back production. During the Great Depression, only high-priced "big books" in the fifty-dollar range still sold; the market collapsed for most mid-priced limited editions selling for ten to twenty dollars.[43] Nearing the abandonment of fine presswork altogether by 1933, Cerf wrote to Richard Ellis of the Georgian Press, "Things are painfully quiet in our Random House division these days, and we plan to do nothing whatever in the way of special editions until the market for such gadgets improves at least 1000%."[44]

BOOKS FOR READING

In 1928, a *Publishers' Weekly* article, "Modern Quarters for Modern Enterprises," featuring a tour of the shared Modern Library–Random House offices (newly redecorated by Lucian Bernhard), suggested that the organizations served "two opposite interests: the utilitarian and the aesthetic."[45] But Cerf and Klopfer knew those interests were not oppositional; there was a specific aesthetic to the utilitarian. Cobden-Sanderson vaguely defined an aesthetically satisfying book as one that effectively and harmoniously delivered an author's text to a reader. The "Book Beautiful" should neither overwhelm the author's words nor swamp the reader's eye with decorative devices; instead, it should present the text in a simple, readable format. But what constituted such a functional book? The answer depended in part on readers' expectations, which largely hinged on their purposes in engaging the texts. Different types of readers desired different qualities in books, and because Cerf and Klopfer envisioned two groups of readers constituting a sizable market for the Modern Library (bohemian intellectuals and urban professionals), they had to balance disparate needs carefully when applying the utilitarian aesthetic.

Based on the success of the Book-of-the-Month Club judges in choosing books for "the general reader," Janice Radway has recreated the reading habits of the professional–managerial class of the 1920s and 1930s. According to her, the judges' reader reports suggest professional–managerial readers turned to literary works primarily for "an experience of total immersion, a sense of being surrounded or embraced by a book, an act of deep-reading." Radway theorizes that deep-reading helped to counter the isolation created by specialized professional activities. Reading as total immersion in a text offered relief from the atomism inherent in modern industrial capitalism by providing a new social space (the text) where individuals could vicariously interact with other types of people.[46]

Under Liveright's management, the Modern Library had catered almost exclusively to students and bohemian intellectuals, two groups inclined to value the text over its physical presentation. For these groups, reading was an act of labor with recreational qualities. Through reading they acquired the literary knowledge necessary for their pursuits. But the majority of professional–managerial readers expected something different from a book: reading literature was primarily a pleasurable act of recreation that also could provide knowledge.

Yet reading pleasure, to a certain extent, depends on the physical embodiment of the text. A book needs quality design and execution to make it easy on the eyes and comfortable to hold. Marred type and awkward, foul-smelling bindings could distract the reader from total immersion. For the "deep-reading" defined by Radway, the book's primary function is to convey the text transparently to the reader's imagination. It also must invite the reader into the text with certain minor luxuries to indicate the recreational aspect. In other words, the book ought to offer sensory triggers to transportation while still straightforwardly presenting the text. The Modern Library (following conventions set up by book designers, reinforced in popular magazines, and touted by respected popular critics) offered the "general reader" a package for transportation. A touch of gold stamping set off on a rich red cover introduced the books.[47] Flexible cloth bindings effortlessly laid open to display clear, black type on opaque white paper. The portable, lightweight volumes fitted comfortably into the average adult hand and could be carried easily to any environment from the bed, to the train, to the beach. The "classy" formality of Adler's title pages announced the texts as elegant delectables for consumption, while the torchbearer served as a trusted insigne of quality.

Klopfer's correspondence with manufacturers reveals his devotion to maintaining the quality behind the trademark. He wrote to the Kennelly Paper Company in February 1931 complaining that the last batch of paper was "decidedly unsatisfactory from the point of view of opacity."[48] He continued, "If that mill cannot improve on the opacity, we will simply have to find another mill to make our paper." Less than two months later he wrote to tell them he was through with their services.[49] Twice in 1930, he berated the Modern Library's long-time binder, Wolff Estates, for lapses in the quality of their workmanship.[50] Although Klopfer selected papers and binding cloths for the series with great care, he was forced to make concessions to economy. Keeping the price down was essential to the success of the Modern Library, and at ninety-five cents a copy (or about sixty cents to most booksellers), every penny of manufacturing costs had to be used effectively. In 1932 escalating gold prices forced a reduction in the amount of gold leaf that could be used on each volume. Klopfer chose to replace a large grapevine motif on the spine with a considerably smaller design incorporating the letters *M* and *L*. To Klopfer, it was more important to use real gold for the stamping than to maintain the larger design with inexpensive false gold stamping. False gold leaf, like the "Croft" leather rejected for honest cloth, threatened the integrity of the series: it would have lacked "class" and displayed poor taste.

Klopfer's careful attention to detail, so conspicuously lacking with Boni & Liveright, maintained the Modern Library's desirability by keeping the physical form of the books in harmony with an historically defined vision of the ideal book. In 1931, the *Nation* printed a diatribe against books "too exquisite to be read." Calling for a return to "functionalism in book-making," critic Henry Hazlitt averred, "I would rather, for sheer convenience, read 'The Decameron' in the little 95-cent Modern Library edition than in the handsome two-volume edition published at $17.50 by Covici-Friede." He praised the Oxford Standard Authors series (an English series similar in format to the Modern Library) for being "compact, durable, reasonably light, able to stand up physically under repeated readings, and admirably printed." To Hazlitt, "fine books" were for "the nouveau riche book collector, who thinks that money can buy even intellectual prestige."[51] A similar vision was expressed in the *Bookman* by Evelyn Harter, also in 1931. Claiming the average reader only wanted "a good story that won't tire his eyes," she called for a functionalist book "in which the words are sharp and clear, in which the line is not too long for [the reader's] eye-span, in which the margins are sufficiently wide so that [the reader's] thumb will not project into the story."[52] Nothing, not even the reader's thumb, should distract attention from the text. Two months later, Harter further explained her ideal book by tracing "a history of the pocket-sized book from Aldus Manutius to the Modern Library" in "Little Sixteenmo, the Good Companion." Her assertion, "men began to wish for books as companions and friends," reflects Radway's idea of how books could overcome isolation — for Harter, a pocket-sized book guaranteed a friend near at hand. She praised the readability and economy of small-format books that, in her opinion, acted through history to democratize literature: "There are still earnest and sincere people who feel that it is a mistake for everyone to know how to read, who admit that literature is best locked in libraries and cherished by a few, but there have been enough enthusiastic believers in the opposite idea to scatter pocket libraries around the world."⁵³ The pocket-sized book served admirably as a textual transmitter, and, unlike an expensive edition, it also functioned through its modest price to open the world of literary experience to the discriminating, "classy" general population.

While *Bookman* and *Nation* editorials treated their self-consciously intellectual audiences to functionalist approaches to bookmaking, Emily Newell Blair, the literary adviser–critic for *Good Housekeeping*, described the act of reading to middle-class women as a full sensory experience. In "Why I Like Books and Some of the Books I Like," she discussed reading Shaw's *Saint Joan* and Blaise Cendrars's *Sutter's Gold:*

> The two afternoons stand in my mind as round gold frames about two pictures, one in the deep tones of an Edwin Abbey, with a single figure of a maid standing out before a background crowded with kings and courtiers, soldiers and priests; the other, with the bent figure of an old man against the gorgeous colors of a Grand Canyon sunset by Thomas Moran. My mind frames them in circles, because each presents to me a complete experience, a complete memory with no broken points, exits or entrances. Yes, I am enthusiastic about this book, about Harry Cimino's pictorial paper jacket, his lovely gold boards, his wood-cut decorations, about the paper and the print, about the chapter divisions and subdivisions, about the short, terse French-formed sentences. . . .⁵⁴

She used these experiences to introduce her brief, highly favorable, review of William Dana Orcutt's *In Quest of the Perfect Book*. Orcutt's collection of essays contained a history of printing that highlighted Aldus Manutius to justify the author's belief in the soundness of Cobden-Sanderson's "Ideal Book." Again, the pocket-sized, simple book stands as a paragon. Blair's sentimental prose reflected her close personal relationship to the books she read, and the "complete experience" and "complete memory with no broken points, exits or entrances" suggested the total immersion of middle-class reading. The rounded, unbroken frames enclosing this experience presented the world of books as something separate from daily life.

In a home-management book written two years later, Blair specifically recommended the Modern Library and other similar series. Their price and format made them ideal for home reading. But at the same time she advised "some volumes *de luxe*" for books toward which the homemaker felt a sentimental attachment.[55] Blair not only delighted in functional books but also felt the need for more ostentatious productions for certain "treasured" stories. The book, for Blair, is a vehicle for the text that can be adorned to delight on multiple levels or be presented in a simple format for in-depth reading.

Hazlitt, Harter, and Blair all agreed on a form-follows-function vision of the ideal book that allowed the reading experience to come to the fore, but their opinions on the functional book differed. For Hazlitt and Harter, it delivered the text comfortably, without distraction; for Blair, it opened doors to full transportation into another world. While Hazlitt wanted only an efficient, portable body for the text, Blair and Harter asked for certain luxuries. Harter admired the Modern Library's "genuine" gold-stamped spine, and Blair delighted in the decorative additions to *Sutter's Gold,* while also recommending the occasional exquisite book. Form might follow function, but surely for Blair, and less so for Harter, if the function was to delight and transport, certain luxuries became necessities. The Modern Library, with its little luxuries as well as its portable, straightforward presentation pleased all three critics.

Seeking to satisfy multiple types of readers by providing little luxuries without distraction from the text, in 1928, Cerf and Klopfer asked Random House's most prolific illustrator, Rockwell Kent, to design a new decorative device for the Modern Library spine. Kent delivered not only a new spine device, but also a redrawing of Bernhard's torchbearer, new endpapers, and suggestions for how the lettering on the spine should be executed.

Rockwell Kent was a shrewd choice to attract the attention of a wider audience *and* to court the intelligentsia and left-wing radicals in New York. In the late 1920s, Rockwell Kent was riding the tide of the most successful period of his life. At age forty-six he had finally achieved commercial recognition for his art. His book, *Wilderness,* and his drawings for *Candide* attracted publishers to his unique book-illustration abilities, and Rolls Royce even asked him to draw a series of advertisements. Moreover, he was the youngest artist represented in the Metropolitan Museum of Art. His presence in the Metropolitan codified his reputation as an established artist, but Kent resented the prestigious institution's general disdain of living artists. He fought for artists' rights when he tried to establish The National Gallery of Contemporary Art—a cooperative venture devoted to the works of living artists. Upon an artist's death, the gallery would auction his or her works and pass any profits on to the artist's heirs as a kind of life insurance policy. His socialist politics, devotion to artists' rights, and deep sympathy for the Russian Revolution made him a hero to left-wing intellectuals.[56]

Cerf felt he was hiring America's foremost commercial designer when he wrote to Kent, "I am counting on you to do a simple but, shall I say characteristic, Kentian design for the back-strip." A design by an artist with Kent's reputation promised to maintain the "class" of the series. Cerf again recognized that class was an expensive commodity; he followed his request with a flattering—and self-congratulatory—exclamation, "I never thought the day would come when the Modern Library would be able to afford to have Rockwell Kent do anything for it."[57] Besides associating the series with Kent, the new design would produce an impressive spot of gold stamping to make the books more attractive to book buyers such as Blair and Harter.

Although the partners wanted something "characteristic," they discussed with Kent the need to appeal to a wider audience then he usually addressed. The correspondence between Kent and Klopfer (who oversaw production) shows a sensitivity to the wants and needs of middle-class America. Though commercially successful, Kent's art was still a little too radical and modern in form for the general public. As Daniel Stark put it so well in *Printers' Ink,* most of the public still liked its art "Norman Rockwellish rather than Rockwell Kentish."[58] Upon completing the designs, Kent wrote Klopfer a two-page letter explaining his attention to audience: "After, I assure you, making more designs for that book-back than there are published works in the Modern Library; after considering and rejecting innumerable pictorial designs, nudes, phallic symbols, and so forth, as either inappropriate to book covers or indigestible to middle western and New England patrons of your publications; I have conceived and executed the somewhat trite, but I feel appropriate, device which I enclose." Kent admits his design has been dumbed down ("somewhat trite") to satisfy a public unused to his controversial style, but his next statement reveals he tried to balance aesthetic tastes: "If you feel that in employing the candle as a part of it I have gone as far in suggestion as may be permitted, please realize that I have shown some restraint in not making that candle of the horrid dipped variety, so much in vogue in modern days." He was willing to cater the overall design to "middle western and New England patrons," but he refused to degrade his phallic symbol by making it overly trendy.[59]

But Kent did not stop with just the spine device. He saw it as his mission to see that all facets of the Modern Library affirmed its status as a cultural entity of high standing. He found Bernhard's torchbearer figure "good in design," but "too grotesque to be in keeping with the serious nature of the Modern Library." He turned his reinterpretation of the torchbearer (blockier than Bernhard's curvy, almost effeminate figure) to face the book's opening and lead the reader into the text: Kent said Bernhard's direction, toward the spine, was "in violation of common sense and precedent in book design" (figures 7a–7d). After referring to the figure as "him," Kent corrected his pronoun usage: "I might better have said It, for I defy you to discover the figure's sex. That's modern enough for you."[60] Modernism, at times, sought to erase gender differences, and the Victorian culture it was revolting against was often characterized in feminine terms. Klopfer surely sensed Kent's irony. With his well-chronicled appetite for women, Kent probably found a genderless society personally disagreeable (the women in his art are usually highly sexed beings, and in 1930 he engraved a party invitation for Cerf depicting a daringly posed nude woman casually spilling a drink toward his own gaping mouth),[61] but he was willing to cater the trademark to the mood of the times. The torchbearer's anatomy, more muscular than Bernhard's original but still gender neutral, not only made the series equally accessible to men and women, but erased any signs of genteel culture. "It" again presented the series as particularly modern in character.

The new Rockwell Kent endpapers display a startlingly different aesthetic from those used under Liveright's management and are a particular manifestation of how Cerf and Klopfer used physical design to present the series in a new light. In 1919, Horace Brodzky had designed pictorial endpapers for the series (figure 8). He foregrounded six powerful workers quarrying two large stone blocks etched "M" and "L." In the distance towers a modern cityscape dwarfing an idyllic country hamlet in the middle ground. The endpapers symbolically present the workers erecting the foundations of a new society from the solid building blocks of the Modern Library. The social–realist aesthetic created by the nude, muscular figures working harmoniously to move enormous stones toward a powerful skyline was congruent with the socialist dreams of the Greenwich Village radicals, as was the idea that literature might form a

FIGURE 7A. Boni & Liveright colophon, 1917. Author's collection.

FIGURE 7B. Boni & Liveright colophon, 1924. Author's collection.

FIGURE 7C. Colophon designed by Lucian Bernhard, 1925. Author's collection.

FIGURE 7D. Colophon designed by Rockwell Kent, 1929. Author's collection.

FIGURE 8. Endpapers designed by Horace Brodzky, 1919. Author's collection.

solid foundation for future civilization. But the taint of class conflict and Brodzky's celebratory depiction of workers failed to mesh with the more conservative values of the professional–managerial class. Then, ironically, the committed socialist Rockwell Kent created a design far more in tune with American middle-class desire. Kent's endpapers featured his torchbearer set in a continuous pattern incorporating the letters *m* and *l* with drawings of open books (figure 9). The "all over pattern," with its short vertical lines stacked horizontally across the page, abstractly presented a wall of books on shelves and flaunted the decorative value of books.

Klopfer and Cerf enthusiastically accepted Kent's overhaul, but the candle device proved impossible to stamp in gold, so Kent designed a grapevine motif.[62] Klopfer expressed his delight in a letter to Kent promising production standards to match the artist's efforts: "Your drawings which we received this morning gave me a real kick. I think they're grand and feel sure that they will do the trick. Even unenthusiastic Elmer deigned to say that he thought the back design was the real thing.

FIGURE 9. Endpapers designed by Rockwell Kent, 1929. Author's collection.

I am going to get really crabby about the stamping, and insist upon their doing first-class work. We'll fix up the lettering and do everything so that the next covers you receive will be complete as you want them."[63]

Their enthusiasm spilled over into the press, overcoming one of the difficulties in the reprint trade: generating media attention. As an original publication, a book evoked free publicity through book reviews and radio programs, but the same title reprinted rarely received more than a simple announcement in the trade press. Kent's makeover and the introduction of the long-awaited cloth bindings stimulated a two-page story in *Publishers' Weekly* to inform booksellers of the new "handsome bindings" and trademark.[64] It also secured the attention of two highly influential radio programs. *Harper's Magazine*'s *Radio Book Program* scheduled a fifteen-minute program to sing the praises of the Modern Library's new format and excellent title selection.[65] The high-profile popular reviewer and literary raconteur Alexander Woollcott, who it was said could "make" a book by recommending it on his radio broadcast, devoted an entire program to the series. Playing off the Harvard Classics "Five-Foot Shelf," Woollcott titled the show "Reading and Writing: A Ten-Dollar Shelf." Asserting that some of the best reading occurs in "snatched time," such as a few moments at the barbershop, Woollcott conjured Dr. Eliot's famous fifteen-minutes-a-day dictate, but he quickly snubbed Eliot's prescription as well as preselected sets by claiming the common man did not want to have his books chosen for him: "My point is that, while he might find it expedient and even necessary to let someone else cut his hair, he does not propose to allow the same fellow the privilege of dictating—even for fifteen minutes—what he shall read." Woollcott then pointed to the Modern Library's advantages—it allowed the reader to select a fitting title, and its price and format dovetailed with the common reader's habits. According to Woollcott, the ideal book was one that could be carried in a pocket or handbag for months, all the while withstanding the hazards of daily life including breakfast spills. After an extended discussion of the fine physical properties of the Modern Library books, Woollcott concluded with his opinion that a ten-dollar bill could provide enough individually chosen reading matter in a fine format to last a season.[66]

Woollcott's concern for matching a book's price and format to reader needs presented a curious paradox: the books that best fitted his demands (inexpensive and well-produced) were dependent on the then-profane notion that books were commodities, a view emphasized by his monetary subtitle, "Ten-Dollar Shelf." In a 1930 *Printers' Ink* interview, Bennett Cerf commented: "We believe that the book which sells at a price of around $1 can be just as attractive in format and dress as much more expensive books. Here we are helped by the good old laws of mass production. Thus we are enabled to use a durable and attractive balloon cloth for covers, to have end papers by Rockwell Kent and title pages by Elmer Adler. In the last analysis I suppose we have a package problem, because dress is as important in selling cheap books as it is in selling packaged merchandise and our covers, end papers and jackets are our package."[67] Mass production meant the artists had to be paid only once for their designs, so Kent's two-hundred-dollar fee could be spread over millions of books. Thus, mass production, so worrisome to cultural critics because it threatened to "standardize literature," made it possible to produce attractive books at a low cost.

The Modern Library's original core audience was highly suspicious of any activity that might demean the sanctity of cultural productions, and books had a sacred quality as cultural icons that could not be fouled without serious repercussions.[68] In the 1920s, middle-class consumers, encouraged by magazines such as *Good Housekeeping,* consciously used books for home decoration. But critics such as Hazlitt deplored those nouveau-riche book collectors with their books too exquisite to read, and nonreading book owners were roundly criticized or lampooned just as Fitzgerald mocked Jay Gatsby's library of unopened editions.[69] Most of Hazlitt's "exquisite books," ironically enough, were handmade, while Modern Library books were unabashedly products of the machine (one advertisement called each volume "a miracle of modern publishing" because modern technology provided such an attractive book at an affordable price).[70] In the machine age, a handmade book calls attention to its own artistic creation, thus subjugating the abstract text to its commodified carrier. At the same time, mass production demands a standardized product that is antithetical to the concept of individualized artistic creation. To many concerned with the fate of literature, books becoming commodities whether handmade *or* mass produced threatened their cultural standing; they either became fetishes of the book form (rather than unobtrusive vehicles for texts) or they standardized the sacred realm of art.

The cultural critics Lewis Mumford and Walter Pitkin feared that mass production, which depended on maintaining product consistency, would lead to the elimination of experimentation in literature. Mumford thought "standards of publishing success" would become "purely pecuniary ones, the author who merely brought honor or glory to the house would be dropped."[71] Walter Pitkin envisioned a future of mass book production that would reduce literature to "slush, trash, blah, and genitals." For Pitkin, mass production of books led directly to the standardization of literary production.[72]

Not everyone agreed with them. Responding directly to Pitkin, Malcolm Cowley maintained that the effect of mass production on book prices was evidence of "an imaginative boldness" and "the first great counter-offensive of the publishers against the forces which have been stealing away their readers and diminishing the social importance of the world of books."[73] Mumford thought the success of the "cheap reprints" like the Modern Library had "precious little to do with mass production," a misconception Cerf was not likely to try to correct.[74] Significantly, Cerf's talk of the "good old laws of mass production" appeared in a trade magazine for the advertising industry, a group he knew embraced the implications of mass production. When discussing the series with audiences threatened by modern industrial forces, Cerf always focused on format, price, and title selection.

JOINING FORCES

As the Great Depression deepened, Random House adapted to the new publishing environment by significantly changing its emphasis. In March 1932, Bennett Cerf met with the lawyer Morris Ernst to discuss the obscenity ban on James Joyce's *Ulysses*.[75] Ernst agreed to contest it in exchange for a small percentage of future royalties. Joyce, desperate for money and excited about opening up the American market, accepted a generous fifteen-hundred-dollar advance from Cerf for exclusive American rights to *Ulysses*. Because only seized materials were admissible evidence in an obscenity trial, Cerf, Klopfer, and Ernst pasted criticism and testimonials from prominent writers such as Arnold Bennett, Edmund Wilson, Ford Madox Ford, and Ezra Pound into a copy of *Ulysses*. They shipped the bulging contraband back to Europe, and then hired an agent to "smuggle" it back through United States Customs. By 1933, customs officials were looking the other way when the blue, Paris paperback copy of *Ulysses* appeared in suitcases: the Random House agent first had to persuade the underzealous customs official to search his bag, then had to call in the official's supervisor and insist the book be seized. The subsequent obscenity trial, presided over by the sympathetic Judge John Woolsey, overturned the ban on *Ulysses,* and Random House published the first unexpurgated American edition in January 1934. Klopfer believed Random House was carrying on Liveright's anticensorship tradition, but Cerf sounded more like Liveright-the-showman when he recounted it: "here was a big commercial book—with front-page stories to help launch it—and it did a lot for Random House."[76]

The move to trade publishing bothered the persnickety Adler who thought Random House should devote all of its resources to promoting fine-press work in America. Cerf and Klopfer amicably bought their friend's shares and merged the corporations.[77] The merger helped the partners move aggressively into trade book publishing by officially linking their corporate names and infusing Modern Library capital into Random House. In June 1933, Liveright, Inc. (as it was then called) descended into bankruptcy. Cerf knew, as did the rest of the industry, of the firm's imminent collapse. Before it fell, Cerf was already actively courting Liveright authors—especially Eugene O'Neill, who he knew would boost Random House's prestige in the literary community just as Nonesuch had in the fine-press world.

In May 1933, Cerf flew to Sea Island, Georgia, to speak in person with O'Neill. By the end of the weekend, he had warmed O'Neill to the prospects of Random House, which prompted Cerf to write a detailed four-part proposal climaxed by "What the Modern Library Can Offer Mr. O'Neill." The proposal offered to employ O'Neill's Liveright editor and close friend Saxe Commins to "be at Mr. O'Neill's service for any help that may be required of him." It also promised to use Random House's fine-press connections to ensure that "all limited editions of Mr. O'Neill's books will, in the future, be handled in the most efficient manner possible and that the typography will be supervised by the best printers in the country." The proposal pointed out: "The fact that Random House and the Modern Library are parts of the same corporation will mean that any reprint editions of Mr. O'Neill's books will be completely cared for, and in short, every possible kind of edition of the books—the limited editions, trade editions, and reprint editions—will be the responsibility of the same firm."[78] O'Neill was impressed by Cerf's personality and by his proposal. A week later he echoed many of Cerf's selling points in a letter to Saxe Commins. The decision to go with Cerf over Coward-McCann was partly attributable to Cerf's "drive and enthusiasm, coupled with keen shrewdness." O'Neill added: "Coward was a trade publisher, pure and simple—but Cerf has more to his publishing than that, a love of beautiful books, an appreciation for good literature, an ambition to keep his firm above the level of the others, to expand only along lines of distinction. That, of course, appealed strongly to me. As for background for my stuff, there is no comparison. Coward has nothing to offer. Cerf has two unique things—Modern Library and Random House."[79] Random House, a relative newcomer to the publishing world connected to the most expensive editions in the country, used its own "class" but also its partnership with a set of inexpensive reprints to lure one of the most celebrated American authors of the day. The partners' long-standing attention to beautiful books attracted both O'Neill and his autocratic wife Carlotta. During Cerf's weekend visit, she discussed bindings with Cerf and tried to convince him that sapphire blue would best suit O'Neill's books.[80] Random House thus acquired Saxe Commins, who became a key editorial voice in the management of the Modern Library. With O'Neill on board and busy with the fight for *Ulysses,* the tireless Cerf sought out and secured Robinson Jeffers, Clifford Odets, and Gertrude Stein for his list.

The partners' next move was to absorb Smith & Haas, admitting Robert Haas into the firm as a full one-third partner. He brought along William Faulkner, Isak Dinesen, André Malraux, and Robert Graves. In a little over three years, Cerf and Klopfer had reacted to the collapse of the limited editions market and transformed Random House from a small distributor to a major literary publishing house.

Haas's entry into the firm completed a unique publishing cycle. When Harry Scherman and Maxwell Sackheim decided to concentrate on developing the Book-of-the-Month Club in 1924, they sold the dying Little Leather Library to Robert Haas and made him the first president of the Book-of-the-Month Club. Assuming wrongly that the club would soon collapse, Haas left it in 1928 to pursue a graduate degree in economics and then, in 1931, formed his own publishing house with Harrison Smith. When Smith & Haas ran into difficulties in distributing its wares, it allowed the Modern Library and Random House to stage a friendly takeover. Haas, who oversaw the final days of the Modern Library's progenitor, the Little Leather Library, and was instrumental in the birth of the Book-of-the-Month Club, became the second vice-president of the Modern Library. He saw only commonality in his activities with the book club and the Modern Library. He, like Cerf, believed the two institutions were pursuing similar aims.

Just as Random House used the Modern Library to help attract O'Neill, the Modern Library began to use Random House's fine-press reputation for advantageous publicity. On the back page of the Spring 1935 Random House–Modern Library Catalog, the new titles in the series were listed over the statement, "The same fidelity to text and attention to every detail of manufacture that characterize books bearing the Random House imprint are lavished—although naturally, on a more economical scale—on Modern Library books."[81] Less directly, Random House helped to establish the reputations of the Modern Library designers by prominently featuring their work in high-profile editions (*Candide* was produced using all three major Modern Library designers: illustrations by Kent, design and production by Adler, and type design by Bernhard). In addition, with the aid of the Book-of-the-Month Club, the trade edition of *Moby Dick* introduced Rockwell Kent to hundreds of thousands of people, many of whom would never have encountered his work outside anonymous advertisements.

BULKING THE LINE

The Modern Library's choice of the handy pocket size, so appealing to critics, presented practical difficulties. Many established literary works of significant length were thus precluded from the series purporting to be "The World's Best Books." In order to accommodate *War and Peace*, Cerf and Klopfer would have been forced either to reduce the type size dramatically and use extremely thin paper or to issue it in two volumes. The first choice was antithetical to the readability they pursued, while the second reduced their readers' convenience. The solution was a larger format, and in the fall of 1931 they released the first three Modern Library Giants: Tolstoy's *War and Peace*, Boswell's *Life of Johnson*, and Hugo's *Les Misérables*. Selling at only one dollar, the still relatively compact format (5 ½" x 8 ½") could easily support over 1,200 pages of text in an appealing type size and with sufficient margins for ease of reading.

The design of the Giants mirrored the regular series, and they were treated as an extension of it. The two formats were usually advertised together, and the Giants' extraordinary value made a more-pronounced appeal to the thrifty. They were touted as "the greatest book value ever offered," and one promotion for *War and Peace* tempted readers: "Hand your bookseller ONE DOLLAR in exchange for ONE OF THE WORLD'S GREATEST NOVELS."[82] In addition to offering longer works, the new format increased the series' value and heft. Despite critical praise for small format books and the success of the regular series, many readers still preferred larger volumes. This was nothing new. A 1917 *Publishers' Weekly* editorial had observed with disappointment: "It is a fact—and we should be very glad to have evidence to the contrary if we are wrong—that the majority of book buyers are influenced in their choice of books very largely by their physical bulk! Of two editions of the same book, each identical in material, each perfectly legible, each bound in identical materials with the same care and taste, each selling for the same price, but one a 16mo and the other a 4to, we believe nine average buyers out of ten would choose the larger book."[83] F. Scott Fitzgerald noted the trend and commented to Cerf, "Even among your clientele the actual bulk of a book, the weight of it in the hand, has something to do with buyer psychology.... Your tendency toward the giant size shows that you [are] alive to this psychological trait in the potential buyer."[84] In the late 1930s, Cerf and Klopfer dropped Rockwell Kent's *Wilderness* from the Modern Library, because the rival Blue Ribbon series had issued the same title at nearly double the physical bulk. Cerf complained to Kent, who had said he "always preferred the Modern Library edition,"[85] "Some day the public will learn that a handy little book can really be more valuable than a bulky tome printed on heavy paper. Speaking in the dual capacity of a private citizen and the head of the Modern Library, I cannot be too fervent with my prayer that the day will be hastened!"[86]

To satisfy public taste, in the late 1930s Cerf and Klopfer hired Joseph Blumenthal of the Spiral Press to modify the physical form of the series slightly. Blumenthal's only significant change was to replace the balloon-cloth bindings with thick, solid board covers. Cerf sent dozens of identical letters informing book reviewers of the Modern Library's more durable new covers. He reiterated his long-held belief that "the Modern Library books are intended to be read and not just to be stuck away in bookcases like the old sets of Balzac and Victor Hugo that everyone used to buy when I was a boy."[87] By dissociating the Modern Library from books produced primarily for display, Cerf reasserted the series' claim to legitimate culture and preempted criticism of their self-conscious "packaging."

Blumenthal's solid boards did more than just increase the heft of the tomes, they also helped to separate Modern Library books from the insurgent "paperback revolution." As had been the case in the late-nineteenth century, critics and many consumers were wary of transformations in the physical form of books. Initially, there was concern that paperbacks were not "real books," a liability it took a generation to overcome. The Blumenthal alterations stiffened Modern Library covers so the books could not be confused with those suspicious new paperbacks appearing on newsstands across the country. Furthermore, his work reinscribed the "class" of the series through its stark contrast with the sensational pictorial covers favored by paperback publishers. Kent's genderless torchbearer, dignified by Blumenthal's cloth-covered boards, connoted good taste and preserved culture's disinterested air.

Although it took four years to settle on a design they felt fitted the series, their obsession with the physical manifestation of Modern Library books dates from the moment Cerf and Klopfer purchased the series. To capture the middle-class, book-buying public, the partners brought to reprint publishing the same attention to design that Knopf lavished on his trade books. Although Liveright's advertisements always mentioned the clear type and "croft-leather" covers, Cerf was able to boast in 1927: "The stampings on Modern Library books are genuine gold. The end papers were designed by Lucian Bernhard, and the title pages by Elmer Adler."[88] Two years later, Modern Library catalogs and advertisements featured Rockwell Kent and later Joseph Blumenthal. Even if the book-buying public knew little of the unique design abilities of the chief artists embodying the Modern Library books, the prominent display of their names promised that expert specialists were working to enhance the books' physical beauty.

CHAPTER FIVE

Selecting the World's Best Books

B ENNETT Cerf knew only careful attention to the selection of quality titles could sustain the Modern Library's long-term growth. Its price and format initially attracted the public, but its lasting success depended on the marketability of its titles. Reflecting on the series' popular appeal, he asserted:

> One might say that the success of a reprint series depends on three factors; the price, the format, the titles. In the beginning the price, if it is low, seems most important, the format comes next, the titles follow. If, however, a series is to succeed, grow steadily and gain for itself increasing popularity, the scale of values must eventually be reversed to read: titles, format, price. This change of values has occurred with the Modern Library.[1]

The partners faced a difficult task: keeping the series up-to-date demanded constant negotiations for reprint rights; maintaining retailers' loyalty required that each title sell well; and holding critics' respect restricted the range of potential titles to "serious literature." They could not afford to try to enhance the critical reputation of the series by selecting prestigious titles that might languish on retailers' shelves, nor could they opt only for big-selling popular titles if they expected the series to remain a respected cultural entity. Believing themselves purveyors to the nation's "civilized minority," the partners built their list to reflect their own cosmopolitan literary tastes. They selected popular titles "in the modern spirit" with a cosmopolitan flair that attracted a significant portion of the professional–managerial class, including the critically demanding members of the intelligentsia. Few titles sold more than seven thousand copies per year, but consistent sales from nearly all their titles maintained the Modern Library as the nation's top reprint series.

Chapter Five

A GREAT CITY OF BOOKS

Sherwood Anderson crowed, "This is something I like doing" to lead off his introduction to the Modern Library edition of *Poor White*. His emotions had gone through a "queer little somersault," ending in a vague feeling of dread and resignation when the manuscript of *Poor White* was first transformed into a printed book, but, he said, he felt only unqualified delight on its reprinting: "There is this book, 'Poor White'—now to be published in The Modern Library, tricked out in a new dress, going to call on new people. The Modern Library is something magnificent. Long rows of names—illustrious names. My book, 'Poor White,' feels a little like a countryman going to live in a great modern sophisticated city." The book's success seemed even to exceed its main character's stellar rise from a dim-witted, Missouri-river-town idler to an industrial genius who could fuel a booming Ohio community. Anderson beamed like a proud papa with his work now enshrined in this pantheon of modern literature. Reiterating his metaphor, he called the Modern Library a "vast city," where his book could overcome its former provincialism. The "new, strange, great city of books" endowed *Poor White* with sophisticated urbanity and "a new time of excitement" in a "new, strong house." Anderson exulted in how new surroundings would attract a broader audience so that *Poor White* "may again live in the life of the imagination other people lead."[2] Anderson's introduction repeats "new" like a mantra to establish this edition as more than just a reprint, rather as a fresh, implicitly exciting affirmation of *Poor White*'s spirit.

Anderson's vision of the Modern Library as "a great modern sophisticated city" succinctly reflected the aims of its architects. Through careful attention to title selection Cerf and Klopfer hoped to create an urbane collection of modern American and European literature enhanced by the latest philosophy, psychology, and criticism, and supported by older titles still "modern in spirit."[3] Taken as a whole, the Modern Library aspired to represent modern thought accurately and thus to capacitate and serve a new cosmopolitan culture.

David Hollinger argues that cosmopolitanism was the single common ideal binding America's otherwise disparate liberal intelligentsia in the first half of the twentieth century. First seriously advocated as America's future promise by Randolph Bourne in "Trans-National America," the cosmopolitan ideal was adopted and cultivated by the country's intelligentsia through the 1920s and 1930s, finally reaching its zenith in the pages of the *Partisan Review* in the 1940s.[4] Embraced by thinkers as politically opposed as Granville Hicks and Ezra Pound, the cosmopolitan ideal represented a position between cultural particularism and assimilationism. Hollinger describes it as:

> The desire to transcend the limitations of any and all particularisms in order to achieve a more complete human experience and a more complete understanding of that experience. The ideal is decidedly counter to the eradication of cultural differences, but counter also to their preservation in parochial form. Rather, particular cultures and subcultures are viewed as repositories for insights and experiences that can be drawn upon in the interests of a more comprehensive outlook on the world.[5]

The cosmopolitan ideal rejected the American "melting pot" which created, in Bourne's words, "a tasteless, colorless fluid of uniformity," but it also rejected the xenophobic cultural nationalism unleashed by World War I. Instead, cosmopolitanism carried a vision of an American culture diversified and enriched by a collection of immigrant colonies within its borders. Bourne believed that "America is coming to be, not a nationality, but a trans-nationality, a weaving back and forth, with the other lands, of many threads of all sizes and colors."[6] Each of America's "national colonies" was inhabited by thinking, intelligent beings who, according to Bourne, held deep respect for their new land and a keen understanding of the past's relationship to the present. But, although cosmopolitanism expounded an openness to a variety of cultural experiences, it most appreciated European cultural achievements to become a quasi multiculturalism dedicated specifically to European traditions.

Anderson's urban metaphor and celebration of the Modern Library's sophistication pointed to the series as an embodiment of this cosmopolitan ideal. The Modern Library gathered from a variety of national traditions and embraced many types of literature to form a "trans-national" series expressive of cosmopolitan taste. In 1929, fifty-three of its titles were British, thirty-five American, twenty-nine French, thirteen German or Austrian, ten Russian, four Italian, three Scandinavian, and one ancient Roman. The series also included several multinational anthologies. No single nationality dominated the series, although an Anglo-American alliance accounted for just over 55 percent of the titles. Fiction made up a solid majority of titles, but drama, poetry, psychology, philosophy, literary criticism, and biography were also represented.[7]

Cerf and Klopfer actively selected contemporary literature and it dominated the series, but they also carved a significant niche for older titles and established classics. When the partners bought the series in 1925, approximately 13 percent of the Modern Library titles had been written prior to 1860, but in a three-year period shortly after they acquired it, they added Greek and Roman classics (*The Iliad, The Odyssey, The Works of Plato, Four Famous Greek Plays,* and *The Satyricon*), medieval and Renaissance masterpieces (*The Decameron, Canterbury Tales, The Memoirs of Jacques Casanova, Don Quixote, The Travels of Marco Polo,* and *Six Plays by Corneille and Racine*), and major Augustan and early Romantic works (*The History of Tom Jones, The Life of Samuel Johnson, Gulliver's Travels, Droll Stories,* and *The Red and the Black*). Each year the series embraced more and more such canonical texts and, by America's entry into World War II, close to 30 percent of all its titles dated from before the American Civil War.[8]

The series maintained a list of over two hundred titles that etched an outline of modern, "serious literature." It supported its early subversive reputation by retaining writers like Émile Zola, Gustave Flaubert, and Anatole France, while also including collections of Marx and Nietzsche. Such writers as Gertrude Stein, Ernest Hemingway, William Faulkner, and John Dos Passos represented American literary experimentation of the 1920s and 1930s. Pearl Buck, John Steinbeck, and Erskine Caldwell illustrated the period's critically esteemed "popular" writing, while the classics traced modernism's philosophical roots.

Cerf and Klopfer asserted the Modern Library's cosmopolitanism and avoided promiscuous eclecticism by chosing works with a constant eye on modernism and its antecedents. Most intellectuals saw modernism (both in the visual arts and literature) as the artistic equivalent of cosmopolitanism. It offered new forms of subjective personal expression centered on fractured identity and it defied genteel prudishness. To critics such as Edmund Wilson it encoded in form and substance the twentieth-century social upheaval. Most older titles were selected because their satire or probing of the individual's plight in society resonated with the modern predicament and anticipated modernism's dominant themes, and as *Publishers' Weekly* proclaimed, Voltaire was "certainly a modern of moderns," as were Butler, Villon, and Dostoyevsky.[9]

As the intelligentsia became more politicized by the economic chaos of the early 1930s, modernism's obsession with form and its adulation of the heroic artist irritated some political radicals, but for others, radical politics and modernism formed a natural alliance.[10] Modernism opened avenues for social criticism to lay bare the shallow nature of philistine life and to expose the personal despair and alienation created by advanced capitalism. For such modernist radicals, poems about the coming revolution or stories of a class-conscious proletariat were inartistic, blunt instruments compared with a modernist unmasking of capitalism's evils, especially one that emerged from a skilled interpretive reading. The critic's role became crucial, for he or she could interpret art and cause it to be transmuted into political action.

The Modern Library assured the wide availability of modernist writings and also featured explicitly radical voices. The 1930s list included the leftist novels of James T. Farrell, John Dos Passos, and John Steinbeck. V. F. Calverton edited three literary and political anthologies for the series, and Max Eastman, Granville Hicks, and Clifford Odets all contributed introductions. The partners offered only fifty dollars for an introduction, but Cerf implied that compensation for the low fee lay in the chance to democratize literature: "The honorarium is nothing to write home about ($50.00 is what we usually pay), but it need not be very long, and we like to think that there is a certain amount of pleasure in helping to launch the first cheap edition of a book that has never sold for less than $3.00 or $4.00."[11] The class-conscious Modern Library promised in its humble way to help meliorate economic inequality.

Along with Klopfer, Cerf was intrigued by leftist causes and was close to being a "fellow traveler" in the 1930s. Cerf hosted a party for Malcolm Cowley, Michael Gold, Henry Hart, and Josephine Herbst to establish a book club called "The Book Union," which was being organized to distribute "proletariat novels" and revolutionary literature to America's workers.[12] When nearly every other New York publisher was fighting the United Office and Professional Workers Union, only Cerf and Klopfer publicly supported their employees' unionization efforts, and Random House was the country's first unionized publishing office.[13] Cerf helped organize International Publishers' tenth-anniversary celebration, and Klopfer's wife Marian worked for the Moscow-controlled firm.[14] In addition, both partners took extended trips to the Soviet Union in the mid-1930s for a firsthand view of communism in action. Though an aggressive capitalist in practice, Cerf proclaimed to critic Isabel Paterson: "Isn't it amazing how the name of Karl Marx, under a shadow for so many years, has suddenly blazoned forth with renewed glory? I think he stands out today as the major prophet of our times."[15]

While the political flavor of the Modern Library corresponded to the partners' convictions, the political volatility of the intelligentsia in the 1930s often called forth all of Cerf's diplomatic skills. Longtime political radical Max Eastman edited an enormously successful Marx anthology for the Modern Library in 1932. The next year he published a stinging attack on Stalinism and the John Reed Clubs, one of the first volleys in an anti-Stalinist schism in America's left.[16] Not yet realizing the impact of Eastman's denunciations, and pleased with the success of the Marx volume, Cerf and Klopfer contracted with him to translate and assemble a companion anthology of Lenin's writings, which Klopfer hoped "would create a great feeling of ill-will in this country."[17] But Eastman's anti-Stalinist views increasingly made him anathema to the organized left, and by the mid-1930s the partners knew that the "ill-will" would come from the Communist Party and that the anthology's most identifiable potential market would refuse to buy anything associated with the disenchanted critic. Eastman, who had become discouraged by the enormity of the task and had spent his six-hundred-dollar advance, later remembered Cerf's diplomatic visit to Martha's Vineyard: "While we were chatting together on the beach after a swim, Bennett began to say something hesitantly—an arresting phenomenon, for he has not a hesitating flow of thoughts. What he said was that since the split with the Trotskyists had grown so bitter, it would cost the firm 'at least two thousand dollars' if I, instead of someone more orthodox, edited and introduced the works of Lenin." Trying to "look pained," a relieved Eastman bowed out of the project and Cerf let him keep his advance.[18] Lenin's works never appeared in the series, and John Strachey even advised Cerf to replace the Eastman-edited Marx volume: "Naturally I dislike the preface very much and think it a complete misunderstanding of Marxism, but then I would. On the other hand, so would all Party Communists."[19] But Cerf held on to the title and its preface knowing that the market for Marx was no longer just the "Party faithful" but readers of all sorts curious about Marxism. Eastman's high-profile split with the organized left advertised his independence from Communist Party dogma and may have given his preface a more objective standing in the eyes of readers among America's civilized minority.

Maintaining a cosmopolitan balance focused on modernism led an exasperated Cerf to tell Alfred Knopf, "We really ought to have a Thomas Mann title somewhere along the line in a series that is supposed to represent the best in modern literature."[20] Cerf was reacting to Knopf's disturbing decision in 1939 to withdraw rights to *The Magic Mountain* and *Buddenbrooks* rather than renew their standard five-year reprint agreements. He first pleaded for *Buddenbrooks,* because losing it "would be a serious blow to the prestige of the whole Modern Library."[21] Failing to persuade Knopf, six months later Cerf wrote to Knopf's chief editor Joseph Lesser: "At the risk of seeming DeGraff-like [sic] in my persistence, I want to beg you and Alfred to consider again the question of THE MAGIC MOUNTAIN. That book is one of the absolute landmarks of the Modern Library series, and I cannot tell you how many inquiries we have received concerning its disappearance from our list." He was being so insistent, he said, because, "I'd rather have it than any other book in print today."[22] This craven pleading went on, and Lesser responded firmly a year and a half later: "Sorry but the answer is 'no' for THE MAGIC MOUNTAIN. Perhaps we can sell you some other title in the near future."[23] Undaunted, Cerf wrote again in July 1942: "I am wondering if, by March of that year [1943], you and Alfred might not be willing to let us put THE MAGIC MOUNTAIN into the Modern Library Giant series.... Quite frankly, we get letters every week in the year demanding to know why this title is no longer in the series, and I'd rather have it back than any other book in print."[24] Lesser remained unmoved: "This title is just too good a back-list item for us to be willing to part with on any arrangement whatsoever. As a trade publisher you must appreciate the necessity of our decision."[25] Not for any lack of effort, the Modern Library could not get a Mann title into the series again until Knopf became a wholly owned subsidiary of Random House in 1960.

Cerf fought so hard for *Buddenbrooks* and *The Magic Mountain* in part because Thomas Mann was Germany's foremost literary modernist and an outspoken critic of fascism. Modernism needed to remain at the series core to satisfy professional–managerial readers anxious to stay abreast of current literary trends. Mann's presence in the series, as an undisputed modern master, could assure readers that they were entirely modern.

The prestige of the series rested on its reputation for presenting the latest cultural developments in a format accessible to a wide market of readers. It had to stay modern to maintain its innovative critical stance even as it satisfied more conservative elements with traditionally canonical works and its overall presentation as a "library" worthy of a nineteenth-century gentleman's home. As a renowned antifascist, whose sprawling critiques of German bourgeois society exemplified the modern novel, Mann was essential reading for "modern" Americans sympathetic to fast-paced, twentieth-century change and critical of oppressive social institutions. Furthermore, most members of America's intelligentsia feverishly embraced Mann's depictions of his heroes' desperate struggles to overcome vapid bourgeois morality.[26]

V. F. Calverton's magazine of radical social thought, the *Modern Quarterly*, heartily approved of the cosmopolitan taste of the Modern Library editors. In its pages, Huntington Cairns, a young lawyer who made a career of fighting censorship, asserted that the Modern Library's "point of view" distinguished it "from all other collections of books," and added, "It is civilized. Urbanity, catholicity, and a certain recklessness are its hall marks. There is also a degree of sauciness, a thumbing of noses, in a collection of books that includes titles so diverse as a detective story by the Baroness Orczy and Walter Pater's *Marius the Epicurean*." The diversity of the series made it "unquestionably the finest," and "unquestionably the most representative, of all collections of modern books." Becoming prescriptive in his enthusiasm, Cairns thought the series "essential" for anyone wishing "to understand modern literature," because it contained "a great number of books which every educated person must read."[27]

Beyond the intelligentsia the cosmopolitan ideal found few followers, and Hollinger points out that it "was of virtually no importance in a national political context," but, according to *Outlook* magazine it defined "the taste and liking of cultivated American readers generally."[28] This magazine addressed to the professional–managerial class asked its readers in 1921 to take "A Test of Taste." *Outlook*'s self-congratulatory poll found little support for high modernism, but it offered "proof of wide diversity of taste and of individual independence" among cultivated Americans. In the end, the "remarkably even division between foreign and American writers" selected by the readers proclaimed "a fairly cosmopolitan verdict."[29]

Providing a more systematic affirmation of the *Outlook*'s conclusions, Douglas Waples synthesized a decade of reading studies in an attempt to create a portrait of America's reading habits during the Depression. Waples differentiated reading into "mass" and "class" categories. "Class" literature was written "with eager conviction upon current social issues, to dramatize the problems of the day in fiction of every hue, and in nonfiction ranging from religion to economics."[30] He refined his definition of "class" literature by incorporating Jeannette Howard Foster's categorization of "good fiction" from her study of "cultural levels." She had grouped the two hundred and fifty most-read fiction authors into six "cultural levels" based on her judgment of their literary sophistication. The top two levels earned the badge of "good fiction," books that either "satisfy in some degree all requirements generally cited for greatness" or whose "understanding and expression is admirable" but still somehow limited.[31] "Good fiction" featured a cosmopolitan list that included twenty-three British authors, ten Americans, and twelve continental writers, nearly all of whom were published by the Modern Library. Foster's library-based study found: "Readers of good fiction are more apt to chose their reading for its quality than for its subject type, that is, they choose good authors from different [genres] oftener than several from the same [genre]."[32] In other words, a person who enjoyed a work of "good fiction" was likely to choose most of his or her reading based on formal excellence rather than theme or subject. As a follow-up, Waples personally conducted another study that determined "good fiction" tended to be favored over "other fiction" by only two statistical groups: the college educated and professionals.[33] The *Outlook*'s 1921 poll and Waples's 1938 analysis of reading studies suggest that the Modern Library's cosmopolitan title selection, with its focus on a wide variety of "class" literature, appealed not only to the nation's intelligentsia but also to most other professional–managerial book buyers.

That "class" literature appealed to both intellectuals and professional–managerial readers eased the difficulty of finding profitable titles, and the Modern Library was proving "serious literature" could attract a substantial market. The partners' primary concern was to produce high-turnover merchandise, and they tried to select only titles that could garner consistent sales without lowering the series' "class." The average title in the late-1920s sold between three and four thousand copies per year, and the best-sellers sold well over ten thousand.[34] In 1928 the partners felt their pool of quality literature was large enough so that they could publicly set a sales quota and promise booksellers that they would replace titles selling under two thousand copies per year.[35] They were willing to give a slow-selling title a chance to catch on but they refused to keep it if it failed to produce steady sales.

The partners showed their hard-nosed commercialism when they dropped *The Great Gatsby*. It had been added in 1934, but five years later the partners were still burdened with stock from their first five-thousand-copy printing and they cut it from their list. Klopfer said removing it "really killed Bennett and myself," and he acknowledged they kept it longer than they normally would have because it was "a great book."[36] Cerf, too, felt bad about the dismal sales, as he explained to Scribner's: "I am sorry to say that we have decided not to reprint THE GREAT GATSBY in the Modern Library edition. The book is one of my personal enthusiasms, but I am sorry to say it has been one of the poorest sellers in the whole Modern Library series." He continued almost helplessly, "I hate to see Scott Fitzgerald's name being forgotten!"[37] Maintaining the title in the Modern Library could have helped keep Fitzgerald's name in the public eye, but only by risking the series' reputation among distributors as a reliable high-turnover commodity.

By 1940 most critics had exiled Fitzgerald from the pantheon of great modern writers, so the discontinuation of *The Great Gatsby* went largely unnoticed, but authors whose reputations were on the rise were coveted despite unimpressive sales. Although the partners described themselves as "ruthless" in discarding titles, they were willing to continue those selling just above the base limit to maintain the series' cosmopolitan appearance. After five years of tepid sales with André Gide's *The Counterfeiters*, Cerf asked Knopf for an extension of reprint rights. Though "this is a book that doesn't sell in any spectacular fashion," Cerf said, "it is a nice one for us to have."[38] It was "nice" because Gide was a major figure for young intellectuals and his reputation was still ascending. *The Counterfeiters* was Gide's only Modern Library volume, as whenever practical, the series wanted one representative title from every important modern writer.

Cerf may have understated Gide's sales potential to dissuade Knopf from rescinding rights in order to publish *The Counterfeiters* in his own Borzoi Pocket Books, as Cerf often muted his customarily optimistic rhetoric when dealing with other publishers. Cerf could secure reprint rights at minimum costs by claiming low-profit potential and good intentions. He apologetically offered Dodd, Mead only a one-hundred-dollar guarantee for two titles to be included in the Modern Library's proposed Freud anthology, because "the volume will be a costly one and obviously no one is going to make very much out of it." To excuse his frugality, perhaps Cerf disingenuously claimed his "primary consideration" was "to popularize" Freud's works.[39] If the Modern Library could boost Freud's marketability, the proposed deal would inflate the value of all of Dodd, Mead's Freud properties. The anthology turned out to be one of the top-selling Modern Library titles of the 1930s.[40]

Cerf expressed public surprise that the Freud anthology sold so well and, after distributing more than one hundred thousand copies in only five years, he confessed, "We haven't the faintest idea why or who are the people that are reading this book so assiduously."[41] Still, it is doubtful that Cerf ever thought the book would not sell well: it was among the first Modern Library Giants, and Cerf wanted the new large format to interest booksellers and the public with popular titles. Moreover, by the time he assembled the anthology, he had already rejected at least two titles on the grounds that the Modern Library imprint could not "put over" a book or "popularize" an author. He told one editor: "The Modern Library is not the medium for popularizing any book, quite regardless of its merits. We have found through bitter experience that the only books that we can sell in this series are ones that have already won their full share of popularity in more expensive editions."[42] Cerf used the same logic to soothe an angry Waldo Frank, who demanded to know why the Modern Library had refused to honor Liveright's earlier promise to include his novel *Rahab*. Offering to meet over lunch to discuss the matter, Cerf told Frank:

> I looked up the sales record for this book and found that over a period of nine months it had sold exactly 36 copies. If there was one thing in this world that I did not want to do, it was jeopardize in any way the good will of this Modern Library that I was paying such a whacking big price for, and it seemed to me absolutely essential that our new titles for the first year or two should be, every one of them, a book known and acclaimed by the public at large. This, Rahab, on the face of it, certainly was not. Furthermore, it has always been our experi-

ence that books that did not already enjoy a wide sale could not be added profitably to the Modern Library; this simply is not the medium for "putting over" an obscure work, regardless of its merit.[43]

Cerf was far more concerned about jeopardizing booksellers' "good will" than alienating the influential critic. To booksellers, the chief virtue of the series was its lack of "deadwood," that is, titles that might add cultural prestige but wasted valuable retail space.

Just as literary merit or critical success could not assure a title's inclusion, neither could the promise of big sales without critical backing. Huntington Cairns suggested the series occupied "a twilight zone in the publishing business," because it uniquely featured good writing with popular sales potential.[44] The series reprinted several 1930s big sellers such as *God's Little Acre, Of Mice and Men, The Good Earth,* and *The Maltese Falcon,* but each of those popular titles also carried the approval of prominent critics. Their success caused the *New York Herald Tribune* critic Lewis Gannett to marvel, "These Modern Library [sales] records show good taste in editorship and good sales can run together."[45]

The policy of selecting only titles with solid critical credentials gave the series standing in the eyes of its authors. Sherwood Anderson's awestruck introduction to *Poor White* illustrated his respect for the series, and Charles Scribner Jr. said Hemingway believed his inclusion provided a welcome confirmation of his talents in the early 1930s and was part of his "growing up."[46] When Scribner's pulled all of Hemingway's reprint contracts in the early 1950s to produce a uniform edition, Hemingway regretted only the withdrawal of the Modern Library's contract: "He winced a little at giving up a long-standing connection with the Modern Library, which had been such a source of pride during his early years."[47]

The partners' ability to select critically acclaimed, briskly selling titles gave the series its standing as an accurate barometer of American literary taste. Huntington Cairns, Lewis Gannett, *Publishers' Weekly,* and *Newsweek* all used the Modern Library's expanding and changing list as an indicator of American's reading habits.[48] More recently the *New York Times Sunday Magazine* has said that the series "served as something like God's own varsity team of great books" for nearly eighty years. The Modern Library had been instrumental in forming America's literary taste, it said, and inclusion in it served as an imprimatur of a work's importance.⁴⁹ The slightly mocking tone of "God's own varsity team" let the reader know that the *Times* knew better than to take "the canon" too seriously, but it also respectfully bowed to the perceived good taste and literary class of the Modern Library's offerings. Cerf and Klopfer were more modest about the significance of the Modern Library imprint and they never saw themselves as "canonizers." They knew through their experience with *The Great Gatsby* that the Modern Library could not create a public for a book or author, but it did provide continued distribution and an additional seal of critical appreciation for an already successful title.

THE SELECTORS

Advertisements and other promotional materials tirelessly alluded to the Modern Library's preeminent commitment to quality title selection, but were silent about how titles were chosen except for vaporous references to "books which critics and public alike have acclaimed as truly great," and the "best works of the best authors" that have "passed the test of time and criticism." Only once did Cerf publicly discuss their choices, during a 1943 radio broadcast of Northwestern University's respected *Of Men and Books* program. To a direct question about the selection of new titles, Cerf responded: "Well, that's a matter of more less of personal choice. My chief partners, Mr. Robert Haas, and Mr. Donald Klopfer, and our head editor, Saxe Commins, and myself very often gather in our office after the day's work is done and discuss the future titles of the Modern Library series. All of us have the Modern Library very close to our hearts."⁵⁰ Cerf's breezy assertion that title selection was a labor of love not included in the "day's work" masked their hard-headed examination of reputation and sales potential in order to humanize the process as reflecting the partners' personal tastes. It is ironical that title selection of the Modern Library so closely followed and praised by America's intelligentsia in the interwar period, was guided primarily by the tastes of two professional businessmen, neither of whom considered himself an "intellectual."

The precocious Donald Klopfer, a college sophomore at the age of sixteen, dropped out of Williams College in 1917. He never resumed his formal education and once marveled: "There's probably no one in trade publishing at my level who hasn't a degree."⁵¹ Drawn to publishing by an aesthetic appreciation of books, he focused his energies on producing a well-made product. When asked if he took "both a sensuous and intellectual interest" in the books he published, Klopfer explained his production-oriented stance: "I'm not a scholar—the intellectual thing is less than that. But I do like lovely books."[52]

Klopfer was self-deprecating when interviewed for Columbia University's Oral History Project and worried that his stories were boring. Even though he cofounded and jointly operated one of the twentieth century's most innovative and successful publishing firms and was a close friend of many of America's most honored authors, he felt he had nothing of interest to offer Columbia's interviewer. Richard Simon remembered Klopfer as "extremely popular" among booksellers and always "pleasant and gracious," but Klopfer claimed an "allergy to personal publicity" and left promotional matters to his more gregarious partner.[53] Klopfer believed his role was to stabilize Cerf's more extravagant personality and to keep the firm on an even keel. Cerf, who never worried about his being boring, remembered their partnership this way: "Donald was always there to say 'Now . . . ,' when I'd come up with some cockeyed scheme, and he'd let me talk about it, and then he'd say, 'That's the most goddamned foolish idea I ever heard in my life.'"[54] Cerf trusted his friend implicitly and respected his judgment in business matters; for a time, only Klopfer's sober judgment could reel in his partner's excessive enthusiasms.

Cerf craved the limelight as much as Klopfer withdrew from it. In Klopfer's words, Cerf "was a terrible ham" who "went out of his way to charm everybody."[55] Cerf characterized his attitude toward life in 1937 to Gertrude Stein: "I still think that my philosophy is the correct one: Have just as much fun out of life as you can while the having is good, and the hell with tomorrow and the generations to come! I believe that this attitude is known technically as having no social conscience. That's me, baby."[56] Despite his devil-may-care assertion, cultural prestige was important to Cerf; still he confessed, "I must admit I am not an intellectual," and even a flattering *Esquire* profile reported he seemed "to have no taste whatever for intellectual discourse."[57]

Henry May claims the word "intellectual" was not used as a noun in the United States until the mid-1910s. The term informally defined a profession for people devoted to culture and the arts. It also had a socialist flavor in denoting "the bourgeois who repudiated his class," and it was clearly associated with Europe, "particularly with the young heroes of novels from Stendhal to Joyce."[58] Most of Greenwich Village's young bohemians were self-styled intellectuals, as were writers for the *New Republic,* the *Nation,* the *Masses,* and the *New Masses.* Adhering to the term's socially minded definition developed in the 1920s and 1930s, Cerf and Klopfer knew they were not "intellectuals," but entrepreneurs devoted to marketing an intellectual product. They saw a clear distinction between their own activities and those of the art-minded authors penning the books they published. In this sense, they identified more closely with Richard Simon and Max Schuster than the two men they most admired, the distinguished Alfred Knopf and the erudite Alfred Harcourt, who did see themselves as intellectuals engaged in business.

Robert Haas's self-conception was not much different from that of the partners he joined in 1934. He, too, was a member of the professional–managerial class attracted by the potential growth of the publishing industry. Educated as an economist, he wanted to find innovative ways to market literature. When his and Harrison Smith's partnership merged with Random House, Haas quietly took over corporate administrative duties, leaving Klopfer in charge of sales and production, and Cerf managing publicity and advertising.[59]

Saxe Commins, nephew of the famous anarchist Emma Goldman, was the only "intellectual" among the Modern Library's key personnel. While studying dentistry at the University of Pennsylvania, Commins had spent his weekends visiting his sister in Greenwich Village, where he had befriended John Reed and Eugene O'Neill. He published his first book with Boni & Liveright, *Psychology: A Simplification,* in 1927, and then abandoned his Rochester dental practice to spend a year touring Europe with his new wife Dorothy. He joined his old friend O'Neill and helped him edit drafts of *Mourning Becomes Electra* and *Dynamo* while also entertaining in his Paris flat the expatriates who gathered in Sylvia Beach's bookshop. Back in New York, he took his first editorial job with Covici-Friede, then joined the sinking ship of Boni & Liveright in 1931.[60] He moved on to Random House with O'Neill on Liveright's collapse, and in Klopfer's word, he "dominated" Random House's editorial decisions until after World War II. Commenting on Commins's devotion to his editorial role, Klopfer said he "was very good, and God, loyal and conscientious—had real integrity too." When an interviewer referred to Commins as "a high priest of literature," Klopfer enthusiastically agreed, "He was. He adored it. He revered it. He was great, just great."[61]

Dorothy Commins sometimes referred to her husband as the Modern Library's director. While he may have been the series' titular head as Random House's chief editor, there is no evidence he exerted any more influence over the series than Cerf or Klopfer (though he probably had a stronger editorial voice than Haas). He thought Cerf was primarily responsible for the series and credited its lasting success to his high critical standards and sure instincts.[62] Commins brought a crucial intellectual perspective to the informal selection committee to make it a fair microcosm of its target markets by the mid-1930s. Cerf, Haas, and Klopfer were solid members of the professional–managerial class. They were interested in literature, but saw themselves as innovative businessmen rather than members of the literati. Commins's reverence for culture and his Greenwich Village and Paris pedigrees neatly made him the singular equivalent of the Modern Library's original bohemian market. As a group, the Random House chief officers probably felt they could select to their personal tastes and closely match their markets' wants. But they were always willing to suppress their own critical evaluations when poor sales proved they had failed to meet the reading needs of America's "civilized minority."

The partners adhered to modern management methods by consulting other experts' opinions to supplement their own "inclinations and hunches."[63] They collected critics' "best books" lists and took counsel from solicited and unsolicited correspondence from university professors and prominent intellectuals.[64] In 1928 Granville Hicks had suggested Somerset Maugham's *Of Human Bondage,* which was added in 1930, and became one of the series' all-time, best-selling titles.[65] Clifford Odets wanted to see Stendhal's *Lucien Leuwen* as well as a collection of "Best American" plays included, but Stendhal was already represented by *The Charterhouse of Parma* and *The Red and the Black* so a third book was not added; the series released a collection of "Best American Plays" in 1951.[66] Edmund Wilson proposed André Malraux's *Les Conquerants* in 1933; his specific request was not met, but a few years later Malraux's *Man's Fate* entered the series.[67] William Lyon Phelps sent a long list of suggestions in 1927, followed by the inclusion of Henry James's *The Turn of the Screw* (1930), Goethe's *Faust* (1930), and Swift's *Gulliver's Travels* (1931).[68] His suggestion for more H. G. Wells may have influenced the decision to publish *Tono-Bungay* in 1931, but the partners ignored his nomination of Bunyan's *The Pilgrim's Progress*. He wanted more George

Gissing and Ivan Turgenev titles, too, but both were already fixtures in the series with two books each. In 1939, James T. Farrell recommended Thomas Paine's writings; a collection had been dropped previously due to low sales, but *The Selected Works of Tom Paine*, which included Howard Fast's popular fictional biography *Citizen Tom Paine,* appeared in 1946.[69] F. Scott Fitzgerald, Heywood Broun, Gertrude Stein, Christopher Morley, and Alfred Kreymborg all petitioned for their own titles, but only Morley's request for *Human Being* was honored (Stein's *Three Lives* was already in the series when she proposed *The Autobiography of Alice B. Toklas* and *Everybody's Autobiography*).[70] According to Cerf, demand from interested readers (probably spurred by the Spanish Civil War) secured a place for Elliot Paul's *Life and Death of a Spanish Town* of 1937.[71]

Because the Modern Library sought many works still under copyright, its selectors were not entirely free agents. During his stewardship, Liveright's lax business ethics had made acquisitions more difficult for the Modern Library, because, as Cerf bluntly explained, "Publishers didn't like or trust him." They feared Liveright would use reprint rights to lure away their authors. Cerf and Klopfer were not publishers of original works until 1933, so few publishers saw them as competitors for future properties. When difficulties did arise, Cerf was always willing to take the "trouble and time to go and woo the publishers." In any case, Cerf pointed out that the Modern Library's customary five-thousand-dollar guarantee against eight- to ten-percent royalties "was pretty attractive" after a book's initial sales had fallen off.[72]

Negotiations for reprint rights were facilitated in part by the partners' reputations as ethical businessmen. Just after the early Random House trade edition of Rockwell Kent's illustrated *Moby Dick* was chosen as a Book-of-the-Month Club selection in 1928 and a five-thousand-dollar check issued for the rights, the club decided to double its normal guarantee for all future selections. The club's director, Harry Scherman, then sent Cerf and Klopfer an additional check with an explanatory note. Perhaps motivated by their own guarantee policy, but more likely seeing an opportunity in the gossipy New York publishing world to dissociate themselves from Liveright's business promiscuity, the young partners decided they ought to honor their original agreement. A shocked Scherman arranged a luncheon with Cerf, Klopfer, and the Book-of-the-Month Club chief officers (it was Robert Haas's first encounter with his future partners), at which a compromise was struck and the partners accepted a seventy-five-hundred-dollar guarantee. The money was not nearly so important to Cerf as preserving the gentlemanly character of his business. After suggesting, "When people are decent, things work out for everyone," Cerf asserted that "the ideal business" is one where "you can work a thing out so that everyone profits."[73] The young partners' willingness to sacrifice a substantial windfall, as well as Scherman's desire to make the club's new policy retroactive, point to the peculiar nature of the publishing business: despite all their overtures toward updating the industry by imbuing it with modern commercialism, both the Book-of-the-Month Club and the Modern Library saw the traditional ethics of the profession as more important than immediate profits.

Klopfer organized a monthly luncheon club, Twelve Against the Gods of Publishing, to cement the partners' relationships with innovative publishers issuing the kinds of books best suited to the Modern Library. The club met at a speakeasy until the end of Prohibition (it moved to the dining room of the Waldorf-Astoria when it, too, became wet in 1933) and served as a liberal alternative to the stuffy Publishers Lunch Club, which, in the past, had denied membership to several Jewish publishers.[74] The "Twelve" consisted of the prominent editorial and management staff for many first- and second-generation Jewish publishers as well as liberal houses such as Doubleday, Doran. Besides Cerf and Klopfer, membership included: Viking Press founders Harold Guinzburg, George Oppenheimer, and Marshall Best; Thayer Hobson of William Morrow & Co.; Simon & Schuster's cofounders Richard Simon and Max Schuster; George Stevens of W. W. Norton; Pocket Books founder and Doubleday, Doran sales manager Robert de Graff; Daniel Longwell, also of Doubleday, Doran; Robert Haas and Harrison Smith (before they merged with Random House); Alfred Knopf; Curtice Hitchcock and Eugene Reynal of Reynal & Hitchcock, publishers of Blue Ribbon Books; Stuart Rose from Little, Brown & Co.; John Farrar and Stanley Rinehart, founders of Farrar & Rinehart; and "Cap" Pierce of Harcourt, Brace & Co.[75] Women were conspicuously absent, even though Cerf's close friend Blanche Knopf and a few other women were becoming prominent members of publishing firms. Also absent were any representatives of the challenged "Gods": Harper's, Macmillan, and Scribner's. A list of authors represented by members of Twelve Against the Gods of Publishing would be impressive indeed, and though Klopfer described a club meeting as a chance to "sit around and discuss the evils of the book business," surely several important reprint deals must have been made at the monthly luncheons.[76]

Informal business clubs such as Twelve Against the Gods of Publishing served multiple functions. Robert and Helen Lynd believed business clubs offered professionals "intangible income," in providing more job satisfaction, boosting personal self-worth, and creating a cohesive community.[77] Speaking specifically of the old Publishers Lunch Club, Henry Holt remembered it as one of the few opportunities he had had to socialize with other publishers; the friendships the club fostered meliorated destructive competition and maintained a congenial atmosphere among New York's older publishing houses.[78] Meetings of Twelve Against the Gods of Publishing brought together up-and-coming publishers in an informal luncheon setting, where they could work out problems, learn of innovations in distribution and production, and form valuable business contacts. In addition, the oppositional stance implicit in the club's name set up its members as heroic underdogs taking on the status quo to bring about cultural change. Twelve Against the Gods of Publishing not only provided a perfect environment for securing reprint rights, it also gave a greater significance to each publisher's activities: bound together, the members could radically change the nature of American book production.

Beyond its friendly, trustworthy owners, the Modern Library had an ace up its corporate sleeve in securing reprint rights: by 1925, when Cerf and Klopfer purchased it, most authors feverishly desired to be a part of the Modern Library. As Charles Scribner Jr. remembered that scene, "For the authors it was a prestigious event to have their books selected by the series, which in turn made it difficult for the original publishers to refuse licensing them."[79] Cerf was willing to elicit the direct support of authors to sway reluctant publishers, as he did in the early 1930s with the new young lions Faulkner and Hemingway.[80] Faulkner, Christopher Morley, and John Dos Passos all expressed their gratitude to Cerf when they first entered the series.[81] So did Clifford Odets, who extolled the handsome Random House trade edition of *Six Plays* as "very fine," then doubled his praise for the simultaneously released inexpensive Modern Library edition, which was "very very fine."[82]

A few authors retained the traditional wariness of reprints, but Cerf tried to reassure them that the Modern Library was "in a rather different category than the ordinary reprint."[83] Cerf wrote to Kenneth Roberts's publisher Doubleday, Doran, "I hope that we might be able to persuade Mr. Roberts that ARUNDEL in the Modern Library will not only sell steadily and well, but might quite conceivably interest many thousands of new readers in all of his other work."[84] Cerf's promise of a new audience failed to sway the best-selling author, but he managed to secure a play for the *Theatre Guild Anthology* from a usually uncooperative George Bernard Shaw. He also persuaded Willa Cather to allow a novel of hers to appear in the series despite her distaste for cheap reprints. Preferring handsome Borzoi books to the typographic disasters most reprinters issued, Cather had decided in the early 1920s not to allow anyone but Knopf to reissue her books. In the mid-1930s she cautiously relented and allowed the Modern Library to reprint *Death Comes for the Archbishop*. The book did well, but after the five-year contract expired, Cather insisted Knopf take back the last reprint she ever allowed.[85]

Knopf proved to be the most difficult copyright holder for the series. He detested Liveright and was hostile to the series from its inception. Just months after Cerf and Klopfer bought the Modern Library, he fired off an angry salvo to them:

> Dear Sirs,
> In view of my conversation in September with Mr. Cerf I read with amazement your advertisement in this week's Nation, in which you feature GREEN MANSIONS by W. H. Hudson as a title in the Modern Library. I expected after my conversation with Mr. Cerf that the relations between you and this house would be friendly and I can therefore but believe that the advertisement in question is a mistake on your part.[86]

The manufacturing clause in the international copyright agreement had left *Green Mansions* unprotected in the United States.[87] Feeling Hudson had been unjustly treated, and perhaps eyeing future rights to his work, Knopf paid Hudson a voluntary royalty on the Borzoi edition. Cerf and Klopfer had no legal obligation to Knopf for issuing the unprotected title, but they nonetheless agreed to pay a small royalty to win his good graces. Knopf softened to the young partners, but he owned the rights to dozens of titles the Modern Library coveted. He maintained his own backlist series and often refused to renew contracts with the Modern Library for titles he believed he could sell himself.

Knopf's Borzoi Pocket Books series, initiated in 1920 to exploit the firm's growing backlist, lacked both the Modern Library's distribution system and advertising budget. Knopf could turn a profit on titles with broad appeal, but the Modern Library, with its greater visibility and commercial force, could take a Knopf title such as Gide's *The Counterfeiters* and maximize its potential by reaching nearly all of its limited market. Marginal titles unable to sustain themselves in a less widely promoted series might still have sufficient demand to remain profitable in the Modern Library. As a result, Knopf could earn money on titles he could not himself successfully sell by leasing rights to the Modern Library.

Knopf was a savvy businessman and always operated a profitable house. That he allowed dozens of his titles to appear in the Modern Library and then refused to renew expired contracts when it might benefit his own reprint efforts, points to the Modern Library's most important contribution to American arts and letters. The titles Knopf licensed were those he could no longer keep in print himself. Without the Modern Library those titles would have gone out of print, and consequently their availability would have been severely limited. Although it never should be thought of as a charitable organization devoted to assuring the wide accessibility of important modern literature, the Modern Library's devotion to the types of literature ignored by other reprint houses kept dozens of important titles with only moderate sales potential in print. Years later, "egghead" paperbacks fulfilled the same function, but before World War II, the only place many modern titles were available was in the Modern Library.

The Modern Library could not "make" a book such as *The Great Gatsby*, but it could assure wide distribution and possibly introduce it to a new generation of readers. Klopfer and Cerf always downplayed the canonical impact of the series, and its notable failures proved they were right to do so, but the critical series stamp of approval impressed a crucial social class. The colophon acted as a cultural adviser recommending over two hundred titles to professional–managerial readers including writers, critics, and educators. Its wide distribution network and aggressive marketing kept marginal titles in print and extended their lives. Through the Modern Library, many authors had one more chance to "arrive." At the same time, it surrounded each of its titles with other respected works and then packaged and marketed them in such a way as to encourage their positive reception among the members of a social class pivotal in defining the canon.[88]

"The Modern Library has played a significant role in American cultural life for the better part of a century," boasted a 1992 Random House promotion: "Young Americans cut their intellectual teeth on Modern Library books." In the same year Gary Giddins remembered how the Modern Library introduced books into his adolescent world that he might never have read had they not "received the Modern Library imprimatur."[89] The series did more than boost the cultural standing of its issues and serve America's young intellectuals, it made many intimidating titles accessible to less intellectually assured readers. To celebrate their first twenty-five years of ownership, Cerf and Klopfer released a list of the all-time, top-selling Modern Library volumes. *War and Peace* led the "Giants" list, followed by *The Basic Writings of Sigmund Freud; Ulysses* came in fifth. *Of Human Bondage* outsold all other titles in the regular series, trailed by *The Brothers Karamazov* and Dos Passos's World War I novel *Three Soldiers*. Also on the list was Proust's *Swann's Way*.[90] Each "best-seller" sold well over a hundred thousand copies, with *War and Peace* and *Of Human Bondage* reaching nearly a quarter-million in sales. These were challenging works, not only in terms of their complexity, but also in their stringent social critiques. For most readers, books such as *War and Peace, Swann's Way,* or *Ulysses* represent formidable tasks not lightly undertaken: their lofty reputations and sheer bulk demand a commitment of time and intellect. But many readers came to trust the Modern Library colophon. That trusted colophon and the inviting format complemented the low price to invite readers to stretch their self-confidence. The cosmopolitan array of the series gently guided many young Americans into a world of literature previously inaccessible as it led a smaller group into a life as an intellectual.

When James Truslow Adams envisioned his American dream at the close of *The Epic of America,* he believed that Americans awakening from a materialistic period were eager for "something more than is vouchsafed to them in the toils and toys of the mass-production age." According to Adams, Americans were turning to culture and he saw indications "of the beginning of an active intellectual life and an intelligent play of thought" in the nation's universities and great libraries. To sustain its democracy and achieve its dream, America had to discover the tools for "the sane and sober criticism of those tendencies in our civilization which call for rigorous examination."[91] At the same time, young Arthur Nelson, who would become a smelter in Tacoma, Washington, was reading books from the Modern Library to continue his formal education that illness had cut short. Nelson credited the belief that "one is defined, not by one's job or class, but by one's beliefs and interests." His family agreed, and they wrote that his extensive library, consisting primarily of Modern Library books, helped him to become a "working class intellectual" and poet.[92] Adams's idyllic vision assumed that twentieth-century democratic self-government demanded a wise, thoughtful population of individuals, like Nelson, who were unafraid to confront stringent social critiques of the modern industrial state. Ironically enough, he thought the profit motive would collapse in a classless society; but while Adams dreamed, the Modern Library, a profit-driven enterprise based on modern marketing and mass production, alone assured the wide availability of affordable texts to sustain the nation's young poets and its "active intellectual life."

CHAPTER SIX

Closing the World's Best Books

During the interwar period Bennett Cerf and Donald Klopfer established the Modern Library as America's premier reprint series. But events after World War II caused its reputation to slip, as both Random House and the reprint market changed dramatically. Cerf and Klopfer were determined to make Random House an industry leader and, preoccupied by this effort, they assigned their editorial staff to supervise the Modern Library. Under this frequently shifting editorship, it slowly lost its focus on modernism and its antecedents. Title selection, distribution, format, and advertising emphasis shifted away from the nation's "civilized minority" to "the academic community broadly conceived." Lower-priced paperbacks, just beginning to assert themselves in the late 1930s, flooded postwar America and opened new markets with expanded distribution systems. In the interwar period, the Modern Library had had few competitors to impede its growth, but by the mid-1950s it no longer occupied a unique niche. Widely available competing quality paperbacks, which could easily undersell the once invincible series, forced it into a reactive stance.

The academic market's rapid postwar growth was a temporary boon to the Modern Library, as editors Saxe Commins and Jess Stein pushed sales by diversifying the series: in 1950, they introduced Modern Library College Editions, and in 1955, Stein founded Modern Library Paperbacks to compete with Anchor Books and Vintage Books. But the fashion in books had changed: expansion ended with the close of the decade, and sales figures started to drop as it became increasingly clear that the Modern Library's format was decidedly old fashioned. Random House marked the fiftieth anniversary of the series in 1967 with an ambitious attempt to rejuvenate sagging sales. When that effort failed, the list was slashed to stave off imminent collapse. The Modern Library was no longer competitive despite Random House's efforts, and production halted in the early 1970s.

THE REIGN OF THE REPRINT

In 1917, most people in the publishing industry still viewed reprints as parasites on trade publishing. The "class" subsequently displayed by the Modern Library's selective list and marketing strategies, however, gave it an integrity that persuaded most trade publishers to reassess the reprint as a healthy "force in publishing." But with Pocket Books' first paperback books in the 1930s, reprints again became controversial. Their cheap manufacture and promiscuity alarmed critics, booksellers, and many publishers who looked askance at the minuscule profit margins they offered. They feared history might repeat itself, and, as the cheap books of the 1880s had flooded the market with substandard works, so might the paperbacks. But fueled by America's seemingly unquenchable thirst for reading during World War II, and further bolstered by the 200 million-plus paperbacks distributed to the armed forces between 1941 and 1946, Pocket Books and kindred paperback lines emerged after the war as sales leaders in the reprint market. Soldiers returned from overseas accustomed to paperbound Armed Services Editions, and many young men and women who had never ventured into bookstores acquired the reading habit, thanks to the Council on Books in Wartime. Council member Robert de Graff hoped they would read as voraciously in peacetime as they had during the war, and his Pocket Books were stationed at newsstands and drugstores across the country to encourage it.[1]

Cerf had considered the mass-market paperback as early as 1936. Allan Lane's Penguin Books had impressed him on a visit to England, and he wrote to his colleagues at home, "The success of this Penguin series makes me wonder again whether we could get away with some similar series in America to retail at a quarter. That's one for Bob Haas to do a little figuring on!"[2] But Haas refused to believe the "tiny margin" could produce profits. He sarcastically suggested an ostrich ought to replace the penguin colophon, that is, Lane must have his head in the sand to think he could make money on such cheap books.[3] Just before the war it was becoming obvious that Haas was wrong. Cerf arranged a cooperative assessment of sales with Grosset & Dunlap and John Day to evaluate the impact of de Graff's twenty-five-cent paperback edition of *The Good Earth*. The title's sales dipped on each of the older company's ledgers, but perhaps no more than could be expected, because Pearl S. Buck's bestseller had been heavily marketed for almost ten years. Pocket Books may well have been reaching a new, yet untapped market not served by the Modern Library or Grosset & Dunlap. Cerf was willing to be patient before taking any concrete action: "As I told Bob de Graff the other day, I think it is this year's figures that will tell the story of what effect his Pocket editions may have on higher priced reprints of the same books. After all, Pocket Books are still a novelty and it is only recently that they have secured nation-wide distribution for them. By the end of this year the novelty angle will have worn off and then, it seems to me, we all should be able to know exactly where we stand."[4]

With Simon & Schuster's financial backing and his experience as head of Doubleday, Doran's Star Dollar books, de Graff established a nationwide distribution network for Pocket Books. He selected titles with large potential markets, bound them in colorful paper covers, and used a rotary press to print enormous runs. By 1941 paperback reprints were already reshaping the industry: in 1929, Grosset & Dunlap led all publishers with eight thousand distributors, but just twelve years later, Pocket Books were available in *eighty* thousand outlets.[5]

Sales statistics showed that at first paperbacks did not affect Modern Library sales. A paperback printed on low-grade, wood-pulp paper, unprotected by solid boards, and, by the mid-1940s, manufactured with a perfect binding (glued spine rather than sewn), had a considerably shorter life span than its Modern Library counterpart. Paperbacks were light, highly portable, cheap, and, like a magazine, disposable. For many readers their ephemeral qualities created an impression that they were not "real" books; they lacked class in their shoddy manufacture, drugstore distribution, and often lurid covers. The Modern Library, on the other hand, still reflected culture's durability and seriousness in its physical form and marketing. Paperbacks were not taking away from other reprint lines so much as opening up huge new markets far too vast to be ignored. In 1944, Random House joined the paperback revolution when it entered into a consortium with Scribner's, Harper's, the Book-of-the-Month Club, and Little, Brown, to purchase Grosset & Dunlap and incorporate Bantam Books to compete with Pocket Books.

Ten years earlier Cerf had been able to use Random House's vertical integration to attract Eugene O'Neill: he could offer a trade edition through Random House, a "deluxe" edition though Random's fine-press connections, and a reprint through the Modern Library. By 1944, Cerf and Klopfer had a new kind of vertical integration to offer: the Random House trade edition, the prestigious Modern Library reprint, plus the added mass-market potential of Bantam Books. The right title could sell to multiple distinct markets, and Random House could deliver it to each discrete segment of the American reading public.

Reprint lines, especially paperbacks, attracted large audiences and through their prodigious sales promised huge profits, but, as was the case with the introduction of dollar books, many critics believed that publishing houses would select works based only on their mass-market appeal. This threat led James T. Farrell to ask, "Will the Commercialization of Publishing Destroy Good Writing?" Sparked by a *Tide* article on how the growing importance of reprint lines made them "the dominating organizations in the book business," the alarmed Farrell enumerated the perils of the mass market. The reprint houses prospered, he said, not because of technological improvements, but because they treated books as merchandise and relied on substantial investment capital to build sophisticated manufacturing and distribution systems. The economics of the new publishing world devoted to a mass market favored a new kind of publisher—one who was a crafty businessman, not an admirer of fine writing. In contemporary publishing, the "best conditions for advancement," he lamented, "are to be found in having a lot of money to invest, in having new ideas for promotion and advertising, in having the charms of a contact man and the inclination to live in the limelight of glamour." On the other hand, good writing needed publishers who were "men with disinterestedness, sympathy for new currents in writing, liberality of view, cultivation and love of books." Such people abounded in the publishing industry, he added, but as employees not publishers.[6]

The most profound threat, according to Farrell, was the publishers' growing dependence on reprints. Because of the low profit margin per unit, paperback reprint lines and most other cheap series demanded high-volume sales. Only books with significant market appeal would be reprinted. Dollar books, like the Modern Library, must sell thousands of copies each year, and a twenty-five-cent paperback must sell tens, or more often, hundreds of thousands. Vertical integration, according to

Farrell, would necessarily drive firms to select books capable of generating profit throughout the chain. For Farrell, this meant that cultural pap must eventually dominate book publishing and push out good books with limited audiences: publishers would acquire new books with their eye mainly on their reprint potential. Worse yet, unable to match the vertical conglomerates' distribution systems and lower prices, small, independent houses would be unable to compete and either be absorbed or driven out of business.

Reviving the critique of the early interwar period, Farrell charged that reprint lines were sold not as books, but as replaceable, mass-produced "pure merchandise." And while the Modern Library had formerly been an exception, it no longer was for Farrell. He exempted "quality reprints" from his charges: "This, of course, does not apply to such reprint libraries as Oxford's World Classics and Everyman's, which are based on quality," but then added: "In the past the same could be said for The Modern Library, but a study of the list of titles dropped and added in recent years indicates that its editors are gradually watering down their stock." The once-languishing Everyman's Library comes in for special praise, and the Modern Library for censure: "The greatest reprint library in existence is probably Everyman's, and its titles include a large proportion of the major literary and scientific works of the ages. The Modern Library, less broad than Everyman's, is also an important reprint library. It, however, is sometimes watered down by such books as the works of Dashiell Hammett which are, at most, a little bit less than classics of the ages."[7] For Farrell, the Modern Library had slipped from the pedestal it once occupied, even though his own *Studs Lonigan* trilogy was still selling briskly in it. The series once stood above the charge of "pure merchandise," and only eight years earlier Farrell had deemed it a "privilege and a pleasure to witness the inclusion of *Studs Lonigan* in the Modern Library," but in publishing's postwar expansion, its editors, he thought, had bowed to commercial interests that cheapened it.[8] Farrell may have been disturbed that an implicit association with Dashiell Hammett tarnished his own book, and for him, the "great city" Sherwood Anderson had been so proud to enter was losing its luster.

Farrell's was not the first salvo directed at the Modern Library's declining editorial standards. Three years earlier, when the series dropped *The Charterhouse of Parma*, the *New Republic*'s literary editor, George Mayberry, in an open letter denounced the decision on grounds that anticipated Farrell's more inclusive condemnation. Mayberry's attention testified to the Modern Library's stature, but it also hinted at cracks that had begun to appear in the formerly irreproachable standing the series enjoyed with American intellectuals. He acknowledged that a general policy of dropping poorly selling titles could "hardly be quarreled with," but he nevertheless felt compelled to denounce "the passing of Stendhal's masterpiece in Scott-Moncreiff's incomparable translation." Mayberry reminded the publishers that Stendhal was "one of the most 'modern' of nineteenth-century writers" who never sought a popular audience but wrote for "the happy few," a category in which the Modern Library's discriminating readers "surely wish[ed] to be classed." Even if Stendhal's select audience did not warrant his continued inclusion for commercial reasons alone, Mayberry believed the series showed "an esthetic shortsightedness" in failing to keep his greatest work in print for "a coming generation of readers."[9] If the Modern Library hoped to continue to be an honored literary institution, it needed to acknowledge its cultural responsibilities. On this occasion it should ignore the profit motive for the greater good of American intellectual life: like Stendhal, the Modern Library should serve the day's "happy few" in anticipation of a more enlightened future when it would receive its reward.

The Charterhouse of Parma for Mayberry was a litmus test, and dropping it indicated that the Modern Library, for all its lofty, self-congratulatory publicity about providing "really good books" to readers, was being driven by the profit motive and not by concern for the common intellectual good. In fact, purging poorly selling titles had long been its policy, but in an earlier atmosphere when the series had been regarded as a quantum improvement over other reprinting programs, this had gone unremarked. As the astounding success of paperbacks began to change publishing and again brought to the fore the question of how reprints affected American intellectual life, the Modern Library's commercial decisions could no longer escape notice, and the halo it formerly enjoyed began to tarnish.

Nor would the issue go away. Two years later *Pharos* reprinted Mayberry's letter in an editorial context that made it less plaintive than condemnatory. The occasion was the little magazine's special issue on Stendhal, featuring an essay by Harry Levin, Harvard's leading literary comparativist. In light of his assertions of Stendhal's significance as a preeminent, anticipatory modernist, the Modern Library's decision to drop

The Charterhouse of Parma seemed especially irresponsible for a series claiming to represent the best in modern literature. And by introducing Mayberry's letter, this is precisely what *Pharos*'s editor accused it of being: by removing the book from its list the Modern Library had "committed" a "cultural outrage against their country." Broadening the condemnation to the series as a whole, the editor sarcastically added that Stendhal had been dropped, because the publishers "thought they were unable to sell it as numerously as such great works as *Life with Father* and *Rebecca*."[10] Clarence Day and Daphne du Maurier watered the stock of the Modern Library, as Farrell was asserting, and, for *Pharos,* the continued presence of their books on its list revealed how bankrupt were the claims of the series to be serving a discriminating audience with "the best." As a little magazine, *Pharos* had a limited readership, but it represented precisely the discerning one that the Modern Library claimed to serve, as more broadly did the *New Republic,* and the magazines' pointed attacks indicated that the series had begun to look suspiciously like a mass-market enterprise rather than an esteemed cultural institution.

Much of the Modern Library's early success depended on its publishing environment. As new independent publishers, Cerf and Klopfer were seen as having bucked tradition and having helped to finish the job of overturning publishing's genteel culture. But by 1946, many of the young publishers who had rallied as the "Twelve Against the Gods of Publishing" had risen to become gods themselves. Simon & Schuster was reaping the profits of Pocket Books and selling millions of copies of Dale Carnegie's *How to Win Friends and Influence People,* Alfred Knopf had become the nation's leading quality publisher, and Doubleday and Company controlled several important reprint lines. The growth of Random House was probably the most dramatic, and by the mid-1940s it was becoming a large diversified corporation. It had moved from its modern offices on East 57th Street into the elegant and dignified Villard Mansion at 457 Madison Avenue, with its spacious rooms, Juliet balconies, grand central staircase, and a handy proximity to other publishers. In their typical fashion, Cerf and Klopfer loved the building, its location, and its history (previously owned by Joseph Kennedy and once occupied by the Free French) because it had "a lot of class."[11] The new offices solidified Random House's stature as an established and prosperous publisher, a reputation backed by impressive sales: the modest publishing house, with total revenue of just under $700,000 in 1937, had grossed $3.2 million in 1946, an extraordinary 470 percent increase.[12]

To a new generation of publishers and magazine editors, the Modern Library was no longer the sacred cow it had been. For example, Farrell's essay appeared in *New Directions 9,* "an annual exhibition gallery of divergent literary trends," edited by the young poet and publisher James Laughlin and published by his New Directions press. In introducing it, Laughlin expressed special concern about the deleterious impact of the mass market on publishing by describing Farrell as one who "has done more than any other writer to call attention to the dangers inherent in the progressive commercialization of the American publishing business, and its sinister linkages with Hollywood."[13] Another critic on the publishing scene was *Pharos,* a fledgling quarterly distributed by New Directions, with each issue "devoted to one important piece of writing or to the work of a single author."[14] Laughlin and *Pharos* belonged to a group of publishers and little magazines that catered to small, self-defined intellectual audiences by publishing works they saw as important but of limited appeal. It was just these sorts of enterprises that Farrell believed would be smothered by the increasing commercialization of publishing.

Random House's transformation into an established, vertically integrated publisher surely fed Farrell's and *Pharos*'s suspicions of the Modern Library's market orientation, but just as troubling was Bennett Cerf, who was becoming the epitome of the publisher Farrell characterized as indicative of the industry's "Hollywoodization." Cerf had long craved attention, and his personality was notorious within the publishing world. Up until World War II, his limited fame was exclusively as a publisher. During the war, however, he became a more conspicuous and generalized public figure: he began to write "Trade Winds," a weekly gossip column in the *Saturday Review of Literature;* published his first best-selling joke book, *The Pocket Book of War Humor;* and hosted a weekly, nationally syndicated radio show *Books Are Bullets.* Although his twenty-odd joke books sold over ten million copies, his greatest fame came as a regular panel member on the television game show *What's My Line?* from 1951 to 1967.[15] His celebrity rated a cover story in *Time* and extended profiles in both the *New Yorker* and *Esquire.* Cerf was able to boast truthfully: "Ask the average man how many publishers he knows by name—it'll be Bennett Cerf."[16] Cerf, it seemed, embodied the qualities that

Farrell had identified as crucial to publishing success but antithetical to nurturing good writing: he had access to investment capital, all the charms of a contact man, and, most of all, loved the limelight.

Farrell was not the only one concerned by publishers' cultural slumming. Without elaboration, Malcolm Cowley said he followed Cerf's career "with not unfriendly disapproval," and Geoffrey Hellman wrote a scathing *New Yorker* profile that focused on Cerf's activities outside the publishing world.[17] His "Descent from Olympus" related how businessmen tainted by the profane world of commerce often redeemed themselves through extraoffice hobbies that promoted high culture. Hellman contrasted a long list of culturally minded businessmen with a damning analysis of Cerf. Each day the management of Random House and the Modern Library put Cerf in contact with some of the world's most distinguished intellectuals and artists, and his efforts gave serious literature a voice in American culture. Yet when Cerf's workday was through, he became "an escapist from culture," recycling jokes for cheap paperback anthologies while hobnobbing with movie stars.[18] Hiram Haydn recalled how Cerf's reputation as a publisher suffered because of his fame: "A charge frequently leveled at Bennett was that he was predominantly a playboy—a celebrity hunter who cared much more about his puns and joke books, his lecture tours, his Hollywood friends, his television show and the entertainment world in general than he did about Random House." Haydn defended Cerf from the charge that he would readily trade Random House for fame, although in a backhanded way, saying that Cerf would "keep Random House, give up all the other things, and die."[19]

While Cerf's publicity-mongering offended some critics, the attention he drew helped to sell books and attract young writers. Klopfer remembered how much he himself had hated publicity: "I had the feeling that you are only judged by the books that you publish. And Bennett was much smarter than that. Bennett knew that you need the publicity, you need the ability to sell the books, you need all the things, the appurtenances that go with it, particularly television and that sort of thing, as that came into existence after we were publishing. It all became very important to us. I would have been terrible at that. He was brilliant at it."[20] Cerf felt he was always promoting his line whatever his activity: "When I talk and tell stories, a lot of them, of course, are about authors whom I know, Random House authors, and I consequently have to mention a lot of

Random House books in the course of a lecture. So I'm selling at the same time."²¹

Cerf's fame may have helped Random House attract talent, but it had a deleterious effect on the Modern Library. Because the series was so closely associated with Cerf, as his intellectual integrity became suspect, so did the series. Had Cerf not been so eager to become a star himself and had he not fit Farrell's mold of the typical new publisher so well, Farrell's indictment of the Modern Library as a contributing force to the Hollywoodization of publishing would not have had the same validity, and *Pharos* could not so easily have turned Mayberry's letter into a personal attack on the series' editors. More significant, Cerf was the innovator behind the Modern Library's success, and his other activities pulled him away from its management at a time when the reprint market's material conditions were changing radically.²² The aura of the series was fading for Cerf as Random House expanded and he entered the limelight. What had once excited his active imagination and benefited from his bountiful energy grew to be a reliable but mundane part of the Random empire.

MORE CHINKS IN THE ARMOR

To suspicious intellectuals turning a wary eye on Cerf and the Modern Library, the imbroglio surrounding the new Modern Library Giant edition of William Rose Benét's *An Anthology of Famous English and American Poetry* in 1946 must have confirmed their fears that the series was not in the hands of a disinterested party. This collection had been a series mainstay for over a decade when Cerf contracted with Conrad Aiken in 1943 to revise its American selection. Aiken was "delighted to hear" that Cerf liked "the idea of modernizing the Modern," then laid out his plan: "My notion would be to keep on the whole the present scheme — i.e., of not too many poets, these being pretty well represented; but a few exceptions if need be. I'll eliminate Max the Bodenheim in toto, reduce Kreymborg to one poem, cut Fletcher somewhat, and Aiken ditto, in order to add considerably to Stevens, Pound, Eliot, MacLeish, Ransom, Marianne Moore, Jeffers perhaps should be in, though as you know I'm no great devotee."²³ Finding no fault with his plan, Cerf urged him to proceed, and in doing so Aiken selected twelve Pound poems. But by June 1945, as Saxe Commins prepared the book for production, the fiercely patriotic Cerf rebelled at the idea of including poems by Pound, who had been formally charged with treason for his anti-American, fascist radio broadcasts from Italy. By then, Cerf was determined not to publish him: "I have devoted the better part of my life to building up Modern Library and Random House lists of which I may feel proud. When I no longer can choose and reject exactly what I want for those imprints, I do not want to remain in the publishing business."[24] Aiken appealed to the sympathetic editor Saxe Commins and threatened to remove his name from the project. After asserting that he was not arguing, but "insisting," he thundered: "This, if you don't know it, is just plain fascism—you are proposing to violate freedom of speech and press, the very things for which the war was fought. You don't suppress good poetry because of a man's political or moral vagaries. Anyway, *I'm* not going to be a party to such, so let's have no more fuss about it."[25] Cerf and Commins then worked out a compromise satisfactory to Aiken wherein they deleted the Pound poems and inserted the following statement in their place:

> At this point Conrad Aiken proposed to include in his anthology the following poems by Ezra Pound: "Envoi" (1919), "The Tree," "The Tomb at Akr Caar," "Portrait d'une Femme," "Apparuit," "A Virginal," "The Return," "The River-Merchant's Wife," "The Flame," "Dance Figure," "Lament of the Frontier Guard," and "Taking Leave of a Friend." He has consented to their omission upon condition that the fact be clearly stated in print that his wishes were overruled by publishers who flatly refused at this time to publish a single line of Mr. Ezra Pound. This is a statement that the publishers are not only willing but delighted to print.[26]

Dropping Pound became a public controversy when *PM* critic Charles Norman wrote an article that he hoped would "shed light on the whole pressing, fascinating question of the artist's place in society." To achieve this, he solicited leading writers and public intellectuals to comment on Pound's role in American letters, among them was Aiken, who related Cerf's refusal to publish Pound.[27]

Lewis Gannett, the high-profile literary critic for the *New York Herald Tribune,* picked up the story in early 1946. Gannett accused Cerf of putting himself on a slippery slope by "acting upon a logic akin to that of the Nazis," the inescapable result of which was, "with such standards, literature goes out the window." Cerf was unmoved, and rebutted with a letter to the *Herald Tribune*. "Damn it, Lewis, the war is not over," he insisted, "every time you parade the work of a man who represents such ideas, especially while he still lives, you are in a sense glorifying him, and giving tacit approval to his point of view." Although he claimed, "I gag at the idea of paying a man like that the few dollars necessary for formal permission to print his lines," Cerf's strongest objection was a moral and political one: "You say I am being emotional about this. Of course I am! How can you help being emotional about the most important struggle in the world today?"[28]

Shortly thereafter, he laid out "The Case of Ezra Pound" in his "Trade Winds" column. Juxtaposed with a Modern Library advertisement plugging *An Anthology of Famous English and American Poetry* as "by far the most ambitious, and most comprehensive, collection of verse to appear in the Modern Library series," Cerf quoted the *Herald Tribune* exchange in full and reported that he was "shaken" to discover that Henry Steele Commager, W. H. Auden, Max Lerner, and one of his own editors, Robert Linscott, all endorsed Gannett's dissenting opinion. Despite this, Cerf remained unconvinced that he was wrong, but he also felt obliged to consider the opinions of people he respected and whose political views he usually shared. Appealing to an idea of cultural democracy, he solicited advice from the *Saturday Review*'s readers before he pronounced a final decision.[29]

Five weeks later Cerf wrote, "It is damn unpleasant to admit a mistake publicly, but I see no way out of it." After receiving close to three hundred letters evenly divided on the issue, Cerf relented and agreed to including the Pound poems. He based his reversal on several points. First, he should respect the opinion of the anthology editor whom he hired to do the job. Second, the poems themselves contained nothing pernicious. Third, he found that the letters supporting his original position "obviously sacrificed all logic for hot indignation." Fourth, he could not see where to draw the line once he started such a policy—should he expunge Marx and Nietzsche from the Modern Library because he disagreed with their political views? And, finally, he felt that a "blasting footnote" deriding Pound the man (not the poet) would be the most effective protest.[30]

Old friend Harrison Smith warned Cerf that his stand against Pound was "dangerous" to his "reputation as a liberal," which Cerf then shored up with his "liberal" justification for changing his mind.[31] He dissociated himself from the political extremes of Pound and Marx, thus implying his location in the "vital center" that Arthur Schlesinger would soon define. His decision, and justification, moved Cerf to the right of his 1930s political stance at a time when many intellectuals had become disillusioned with Marxism and embraced liberalism instead. In the 1930s, many had seen him as a fellow traveler trumpeting Marx as "the major prophet of our times," but the Pound episode brought forward the new face of the benignly tolerant liberal.

Cerf was protecting more than his own reputation; he was also protecting Random House's as a first-rate publisher with class. When W. H. Auden first heard of Cerf's determination to expunge Pound, he threatened to sever his connections with Random House. Auden used Gannett's logic, though more forcefully, in an early February letter to express his "surprise and dismay" over Cerf's position. He argued, "Once you accept the idea that one thing to which a man stands related shares in his guilt," then "you will end, as the nazis did, by slaughtering his wife and children."[32] Cerf sent a draft of his February "Trade Winds" column, and begged Auden "to please read the enclosed column which gives the whole story as we see it, then review your own attitude in the matter, and then write to me again."[33] Auden replied with a considered response but refused to reverse his decision to seek a new publisher.[34] Cerf then appealed to Auden's self-interest by sending a summary of sales with examples of how Random had helped his career.[35] Just a few days before his first "Trade Winds" column hit the newsstands, Cerf wrote to Auden: "As a matter of fact, I am inclined to the belief that the right way to handle this whole Pound business is to print his poems in the anthology and *then* run a footnote, saying what we think of the man himself."[36] Auden wrote back, "Of course, if you change your mind, I shall be delighted to change mine, and on the day you publish the poems, I hope you will tear up my original letter."[37] When Cerf reversed himself on March 4, he offered to destroy Auden's letters and added, "[I] hope that we'll do nothing to arouse your ire for the next ten years."[38] Auden graciously responded, "Many thanks for your letter and its welcome news. I congratulate you. Decisions are hard enough to take, to change them is even better."[39]

In retrospect, Cerf's reversal was not based so much on his moral beliefs as on his business sense. He later recalled the episode with regret: "I decided that when people I respected, like Lewis Gannett . . . told me I was wrong, well then, I must have been wrong," but then he expressed his misgivings: "I still in my heart don't think I was, but I had to admit that I was overwhelmed by people who felt the other way."[40] Excluding Pound would have cost Auden and the goodwill of critics like Gannett. Instead, by including Pound, Cerf took a public stand for the primacy of poetry over politics and, for a moment, he could foreground his "liberality of view" and his commitment to literary ideals.

The Pound business resurfaced three years later when the Fellows of the Library of Congress in American Letters awarded him the first Bollingen Prize for Poetry for his *Pisan Cantos*. Pound was still under indictment for treason and, at the time, committed to St. Elizabeth's Hospital for the criminally insane in Washington, D.C. The award divided America's intellectuals, and a hotly contested debate raged in four important venues: the *Partisan Review* devoted its May 1949 issue to it, with the majority of the essays condemning the decision; Dwight Macdonald responded in *Politics* with his bold statement that the award was "the brightest political act in a dark period"; the *Saturday Review of Literature* published two invectives against Pound written by Robert Hillyer, who had supported Cerf three years earlier; and *Poetry: A Magazine of Verse* responded with *The Case against the Saturday Review of Literature,* which reprinted several attacks on Robert Hillyer.[41]

Although Pound scholars link the two events, one incident leading to another, the actors in the Bollingen Prize controversy seemed to have forgotten the hullabaloo surrounding the Modern Library's anthology.[42] Never was it even mentioned. The 1949 debate began with Pound's fascist politics but soon shifted to discussions of modern poetry, New Criticism, and anti-Semitism in modern literature. The Modern Library incident had been seen as a test case on political censorship. None of the major voices in the Bollingen Prize debate thought Pound's poetry should be suppressed; they were far more concerned with the question of whether the *Pisan Cantos* were good enough to be called the "Best" American poetry of 1948, or whether such a prize awarded by the Library of Congress should be given to a treasonous poet who was an American only by accident of birth. Cerf stayed out of the affair. During its height, he continued his usual gossipy "Trade Winds" banter about the book trade, while also weighing in with two columns devoted to the Pennsylvania Railroad's degenerating passenger services. He avoided stirring up old memories or mixing the Modern Library in a debate that pitted many Random House authors against one another, while also dividing the series' long-standing core audience. In this instance, Cerf uncharacteristically rejected the axiom that all publicity is good publicity and apparently was glad to have his own controversy over Pound forgotten.

REACTING TO A NEW MARKETPLACE

By the close of World War II, Pocket Books, Penguin Books, and Bantam Books were creating new casual readers, and the paperback revolution made significant inroads into the professional–managerial-class audience Cerf and Klopfer had so assiduously cultivated and counted on for continued growth. Modern Library sales did not drop, but Cerf and Klopfer watched and participated with Bantam in the rapid expansion of the paperback's market dominance. By the late 1940s, as Jess Stein, head of the Random House reference and college textbook department, began to gain more editorial control over the series, the Modern Library ceded much of the "civilized minority" to the insurgent paperback revolution to concentrate on a smaller but still extremely profitable niche market, the academy.[43]

Immediately after the war, college and university enrollment skyrocketed. In 1930, just over one million full-time students were enrolled in the nation's colleges and universities, a number that had more than doubled by 1948 and continued to climb through the 1950s as the GI Bill funded millions of veterans' college educations.[44] At the same time, the Modern Library's long-established core intellectual audience also entered the academy. Russell Jacoby sees the intellectual generation born around 1920 (Alfred Kazin, Daniel Bell, Irving Howe) as "transitional." Its members "grew up writing for small magazines when universities remained marginal," but in the 1950s "they often accepted university positions, which looked better and better as the nonacademic habitat diminished." For the generation born in 1940, the "identity of universities and intellectual life was almost complete."[45] The university offered a stable paycheck, and as enrollment grew, so did the number of faculty, from just over one hundred thousand in 1932 to nearly a quarter of a million in 1950.[46]

Random House was not the only trade publisher to notice the enormous potential in the academic expansion. In 1948, Rinehart and Company issued their first Rinehart Editions. In a memo to all salesmen, Lewis Miller outlined this new initiative and its impact on the Modern Library:

> An important percentage of our Modern Library business derives from their use as texts in colleges. In the past two years, there has been a noticeable curtailment of these sales due in great measure to the entry into the field of the Rinehart Editions, published by Rinehart & Company. Rinehart Editions, now have 35 titles and we understand that approximately 15 additional titles will be launched this year. In the main, the Rinehart Editions duplicate Modern Library titles. The retail price of the Rinehart Editions is 50¢, 65¢, or 75¢, depending on length. The Rinehart Editions are sold exclusively through college bookstores at a discount of 20%. Although professors and college bookstore proprietors are extremely favorably disposed to the Modern Library, it is quite clear that the low price of the Rinehart Editions has been forcing many schools to select Rinehart Editions in preference to the Modern Library.[47]

This erosion in adoptions made the Modern Library's entry into the field with a similarly priced series "mandatory," and in 1950 Random House announced the new Modern Library College Editions. Promotional catalog copy urged college bookstores and instructors to "LOOK TO THE MODERN LIBRARY COLLEGE EDITIONS FIRST," then leveraged the esteemed brand name by drawing on the series' illustrious past to legitimate the new editions: "For more than a generation, the Modern Library has been the most popular source of inexpensive reliable editions of the best books of all times. There is hardly a literate person in the United States today who has not at some time in his life benefited by the easy availability of good books in the Modern Library." Selling at sixty-five cents, each new compact, paperbound book featured an introduction by "an outstanding teacher and critic" and appended recommended reading lists to enhance their attractiveness to the college market.[48]

The Modern Library was determined to win back business lost to Rinehart. All the initial title selections, such as *Pride and Prejudice, Jane Eyre, Crime and Punishment, Tom Jones, The Scarlet Letter, Moby Dick,* and several Greek classics, were in the public domain. Using "the domain stuff" reduced costs so the series might "choke off competition."[49] In addition, publishers had traditionally offered books to college bookstores at a 10 or 20 percent discount, assuming that the "selling" was already done by the company travelers who sent examination copies and then called on instructors to persuade them to adopt the texts. The Modern Library offered its new editions at a 40 percent discount to college stores. Cerf himself boomed the series at the National Association of College Stores. The plan excited attention and, aware of the potential profit they represented, the trade association supported the new editions by distributing promotional letters to its membership.[50]

In conjunction with college store promotions, the Modern Library developed an advertising strategy to take full advantage of the academic market. The new line's editor, Jess Stein, wrote to Cerf: "The attached list shows the magazines in which I recommend advertising and the issues in which I think the ads should appear. The total cost for this program is slightly over $1,000. The first periodical (*PMLA*) reaches the scholarly professors; the second (*College English*) reaches the professors who are predominantly interested in teaching techniques; the third (*CEA Critic*) reaches somewhat of a hodgepodge of professors; while the fourth and fifth (*Kenyon Review* and *Sewanee Review*) reach, as you know, the more literary professors." Stein concentrated full-page ads in the spring and fall seasons "when most of the consideration of textbooks for the following semester is underway."[51] An advertisement in the *Kenyon Review* reiterated the Modern Library's historic importance and then introduced the new series: "Now there is a new series in the Modern Library, prepared specifically for the classroom—the Modern Library College Editions, priced at 65¢ a book in sturdy, flexible binding." The advertisement never referred to the "sturdy, flexible binding" as paper, and the books were further dissociated from cheap paperbacks by touting the introductions as "penetrating critical discussions" by people who are both critics *and* teachers, with each volume also including "necessary biographical and bibliographical data." Even though the *Kenyon Review* was a literary review, not an academic journal, "faculty members anywhere" were invited to send for complimentary examination copies.[52] To emphasize their serious purpose, the advertisement lacked graphic embellishment and included no appeal to recreational reading—a feature Modern Library advertisements had traditionally stressed.

The sales force showed immediate concern that the College Editions were only being offered to the college market. The Modern Library hesitated to put the new series in trade stores where it would compete with the regular $1.25 line and produce sales with lower profit margins, bad both for the Modern Library and for the bookseller. But sales agent James Russell feared the marketing strategy might stunt the new series. He wrote to Miller: "I am a little disturbed about CML. As nearly as I can determine our text orders are coming through in good shape, but I have observed the Rinehart people making a big play with their Classics in trade bookstores, inviting promotions etc. I appreciate our wanting to hold back so as not to upset the $1.25 sales, but don't like to see a competitor get the jump on us with a paperbound line."[53] Russell's concern helped to persuade Miller that the regular book trade should be included: Miller acknowledged the risk of cutting into the regular series sales but admitted, "it's better to compete with yourself, than let the other fellow take business from you." He reasoned that while the new series will "very likely" hurt the sale of the regular series, "the sum total of the sales of the *two* lines should be much greater than the total of any *one*." To allay booksellers' concerns that the Modern Library was purposefully trying to undercut their profits, he asked his sales force to emphasize that competition from Rinehart compelled the issuing of the cheaper new line.[54]

The College Editions were an immediate success. In the first three weeks after announcements were distributed to college instructors and bookstores, 1,128 reply cards for over 5,000 examination copies were returned. The Modern Library sold over 80,000 copies during the fall semester, grossing $43,000. Sales more than doubled in 1951, and tripled by 1957.

The College Editions were not the first experiment in diversifying the line. Twenty years earlier, the Modern Library had introduced its Giant series, books in a larger format, averaging over a thousand pages and selling for only five cents more than the regular series. Directed at the same market with the same marketing philosophy, the Giant format was not meant to compete with the regular series or appeal to a new audience, but to offer attractive texts otherwise impractical to produce because of their length. The College Editions, on the other hand, consisted of the same titles as the regular series but packaged and priced for an emerging market. In this aspect, they were very much like the unsuccessful "Illustrated Modern Library" initiated in 1943.

This changed emphasis in the series' lines illuminates the Modern Library's retreat from the broad professional–managerial-class audience it had pursued until World War II. In 1943, Random House contracted with Harry Abrams of the Book-of-the-Month Club to edit the Illustrated Modern Library. Abrams was to reissue select Modern Library titles with original new illustrations in deluxe bindings and slipcases. The series targeted book collectors of limited means with "collectors' editions" that were far less expensive than the successful and popular Limited Editions Club volumes. Designed as artistic showpieces, they were not marketed for reading, but as books "created so that the booklover of modest means may acquire beautifully illustrated and designed books of enduring worth for his library." An advertisement stressed their physical virtues: "No two books will look alike. Each is a creation in itself, interpreting in its format and in its illustrations the spirit of the text. All books are complete and unabridged and are profusely illustrated with paintings, drawings, lithographs or woodcuts. They will be beautifully bound and individually boxed, stamped in 24 carat genuine gold."[55] Cerf viewed their audience as aesthetically conservative, so he was delighted to hear from Abrams that America's foremost book designer Bruce Rogers had agreed to design *The Autobiography of Benjamin Franklin,* and he was equally happy to learn that established book illustrator E. McKnight Kauffer would execute *Green Mansions.* On the other hand, judging a public wary of avant-garde aesthetics, he reacted against Abrams's attempt to secure Salvador Dali's services. Defining the series' prospective audience, he exclaimed: "For the life of me, I can't see Salvador Dali as an illustrator for a series like ours. His stuff is caviar and I think the general public wouldn't know what the hell he was driving at. He might make a really honest effort to give us the sort of thing that we want but, try as he might, I am sure that his surrealist didoes would creep in. I am open to conviction on this point, but my first reaction is 'for God's sake, no.'"[56] The series sold well, but wartime paper rationing restricted production almost immediately. To circumvent the paper regulations, Random House contracted with textbook publisher A. S. Barnes to publish the series, with Random House's editorial supervision. The Illustrated Modern Library's initial price of $1.35 could not cover expenses, so it was raised to $2.00 in 1946, and then to $2.50 in 1947. High postwar production costs assured its demise, and no new titles were added after 1947. By 1952 the stock was completely sold out and the series officially went out of print.[57]

The collapse of the Illustrated Modern Library and the concurrent rise of the College Editions solidified the strong connection between the Modern Library trademark and the academic market. For the next several years the series would concentrate on college markets and, except for the periodic announcement of new titles in the *New York Times Book Review*, abandon nearly all promotions directed toward those outside the academy.

KEEPING COMPETITIVE: MODERN LIBRARY PAPERBACKS

The paperback revolution curtailed growth but it did not dampen the Modern Library sales bolstered by the college market in the 1940s or early 1950s. By contrast, the Grosset & Dunlap clothbound reprints, which always featured best-sellers and other popular fiction, had "dwindled to nothing" by 1946.[58] Although early paperbacks could not kill the Modern Library, they confined its market and precluded any hopes of expanding into the mass market. Random House depended on Bantam to fill that niche. Cerf recalled that the Modern Library "grew by leaps and bounds" in the beginning, but "when paperbacks came into favor, we were lucky to hold our own, and it was only by adding important new titles that we could keep The Modern Library going ahead."[59] The Modern Library's core market was not seriously threatened until Jason Epstein, a twenty-five-year-old "brilliant boy" in the publishing world persuaded Doubleday and Company to found Anchor Books, the first "egghead," or "quality," paperback series, in 1953.[60] Starting with a book he had treasured in its Modern Library edition, *The Charterhouse of Parma,* Epstein hoped to capture 10 to 15 percent of college students and instructors as well as the "intellectual" segment of the general public with his moderately priced paperbacks. The sixty-five to ninety-five-cent price, considerably higher than the twenty-five cents for a "mass-market" paperback, allowed for press runs of twenty thousand, rather than the one to two hundred thousand Pocket Books or Bantam required to assure profitability. Anchor Books was quickly followed by Knopf's Vintage Books, a similar "quality" line that drew on Knopf's powerful backlist and was also directed at an academic market (the first ten titles were selected by canvasing college and university faculty).[61] When Anchor Books won the prestigious 1954 Carey-Thomas Award for creative book publishing, *Publishers' Weekly* was forced to rethink its regular "Mass Market" column. It had equated "mass market" with the cheap paperback format, but the new "quality" lines offered the same range of titles that regularly appeared in the Modern Library and were marketed with that quality Bennett Cerf would call "class."[62] Although Pocket Books and the New American Library packaged their fiction in sensational covers and sold them on newsstands and in drug- and even grocery stores, but not in bookstores, Anchor and Vintage both presented their higher priced paperbacks as superior literature for people with discerning taste. They eschewed the wire racks of the newsstand for displays in bookstores and other traditional outlets. Advertisements were typographic and ran in such magazines as *Partisan Review* and *Kenyon Review*. Printed on regular book paper rather than cheap wood pulp, and with dignified cover art, the books were designed to become part of "the permanent collection of the serious reader."[63]

Anchor and Vintage's success created pressure on Random House to maintain its market share, and it responded in 1955 with the Modern Library Paperback Books line. Echoing his earlier analysis of the College Editions, and reemphasizing that the Modern Library was no longer an innovator but had been forced into a responsive mode, Lewis Miller described the new series "as a defensive measure," designed to "stake our claim and take a look-see."[64] It was a very cautious "look-see": no advertisements to the trade or the public introduced the series, and even a Modern Library advertisement in the *New York Times Book Review* one month later made no mention of it.[65] Only *Publishers' Weekly* acknowledged the new line with its summary announcement: "The cheaper books are aimed at bringing to a wider audience the most popular titles in the regular Modern Library series as well as other titles from the publisher's regular trade list which have gone out of print but are still in demand."[66] The first volumes, including two each by Faulkner and Dostoyevsky, Fielding's *Tom Jones,* Thackeray's *Vanity Fair,* Swift's *Gulliver's Travels,* Plato's *Republic,* and Cerf's own *Great Modern Short Stories,* distinguished the series as a "quality" line that would compete directly with the regular series, but possibly stem Anchor and Vintage's encroachment into the Modern Library's market.

Despite the absence of advertising, sales took off immediately and continued to expand: they rose 58 percent over the previous year in 1957 (to $125,000 from $79,000), and in the first two months of the next year another 63 percent over the same period in 1957 (to $32,000 from $19,000). These sales figures were "vocal beyond any memorandum," and, shedding the "look-see" attitude, Miller asserted, "From here on in the policy is Up and At Em."[67]

Cerf solidified the "Up and At Em" commitment to the paperback line by wooing Jason Epstein to Random House as the Modern Library's new editor in late 1958.[68] Epstein inherited a Modern Library that had become a trademark for four products: the somewhat stodgy College Editions, the "egghead" paperback series, the larger-format Giants, and the once-indispensable clothbound regular series. By transforming the Modern Library into a differentiated product line and energizing it with Epstein, Random House hoped it could hold its own among its traditional audience.

Like Anchor Books, the paperback series was consciously designed to be instantly distinguishable from mass-market paperbacks. Epstein's editorial notes for a 1959 meeting outlined design elements for each new title. He suggested consulting with the author of *The Way of Chinese Painting,* Mai-Mai Sze, herself a painter, about cover art. For *Fathers and Sons,* he wanted "a big, flat drawing in a humorous, ironic rather bitter cartoon type," and he suggested a woodcut by Leonard Baskin for Edgar Goodspeed's translation of the *Apocrypha.* Less specific about the cover for Bernard Malamud's collection of short stories, *The Magic Barrel,* he did stipulate that it "must look like a higher-priced paperback ... as far from the Bantam-type as possible."[69]

Epstein saw Anchor Books and the various Modern Library lines as similar products with nearly identical target audiences, but he believed the Modern Library was suffering from inadequate publicity. He told Cerf that the Modern Library needed to "remind its academic readers" that it included very good editions of major English poets and of most modern philosophers, because this was something "a lot of people seem not to know." He suggested advertising in literary and academic journals: *Partisan Review, Hudson Review, Commentary, Kenyon Review, College English,* and *PMLA,* nearly the same array that has introduced the College Editions. These magazines, with their small, "highly specialized" combined circulation, reached "the center of the market for Anchor books and Modern Library books."[70] An advertising schedule for 1959 indicates that Cerf expanded Epstein's tight audience focus, but only slightly: advertisements appeared in the six journals Epstein suggested with additional ones in the *Reporter, Evergreen Review,* as well as the two longtime Modern Library allies, the *Nation* and *New Republic.*[71] Notably absent was the *New York Times Book Review* with its large, more generally defined readership that the Modern Library had formerly courted.

Epstein fondly remembers the Random House he joined in 1958 as an intimate and personal company that had only recently become a leading American publisher. Still comfortably ensconced in the north wing of the Villard Mansion, the company's phone directory "didn't fill a sheet the size of a postal card." Authors came and went, or they spent the night in his office. W. H. Auden would wander in wearing a "torn overcoat and carpet slippers," and Terry Southern, too, worked on his Random House projects wherever desk space could be found. Epstein acknowledged that the "revolutionary" tag enjoyed by Random House in the 1930s was an anachronism, but he still likened the company to a "guerrilla army" living among the people.[72] Much would change in the following years. In 1957, Random House's total sales were $7,786,202, more than double the 1947 level and eleven times the total from 1937. As its sales climbed and its net worth grew, Cerf and Klopfer became concerned that, if either partner died, tax laws would block the other's ability to retain control of the company. In 1959 they offered 30 percent of Random House at $11.25 a share on the New York Stock Exchange. After one day, it was selling at $14.00, and within a year at $45.00. Cerf and Klopfer, who had never paid themselves much salary and had poured all their profits back into the firm, were suddenly millionaires, and Random House was a major, publicly owned corporation. Cerf remembered the event as momentous: "This marked a big change, since the minute you go public, outsiders own some of your stock and you've got to make periodic reports to them. You owe your investors dividends and profits. Instead of working for yourself and doing what you damn please, willing to risk a loss on something you want to do, if you're any kind of honest man, you feel a real responsibility to your stockholders. It was a very important decision."[73] Epstein recalled that the "mood subtly changed" at Random House after it went public. Cerf fretted every time the stock fell, and his fame heightened his torment: "Like all celebrities, Bennett thrived on applause, which he imagined now depended upon rising quarterly profits."[74] To keep the stock rising and to encourage investors' trust, which Cerf took personally, the partners needed to expand the business. The next year

Random House bought out Knopf, and in 1961 it purchased Pantheon, a line Klopfer hoped would add a "touch of class" to the corporation's changing image.[75]

As the company grew, the Modern Library diminished in importance. By 1961, Random House operated a successful reference division highlighted by *The American College Dictionary* and the *Random House Dictionary of the English Language,* a spectacular children's book division that included Dr. Seuss and Landmark Books, a school textbook line, Bantam Books, Pantheon Books, as well as the many formidable Knopf lines including Vintage Books.[76] The series that gave birth to Random House accounted for nearly half of the company's total sales in 1937. By 1957, all the lines under the Modern Library trade name amounted to only 23 percent. When the Paperbacks were merged into the better-established Vintage line, the Modern Library's financial heft became even more insignificant, and the commitment to the trademark was waning. Without its paperback line, the Modern Library did not offer much potential for future growth, which surely acted as a psychological impediment to active involvement in the series, especially in the new atmosphere of a publicly owned company. While several important titles entered the series as a result of the merger with Knopf, including books by Camus, Kafka, Gide, and Cather, Epstein, who had made his name with Anchor Books and was committed to "egghead" paperbacks, saw Vintage as far more worthy of his creative talents. Despite their deep affection for the series, Cerf and Klopfer's need to expand left little time for the segment of their empire that could no longer repay their attention.[77]

Worried about the fate of the Modern Library, which had lost its special identity, Random House managing editor Tony Wimpfheimer initiated talks with designer Neil Fujita and the public relations firm of Ruder & Finn in early 1966.[78] Ruder & Finn's preliminary report expressed the opinion that "there is no question that the Modern Library represents an enormous potential and that, for a variety of reasons, this potential is not being realized at the present time." Citing a change in the nation's zeitgeist, it reported that when the series started, and as it developed and matured in the 1930s and 1940s, "the word 'library' meant something," then elaborated:

> Young men and women were interested in building their own collections of books and there was something permanent about having a

Modern Library title. It was an idea that was in tune with the spirit of the young college students and adults in the 30's and 40's.

Today, of course, the situation has changed radically. With the advent of paperback books, one tends to think of the Modern Library last rather than first. Even those of us who have fond recollections from our college days and who have libraries that we continue to build don't give a high priority to Modern Library editions. Either we want an inexpensive paperback book which we know we will throw away in fairly short order, or we want to spend more money for a deluxe edition which will be a handsome one.

The report then located the Modern Library in a no-man's land in the current market: "Modern Library appears to fall between these two choices." It no longer conformed to a changed sense of the ideal book that other reprint lines now embodied: "The second fact is that the Modern Library is no longer modern by contemporary standards of book publishing. On the contrary, it is distinctly old-fashioned.... The series is considered *less* up-to-date and *less* attractive and appealing to modern tastes, and does *not* imply permanence as distinguished from paperbacks."[79] The report offered a host of solutions that centered on redesigning the books and presenting them as deluxe editions suitable for a fine home library. This was a step back to the philosophy of the aborted Illustrated Modern Library, and one that would have abandoned the lucrative academic market for a last shot at a broad middle-class audience. The fresh presentation was to be accompanied by a sweeping public relations campaign designed to reawaken the American public to the joys of building a distinguished home library. Stirred by advertisements, informative booklets, and press releases, the American public would once again long for substantial books in attractive wrappings.

The report met with mixed reactions at Random House. Everyone agreed that the series needed to be spruced up if it were to survive. The type was badly worn, many of the introductions were out of date, and the jacket and cover designs smacked of a bygone era. The editors disagreed on the strategies outlined by Ruder & Finn. Tony Wimpfheimer and Sidney Jacobs were both sympathetic, but Dick Krinsley reported: "I can see no purpose in adopting Ruder and Finn's proposals on behalf of the Modern Library. I do think we have a marketing problem as well as others, but for the life of me I can't see why the solution of these problems lies in the field of public relations.[80] Epstein was equally unimpressed and he balked at the idea that the Modern Library could ever again hope to appeal to a broad market: "It seems to me that David Finn's proposal does not answer our main problem, which is to revive interest in the Modern Library within its basic market, which is to say the academic community broadly conceived."[81] Ruder & Finn wanted to open the Modern Library's market, but for Epstein, the ideal of the "civilized minority" had collapsed into the more specific "academic community broadly conceived." Cerf and Klopfer saw the original "civilized minority" as the nation's movers and shakers, people capable of creating a cultural flowering. In a retreat from the cultural ambitions of the 1920s and 1930s, the Modern Library no longer was willing to present itself as a vehicle for cultural change. Instead it rejected Ruder & Finn's public relations extravaganza, but accepted a major redesign of the series. It had undergone a host of minor design changes in the previous four years and it was losing the distinctive look that had made it so attractive to book buyers for nearly fifty years. The gold stamping on the cover was twice changed, the title lists disappeared from the inside of the dust jacket, edge staining was abandoned, and the torchbearer symbol was changed slightly. As Gordon Neavill points out, the changes did little to help the series that "was losing its position as an institution of American intellectual life."[82] Neil Fujita redesigned the torchbearer, replaced gold stamping with silver, and modernized the dust jackets. The predominant feature was no longer the torchbearer, but an adaptation of the "*ml*" motif Rockwell Kent had used for his endpaper design. Kent's torchbearer was maintained on the title page, but Fujita's blockier, less articulated torchbearer was stamped on the cover.

No significant editorial changes were made, much to the dismay of editor Thomas Lowry who had suggested "beefing up the Modern Library line by giving it a new job to perform that is not already being performed by either trade editions of books or reprint editions." Lowry thought "packages" of authors the likes of Elizabeth Bowen, Willa Cather, E. M. Forster, André Gide, John Hersey, Franz Kafka, Thomas Mann, Mary Renault, Isak Dinesen, William Faulkner, Oscar Lewis, James Michener, J. R. R. Tolkien, and John O'Hara might change the character of the series and give it a distinctive new identity. For Lowry, the design changes were insignificant without a new editorial policy to make the product more appealing: "My feeling is that we have to give

Modern Library a job to do if it is to flourish and if we are to function as anything more than people who worry about when to put IN COLD BLOOD into the line and whether or not to put THE MAGIC CHRISTIAN into it at all."[83] Lowry's suggestions were not adopted, and the Modern Library became a repository to prolong the lives of backlist items. The editors were no longer making important decisions about the shape and character of the series, but merely acting as go-betweens for the trade edition and the reprint.

Harkening back to earlier promotions, to reintroduce the series to the "academic community broadly conceived" and to celebrate the fiftieth anniversary of the series, Random House sponsored a contest expressly designed to encourage their audience to inspect the Modern Library list and familiarize itself with its makeup. Working with a budget of just under ten thousand dollars, it ran a four-page insert in two magazines, the *New York Review of Books* and the *New Journal,* and distributed the insert to bookstores across the country. With a gimmicky headline, it invited readers to "Let Marcel Proust Put You in the Driver's Seat!" Referring to James Thurber, Franz Kafka, Lewis Carroll, John Dewey, Charles Darwin, Thomas Mann, and Fyodor Dostoyevsky, as "Jim, Franz, Lew, John, Chuck, Tom" and "Fyodor," it asked readers to study twenty-one David Levine caricatures of international literary figures, then to list the Modern Library titles by each of them. The lucky winner would receive a fiberglass replica of a 1931 Model A Ford touring car, a "dilly" of a prize that, according to the advertisement's editorial voice, "Marcel and the rest of us feel . . . is singularly appropriate since it represents style and value that never go out of date . . . very much like the Modern Library."[84] The series that had once been so concerned with being particularly "modern" while maintaining an air of legitimate culture—distaining false gold leaf as lacking class—offered a replica of a past era to represent "style and value" and then equated a fiberglass imitation with the Modern Library.

While the contest spurred momentary interest (according to a press release, six thousand entries were returned from "college students, professors and instructors, and from people in the professions"), the overall redesign and the contest publicity failed to excite long-term interest and it also failed to deliver sales.[85]

Despite the enormous investment in the series in 1967, by 1971 net sales of the Modern Library amounted to $1,080,000, a 40 percent decline from 1957. Worse yet, sales accounted for only a little over one percent of Random House's gross, and after production, promotion, and distribution costs, the Modern Library contributed only $85,000 to overall profits and overhead.[86] Cerf retired in late 1970, thus eliminating one impediment to an aggressive response to the series' failing sales.[87] In February 1971, Epstein asked Larry Kirshbaum to circulate an aggressive "drop list" as a last-ditch effort to save the series before it moved into the loss column. The Modern Library Committee headed by Epstein recommended dropping 118 of the 306 Modern Library titles in print.[88] The drop list pushed aside any pretension of keeping the series up to date. Only ten works of fiction written since World War II remained, and only three books among them (Gore Vidal's *Julian,* William Styron's *Confessions of Nat Turner,* and Joseph Heller's *Catch-22*) were written after 1960.

The commitment to maintain the series was not based on its profit potential, but loyalty to its historic contribution to Random House: "While the committee recognizes that Modern Library is not as profitable as the overall Reprint classification, the editors involved feel that the prestige and quality of the line warrant its continuation."[89] The attached memo continued by noting the precarious situation the once-hardy series occupied: "In order to maintain a minimum profitability in 1972 it may be necessary to raise prices next January. For the current year, however, the committee feels that any further remainder sales or price increases would kill the line." The plan met with some resistance, and there was wrangling at Random House over which titles to drop. One memo gleefully trumpeted the "Good News!" that permission had been granted to eliminate three titles not originally on the drop list, *The Philosophy of David Hume, Collected Tales and Plays of Nikolai Gogol,* and a collection of Thucydides, but then reported disappointedly that "we must however maintain" two titles slated for exclusion, Dreiser's *Sister Carrie,* and a collection of Somerset Maugham's stories.[90]

The final decision to drop titles probably came from Klopfer who, like Cerf, still clung to the series.[91] Less than a year earlier, John Simon had tried to clear with Cerf the elimination of "titles by house authors which we keep in the Modern Library to please them and please us."[92] Included on the list were O'Hara, Michener, Styron, Updike, Mann, Hersey, Moss Hart, and Truman Capote (all major Random House or Knopf authors). None of the titles was dropped even though they were all suffering from low sales. The long-standing policy of eliminating deadwood to keep each title selling had collapsed as the series aged and its importance to the corporation diminished. The Modern Library was fast becoming Random House's "vanity press," maintained only to please Cerf, Klopfer, and authors who published under the Random House umbrella.

Despite the cutbacks and the stated commitment to the series' prestige, by the mid-1970s it was nearly finished, and there were no new printings until 1977 when a furtive effort was made to revive it.[93] The titles lingered in bookstores for another fifteen years until, in 1992, Random House successfully relaunched the series as a set of distinctively designed classics and near-classics suitable for a permanent home library.

During a 1976 interview Donald Klopfer gestured to a set of Modern Library books adorning his office, then situated on the twelfth floor of Random House's "nondescript glass building on Third Avenue," and said: "There is the Modern Library over on those shelves, over there, and it's almost finished, being phased out, because of paperbacks—perfectly sound, just as it should be. I regret it because I love it. After all, it's my baby. But the so-called egghead paperback has put us out of business." He continued with empirical evidence to back up his claim: "for exactly the same price, we sell about eight times as many in paper as we do in that nice cloth bound book. Because the fashion has changed, that's all. Young people aren't interested in cloth bound books. Colleges, students of all sorts."[94] Instead of cursing the "Gods of Publishing," Klopfer remained an optimistic pragmatist and he applauded the paperback as "the greatest thing for publishing that we could have."[95] Paperbacks fulfilled one of the Modern Library's early promises: they opened new markets and successfully delivered books to casual readers pining for "something to read."

Klopfer suggested that, for a new generation who had grown up with Pocket Books and other kindred imprints, paperbacks were more desirable than clothbound books. Cloth seemed stuffy, ostentatious, and old fashioned, but a contemporary paperback conformed to its reader's physical needs. The average reader's "ideal book," once so well encapsulated in the Modern Library, evolved into a more portable, malleable, and less permanent package. The format so important to the Modern Library's success became outdated and resulted in the series' slow decline. But just as important, the conceptual framework that helped to create the series' success became outdated when it no longer received Cerf and Klopfer's close attention. "Modern" lost its meaning as the series came to resemble a college English reading list rather than a list of required reading for a "modern" person. Ironically, however, most of the Modern Library choices still sold well as the series collapsed, but in other formats and other series more "modern" in character.

Epilogue

In 1992, Random House unveiled the new Modern Library. Perhaps symbolizing a series forever young, Modern Library #1 was Albert Boni's original first selection, *The Picture of Dorian Gray*. The physical format of Wilde's once scandalous novel mutated only slightly: somewhat larger than its predecessor, it sported a matted gray and silver pictorial jacket over a gray cloth cover gold-stamped with Lucian Bernhard's trademark. With a nostalgic reference to the torchbearer as the "dame running away from Bennett Cerf," a Random House prospectus focused on the legacy of the series "as America's most distinguished publisher of the world's best books." It then staked the series' claim on the nation's cultural landscape: "The series shaped [young Americans'] tastes, educated them, provided them with a window on the world. Many of the country's celebrated writers are quick to attest that they 'grew up with the Modern Library.'"[1]

The new series shares its predecessor's brand name and trademark, but its appeal is fundamentally different. The paperback revolution's gradual overthrow of the original Modern Library proved most book buyers will now choose a paperback book. The 1930s values of price and format no longer worked: at $12.50 the hardbound *Dorian Gray* could never compete with the flexible Vintage edition shelved next to it at one-third the price. New Modern Library books are luxurious editions of reader favorites that provide a more intimate tactile pleasure for special reading experiences. They resemble the "volumes *de luxe*" *Good Housekeeping* critic Emily Newell Blair recommended for treasured titles.[2] A first-time reader of Jane Austen's *Emma* will likely choose a Signet Classic or some other inexpensive paperback edition, but a lover of the book looking to revisit his or her favorite literary character might very well opt to spend a little extra for the new Modern Library edition's dignified elegance and permanence. A *Vogue* review commented that they "make great gifts" and then stressed the books' sensuous qualities by proposing, "They're just the thing to leave open by the bedside as a lubricant to a cerebral seduction."[3]

To arouse public interest and reinforce the Modern Library's association with treasured texts, Bennett Cerf's son Christopher led the series' editorial committee in compiling a list of the one hundred best twentieth-century novels in English. Released on July 20, 1998, "The List," as it quickly became known, was an instant sensation. The Modern Library site on the World Wide Web experienced a 7,000 percent increase in traffic over the following weeks, and its readers' bulletin board, "Forum," had nearly 3,000 postings on the topic within two months. For those wanting to initiate structured discussions, the Modern Library offered a series of "Talking Points" to guide intelligent debate.[4] *Newsweek* enthused: "You keep hearing that we live in a post-literate age, but how do you explain what went on last week? As the mass media kept tabulating home-run totals, the Dow Jones industrials and the number of consecutive days above 100 degrees, a surprising number of people were obsessing over a list of the century's 100 greatest English-language novels."[5] And people were not just talking: amazing as it seems, four of the list's most honored titles shot onto Amazon.com's best-seller list.[6]

To Cerf's delight, the controversy inspired a spate of editorials and commentaries. Newspapers quibbled with the rankings on the list, while others rejected them altogether. A publishing conclave at Radcliffe College issued its own counterlist. Many pundits were shocked to see "the often impenetrable" *Ulysses* at the head of the list, and panel juror William Styron marveled that *Brave New World* could rank among the top five.[7] He was aghast to find *The Magnificent Ambersons* and *Zuleika Dobson,* both "toothless pretenders," on the final list. Critics pointed to the panel's demographics (racially white, 90 percent male, with the average member's age at 68.7) to explain the list's glaring omissions.[8] Toni Morrison was the most notable absentee, but the panel also snubbed Doris Lessing and Nadine Gordimer. Besides slighting women and authors born outside Great Britain and the United States, the panel had selected only four titles published after 1975. Literary expression, it would seem, peaked about 1940, when most of the panelists were entering adolescence. For those born after 1950, the *New Yorker* pointed out, the books are still "completely recognizable," because "these are the books your parents read."[9] Styron conceded most of the list's "old fogies" such as James T. Farrell, Thorton Wilder, and Arnold Bennett, probably did not belong, but he "cheerfully" assented to the charge that "the list is 'weird,'" because it taught the simple lesson "that all lists are weird, but each list is weird in its own way."[10]

USA Today's critique of the Modern Library list resonated with the critical outrage of the 1920s against "book ballyhoo." In "Rank Rankings Make the List," the editorialist charged that the ranking "formula" went unexplained to hide the fact that the final pecking order could have been dictated by Random House's "dust-jacket designers." The list was based on the premise: "if you want the public to talk about real *lit-rah-chure*, you have to lie to the poor schmoes." Mocking the Modern Library's cultural pretensions, the paper charged the ranking process gave the audience less credit than "modern pro-wrestling." The list's sin was not its white male bias or its neglect of recent literature, but its assumption of an ignorant, gullible public. The Modern Library, according to *USA Today*, shamelessly perpetrated a "piddling fraud" to sell its books.[11]

Although *USA Today* certainly took the list seriously, Christopher Cerf found its attendant hoopla amusing. He admitted the list's creation was "to some degree a scam" but, sounding like his father, he continued, "I mean that in the best sense of the word."[12] The list was designed to get people interested in the concept of the "best books," and Cerf thought a heterogeneous board and equally diverse list would fail to evoke the controversy he wanted. Random House's editor-in-chief Ann Godoff was right in thinking the list would "bring The Modern Library to public attention."[13] The "neat game" the list provoked justified its existence for Cerf: "What is most remarkable about the list is that it has brought the novel into the nation's headlines and conversations."[14]

The "best novels" list and the subsequent best nonfiction list, released with much less fanfare the next year, are marketing techniques that fit the modern strategic promotions Cerf and Klopfer helped bring to publishing. The lists were designed to create brand-name recognition and link "the Modern Library" to sanctified culture for a specific audience. One analyst asserted the fiction list "was pitched toward the demographic market that everyone's trying to get—white, middle class, upscale—people who read The New Republic and Harper's," those most likely to give books as gifts, choose to reread treasured authors, or try to overcome their cultural illiteracy.[15] Random House tried to negotiate reprint rights to all one hundred titles, and it planned to release them over the next several years to keep the series in the public eye. The logistics proved too difficult, but had the effort succeeded, "it would have

FIGURE 10. Advertisement featuring "toothless pretenders" from the 100 Best Novels list. From *New Yorker,* 5 October 1998. Joseph Regenstein Library, University of Chicago.

been a publicity masterstroke—the best novels of the century, all available from the Modern Library."[16]

In 1930 Cerf and Klopfer had approached professional–managerial readers by promising to satisfy their already defined aesthetic taste. The Modern Library delivered the crucial texts of modernity—the classics that remained contemporary and the moderns that would become classics. The 1998 "best novels" promotion told readers what they *ought* to read. At the same time that the series offered insecure readers a sanctified list, it also reassured more savvy readers that it was well aware of its own absurdity. Six weeks after the list's release, an advertisement (figure 10) prominently placed alongside the *New Yorker*'s table of contents asked, "Have you read the 100 Best Novels of the 20th Century?" The answer, of course could only be "no," for not even the panel members had read the entire list, and the *New Yorker*'s editorial director could only claim intimacy with two-thirds of the titles.[17] The Modern Library helpfully offered five titles under the command, "Start with These." At the bottom of the page, Lucian Bernhard's leaping torchbearer danced above a newly designed "100 BEST NOVELS" logo. The text of the advertisement offers readers a chance to overcome cultural deficiencies, but its illustrations mock the entire notion. Only three weeks after William Styron labeled Booth Tarkington's *The Magnificent Ambersons* and Max Beerbohm's *Zuleika Dobson* "toothless pretenders" in the magazine's "Talk of the Town" column, the Modern Library impudently displayed the two most controversial titles as the *first* must-reads on the "best novels" list.

In a way the "best novels" tie-in is strikingly similar to the Modern Library's 1926 promotion that teased *New Yorker* readers with the series' "worst sellers": both assert the series' claim to legitimacy while gently ridiculing its own pretensions. The 1926 promotion, however, accentuated the series' currency and presented its books to thoroughly modern individuals. The 1998 "best novels" list and advertisement offered a pantheon sanctified by septuagenarian intellectuals. The original Modern Library was up-to-date, but the "best novels" list is particularly dated. Jane Smiley called the list "an artifact of the 1950s" and she found it "depressing to think that at this late date there's [sic] still people who think of literature in terms of a kind of hierarchy rather than a map."[18] *Newsweek* summed up a similar sentiment in its headline, "The Dated and the Dead," and *U.S. News and World Report* referred to the list as "grandpa's favorite books."[19]

In the 1920s and 1930s the "World's Best Books" were selected to represent the finest works of the moment and to make available the key documents of a literary revolution. Many of those very titles were featured on the series' "best novels" list, but when Albert Boni, Horace Liveright, Bennett Cerf, and Donald Klopfer selected the "World's Best Books," the titles carried a distinctly different cultural cachet from that of today. Modernism's literary rebellion is now what the Harvard Classics denominated "the mysterious thing called 'background.'" But the Harvard Classics' publisher always presented the set with a grave seriousness. Christopher Cerf's willing admission that the "best novels" list was a scam and the ironically playful *New Yorker* advertisement recall a legacy of clever marketing that satisfied multiple audiences and helped to make the Modern Library one of the most respected publishing ventures of the twentieth century.

Notes

Introduction

1. William B. Liebmann, "Random House; Or Fun and Profit in Search of Excellence," *Columbia Library Columns* 20 (February 1971): 4.
2. "Merchants Gone Mad," *Publishers' Weekly* 118 (25 October 1930): 1847.
3. Gimbels advertisement, *New York Times,* 13 October 1930.
4. As late as 1930, most people in the publishing industry believed there were only around two hundred thousand book buyers in the entire country. Charles Lee, *The Hidden Public: The Story of the Book-of-the-Month Club* (New York: Doubleday, 1958), 25.
5. Surprisingly little has been written about the Modern Library from a scholarly standpoint—surprising mainly because so many twentieth-century academics had relied on Modern Library editions in their adolescence and college years. The key exception is Gordon B. Neavill's doctoral dissertation for the University of Chicago's School of Library Science in 1984. Drawing on the Random House archives at Columbia University, Neavill constructed a detailed history of the Modern Library focused on its success as a dealer in literature. Neavill examined how individual titles sold; changes in the makeup of the Modern Library list; distribution practices; the struggles to keep the business operating smoothly through the Depression and World War II; the impact of the paperback revolution on the series; and a brief discussion of the Modern Library's "impact on American cultural life," in which he asserted that the Modern Library helped to "democratize literature." See Gordon Barrick Neavill, "The Modern Library Series" (Ph.D. diss., University of Chicago, 1984). In addition to Neavill's work, George M. Andes published a detailed descriptive bibliography. Information on the physical design and layout of the series, as well as a listing of each title in the regular series with information regarding its first appearance are provided in Andes, *A Descriptive Bibliography of the Modern Library Series, 1917–1970* (Boston: Boston Book Annex, 1989).
6. Huntington Cairns, "The Modern Library," *Modern Quarterly* 5 (Fall–Winter 1928): 121; Modern Library Catalogue, Fall 1928, Random House Collection, Rare Book and Manuscript Library, Butler Library, Columbia University, New York (hereafter cited as RHC). The Modern Library was

inconsistent in its spelling of "catalog–catalogue," as was Bennett Cerf. Until 1929, when they settled on "catalog" both spellings appear.

7. Pierre Bourdieu finds a reversal of the economic world in the field of cultural production. Authors who succeed materially (acquire financial capital) usually suffer from a lack of prestige (symbolic capital). Because prestige is so important in the cultural field, literary production is "a generalized game of 'loser wins,'" based on "a systematic inversion of the fundamental principles of all ordinary economies." See his *The Field of Cultural Production: Essays on Art and Literature,* ed. Randal Johnson (New York: Columbia University Press, 1993), 39.

8. Malcolm Cowley claims the battle for control of the literary landscape was won by 1930. In 1937 he wrote, "By that time [1930], the genteel critics were fighting rearguard actions to protect their line of retreat. The 'young intellectuals' were mopping up territory already conquered." See Malcolm Cowley, "The Revolt against Gentility," in *After the Genteel Tradition: American Writers since 1910* (New York: W. W. Norton, 1937), 23.

9. For a typical indictment of prepackaged, marketed culture, see Robert L. Duffus, "An Outline of 'Culture,'" *Bookman* 64 (December 1926): 433–36.

10. "Has America a Literary Dictatorship?" *Bookman* 65 (April 1927): 191–99.

11. Janice Radway, *A Feeling for Books: The Book-of-the-Month Club, Literary Taste, and Middle-Class Desire* (Chapel Hill: University of North Carolina Press, 1997), 259. For an extended discussion of "middlebrow culture," see Joan Shelley Rubin, *The Making of Middlebrow Culture* (Chapel Hill: University of North Carolina Press, 1992). Rubin defines "middlebrow" as a taste culture guided by a reverence for established canons of culture and the quest for "self-culture." Like Radway, Rubin traces "middlebrow culture" to twentieth-century commercialism in book production, promotion, and distribution.

12. According to Van Wyck Brooks, neither the highbrow's otherworldly idealism nor the lowbrow's practical nature was altogether bad, but their polar isolation precluded a healthy American culture capable of integrating the ideals of art and beauty into practical life, in his "Highbrow and Lowbrow," in *America's Coming-of-Age* (New York: B. W. Huebsch, 1915), 35.

By 1920, "highbrow" had become a common term of disparagement. Henry Seidel Canby considered highbrow "provincial," because its "fussing in little areas" was as limited as lowbrow culture's lack of sophistication. See his "Highbrow and Lowbrow," in *Definitions: Essays in Contemporary Criticism,* 2d series (New York: Harcourt, Brace and Co., 1924): 128–31. For a similar view, see Grant Showerman, "Liberal Culture in Action," *Nation* 110 (31 January 1920): 134. A 1934 essay on language usage in *English Journal* noted, "Correct, vigorous, colorful English is considered 'highbrow' by the masses—and no more fatal verdict could be rendered." Quoted in J. M. Steadman Jr., "Affected and Effeminate Words," *American Speech* 13 (February 1938): 14.

Lowbrow fared no better. Mary Ellis Opdycke called "lowbrow" entertainments the "bastard children" of the arts, produced to meet the "direct demand" of "mass civilization." Opdycke admitted enjoying the popular arts, but averred that only fleeting "popular success" bestowed the laurel on the lowbrow. She added, "The public, mopping the beads of excitement from its brow, as it stands yelling its enthusiasms for Tinney [*sic*] or Jolson or Babe Ruth, will all too quickly wipe the laurel wreath away." Her description of a sweating, emotional mob clearly separated lowbrow arts from the legitimate arts absorbed in quiet contemplation by disinterested individuals. See Mary Ellis Opdycke, "Laurels for Low-Brows," *New Republic* 39 (2 July 1924): 155–56.

13. Besides the work of Rubin and Radway on middlebrow culture already mentioned, the study of taste categories and their attendant "taste cultures" is most fully realized in the works of five writers. Russell Lynes first systematically mapped out America's dominant taste categories in *The Tastemakers* (New York: Harper and Brothers, 1954). Dwight Macdonald published his stinging critique of the "midcult" in "Masscult and Midcult," first as two parts in the *Partisan Review* (Spring and Summer 1960) and then combined in his *Against the American Grain* (New York: Random House, 1962), 3–75. Herbert J. Gans took Lynes's five basic groupings and expanded them in his sociological study of American taste, *Popular Culture and High Culture: An Analysis and Evaluation of Taste* (New York: Basic Books, 1974). Lawrence Levine provided an historical examination of the basic division between high and low culture in *Highbrow/Lowbrow: The Emergence of Cultural Hierarchy in America* (Cambridge: University of Harvard Press, 1988). By far the most exhaustive study is Pierre Bourdieu's *Distinction: A Social Critique of the Judgement of Taste* (Cambridge: Harvard University Press, 1984). In each instance, taste is interrogated as a key marker of social distinction. Bourdieu and Levine make the case that this marker is used to legitimate and naturalize economic class distinctions. "Good taste" and "high culture" belong to the upper classes, while the masses satisfy their barbarian tastes with "low culture." The interwar desire to transcend taste categories altogether suggests a desire to escape social hierarchies and conforms to the young intellectuals' infatuation with socialist movements.

14. "Highbrow," according to an *Atlantic Monthly* advertisement, could mean "intelligent, authoritative and informative," or, more commonly, "dull, academic, pretentiously intellectual." In either case, highbrow was a meaning-

less "tag of a standardizing age." See *New York Times Book Review,* 3 November 1929, 23.

15. The mixed regard for Arnold's vision of culture is articulated in Katherine Fullerton Gerould's gradual movement away from a strict Arnoldian concept. In "The Extirpation of Culture," *Atlantic Monthly* 116 (October 1915): 445–55, she defended the Arnoldian tradition, but twelve years later, in "What, Then, Is Culture?" *Harper's Monthly* 154 (January 1927): 190–95, she claimed Americans err when they think of culture only as knowledge of the best that has been thought and said. She still favored the masterpieces, but she also included a spiritual sensitivity and the ability to find beauty in unexpected places in her definition. Interestingly enough, her first essay was attacked in the *New Republic* as the rantings of an "angry daughter of the Brahmins." See "Books and Things," *New Republic* 4 (9 October 1915): 265. In addition, F. M. Colby in "The Taboo of Culture," *Harper's Monthly* 141 (September 1920): 540–42, claimed that most Americans dislike "culture" because they think of it as an affected love of the classics. Although Colby did not use the term "highbrow," he believed most Americans found culture pretentious, dull, and academic. He hoped a natural, unpretentious relationship with the arts might one day develop in the United States, as he maintained it had in France, to erase the "taboo of culture."

16. Arnold, of course, had a more sophisticated view of culture than simply that of a static canon of works. As Raymond Williams points out, Arnold combined two definitions of culture: first, "the independent and abstract noun which describes a general process of intellectual, spiritual and aesthetic development"; and second, "the independent and abstract noun which describes the works and practices of intellectual and especially artistic activity." Williams points out that the second meaning came to dominate the way Arnold was understood. Arnold's definition of culture as "the best" lends itself to the construction of prescriptive lists and sets. See Raymond Williams, *Keywords: A Vocabulary of Culture and Society* (New York: Oxford University Press, 1985), 90–92.

17. Randolph Bourne, "Our Cultural Humility," in *History of a Literary Radical* (New York: B. W. Huebsch, 1920), 33, 38, 42.

18. John Erskine, "Culture: The Interplay of Life and Ideas," *Century Magazine* 116 (May 1928): 83–85.

19. John Dewey, "The Crisis in Culture," *New Republic* 62 (19 March 1930): 123–26.

20. Stark Young, "No Culture but the Opera," *New Republic* 65 (14 January 1931): 346–47.

21. Warren Susman sees the "popular 'discovery' of the concept of culture" as one of the most significant features of the 1930s. He points out that the "sense of awareness of what it means to *be* a culture" pervades the decade's discourse: "It was during the Thirties that the idea of culture was domesticated, with important consequences. Americans then began thinking in terms of patterns of behavior and belief, values and life-styles, symbols and meanings." The concepts of "The American Dream" and an "American Way of Life" emerged as Americans began to search for their own "Patterns of Culture." Culture was still used in its old sense, but its new meaning gained currency as Americans sought to understand their modern predicament. Warren I. Susman, *Culture as History: The Transformation of American Society in the Twentieth Century* (New York: Pantheon Books, 1984), 153–54.
22. For an extended discussion of intellectual critics' worries about the debilitating effects of modern commercialism on the national character, see Thomas L. Hartshorne, *The Distorted Image: Changing Conceptions of the American Character since Turner* (Cleveland: Case Western Reserve University Press, 1968), 79–117.
23. Edward Sapir, "Civilization and Culture," *Dial* 67 (20 September 1919): 233.
24. The concept of cultural pap is central to Radway's discussion of the Book-of-the-Month Club's history. See especially the section "Gender and the Transformation of Literary Production," in her *A Feeling for Books,* 210–20.
25. Lewis Mumford, "Publishing, Old and New," *New Republic* 64 (1 October 1930): 178.
26. Duffus, "Outline of 'Culture,'" 435–36.
27. James Truslow Adams, *The Epic of America* (Boston: Little, Brown, 1931): 404, 406, 415.
28. Robert L. Duffus, *Books: Their Place in a Democracy* (Boston: Houghton Mifflin, 1930), 119.
29. See Cowley, *After the Genteel Tradition,* 240. (Cowley got the year wrong in citing 1918, but he corrected his mistake for the Crosscurrents reprint [Carbondale: Southern Illinois University Press, 1964]). Henry F. May, *The End of American Innocence: A Study of the First Years of Our Time, 1912–1917* (New York: Alfred A. Knopf, 1969), 293.
30. Charles Scribner Jr., *In the Web of Ideas: The Education of a Publisher* (New York: Scribner's Sons, 1993), 8. Sontag discovered the series in a stationery store in Tuscon as a teenager. See Joan Acocella, "The Hunger Artist," *New Yorker* 76 (6 March 2000): 72. Dillard describes running her finger along the shelves of the public library searching out the Modern Library logo in *An American Childhood* (New York: Harper & Row, 1987), 84. Bellow describes

his young autobiographical character's obsession with Modern Library volumes in *Humbolt's Gift* (New York: Viking Press, 1975), 76–77. See also, Ernest Hemingway, Piggott, Ark., to Bennett A. Cerf, New York, 26 December 1930, in Bennett Cerf Papers, Rare Book and Manuscript Library, Butler Library, Columbia University, New York (hereafter cited as BCP); William Faulkner, Oxford, to Bennett A. Cerf, New York, 15 April 1931, BCP; and John Dos Passos, Provincetown, to Bennett A. Cerf, New York, 23 May 1938, RHC.

31. The Modern Library's founding was one of only four items placed on the timeline to represent the 1910s. See *New York Times Book Review,* 6 October 1996.

32. Radway, *A Feeling for Books,* 259.

Chapter One

1. Walker Gilmer, *Horace Liveright: Publisher of the Twenties* (New York: David Lewis, 1970), 6.

2. Throughout this chapter I use the terms "modern," "modernism," and "modernist" on a way that broadly reflects how the terms were bandied about in the first decades of the twentieth century. Many people used "modernism" to describe twentieth-century literature that explored the fractured inner psyches of individuals caught in social constraints; others applied it oppositionally to any work that challenged the genteel tradition. Unless I state otherwise, I follow the latter usage. For a good general discussion of the confusion surrounding the three terms, see Irving Howe, "The Idea of the Modern," in *Literary Modernism,* ed. Irving Howe (Greenwich, Conn.: Fawcett, 1967), 11–40.

3. Charles A. Madison, *Jewish Publishing in America: The Impact of Jewish Writing on American Culture* (New York: Sanhedrin Press, 1975), 254. See also Alfred A. Knopf, "Some Random Recollections: An Informal Talk Made at the Grolier Club, New York, October 21, 1948," in *Portrait of a Publisher* (New York: Typophiles, 1965), 6–7. Apparently Knopf was only able to get the job after trying every other publisher in New York City. He got a job at Doubleday's Country Life Press on the strength of a letter of recommendation from the owner of the Long Island Railroad, at a time when Doubleday was lobbying for an LIRR stop at his printing plant.

4. *The Reminiscences of Ben W. Huebsch* (1965), 48 and 35, in the Oral History Collection of Columbia University.

5. Madison, *Jewish Publishing in America,* 253–54.

6. There is a significant body of work, both personal recollections and academic studies, documenting the lives and loves of the Greenwich Village radicals. See Rick Beard and Leslie Cohen Berlowitz, eds., *Greenwich Village: Culture and Counterculture* (New Brunswick: Rutgers University Press, 1993); Alexander Bloom, *Prodigal Sons: The New York Intellectuals and Their World* (New York: Oxford University Press, 1986); Terry A. Cooney, *The Rise of the New York Intellectuals: Partisan Review and Its Circle* (Madison: University of Wisconsin Press, 1986); Robert E. Humphrey, *Children of Fantasy: The First Rebels of Greenwich Village* (New York: John Wiley & Sons, 1978); Lawrence Langner, *The Magic Curtain: The Story of a Life in Two Fields, Theatre and Invention* (New York: E. P. Dutton, 1951); and Jack Selzer, *Kenneth Burke in Greenwich Village: Conversing with the Moderns, 1915–1931* (Madison: University of Wisconsin Press, 1997).
7. Gilmer, *Horace Liveright,* 10.
8. Bennett Cerf, *At Random: The Reminiscences of Bennett Cerf* (New York: Random House, 1977), 41. Cerf refers to Stephen Birmingham's *Our Crowd: The Great Jewish Families of New York* (New York: Harper & Row, 1967).
9. Quoted in Tom Dardis, *Firebrand: The Life of Horace Liveright* (New York: Random House, 1995), 98.
10. Information on the Century Club blackball incident is from *The Reminiscences of Ben W. Huebsch,* 461–64. Random House editor and cofounder of Atheneum Publishers Hiram Haydn reports that both Cerf and Knopf were also denied admission to the Century Club, but adds that it may well have been "a matter of personality." See Hiram Haydn, *Words and Faces* (New York: Harcourt, Brace, Jovanovich, 1974), 70. Both Dardis and Gilmer offer extended discussions of the anti-Semitism focused on Liveright.
11. Henry May, *The End of American Innocence: A Study of the First Years of Our Own Time, 1912–1917* (New York: Knopf, 1969), 293.
12. For a good discussion of the two contrasting social worlds of the Village at a slightly later period, see Caroline F. Ware, *Greenwich Village, 1920–1930: A Comment on American Civilization in the Post-War Years* (Boston: Houghton Mifflin, 1935), 3–8 and 105–26.
13. May, *End of American Innocence,* 284.
14. Quote from Susan Glaspell in Beard and Berlowitz, *Greenwich Village,* 196.
15. Gilmer, *Horace Liveright,* 3.
16. Langner, *Magic Curtain,* 75–76.
17. Ibid., 94–95.
18. Van Wyck Brooks, *America's Coming-of-Age* (New York: B. W. Huebsch, 1915), 7, 35.

19. Randolph Bourne, "History of a Literary Radical," *Yale Review* n.s. 8 (April 1919): 473–74, 479, 482, 484.
20. Ibid., 483.
21. Langner, *Magic Curtain*, 90.
22. Harry Scherman Oral History, *Book-of-the-Month Club Project* (1956), 20, in the Oral History Collection of Columbia University.
23. The books are 3 ⅜ by 4 inches. Most are limited to the 96 pages that make up three signatures (32mos), but some longer volumes have a fourth signature and 128 pages. For more bibliographical information on the series, see G. Thomas Tanselle, "The Little Leather Library Corporation's 'Fifty Best Poems of America,'" *Papers of the Bibliographical Society of America* 62 (1968): 604–7. I am in debt to Sidney Gissman for allowing me to examine her personal collection of LLL volumes.
24. Liveright's early career is well documented in Dardis, *Firebrand*, 3–44.
25. "Socialism in action" quoted in ibid., 136.
26. Ibid., 49–50; and Langner, *Magic Curtain*, 199.
27. Announcements, *Publishers' Weekly* 91 (2 June 1917): 1797.
28. Dardis argues that Liveright's overbearing personality would never allow him to watch idly while Boni made all the decisions, in *Firebrand*, 55–56.
29. Modern Library advertisement, *Dial* 63 (8 November 1917): 432.
30. Gilmer, *Horace Liveright*, 11.
31. Boni & Liveright advertisement, *Publishers' Weekly* 92 (3 November 1917): 1466–67.
32. Information on Boni & Liveright advertising placement is found in Boni & Liveright advertisement in *Publishers' Weekly* 92 (6 October 1917): 1132.
33. Boni & Liveright advertisement, *New Republic* 13 (17 November 1917): 15.
34. "Books at a Bargain," *Independent* 91 (8 September 1917): 400. Like *Outlook*, *Independent* was a socially progressive popular magazine directed to the nation's "general readers."
35. J. B. Kerfoot, "The Latest Books," *Life* 70 (23 August 1917): 311.
36. "Notes," *Nation* 105 (20 September 1917): 322.
37. Quoted in Boni & Liveright advertisement, *Life* 70 (18 October 1917): 642.
38. Quoted in Boni & Liveright advertisements, *Publishers' Weekly* 92 (7 July 1917): 3; (18 August 1917): 518.
39. "The Modern Library," *Bellman* 22 (30 June 1917): 721.
40. Raymond Howard Shove, *Cheap Book Production in the United States, 1870–1891* (Urbana: University of Illinois Library, 1937), 4.

41. John Tebbel, *A History of Book Publishing in the United States,* vol. 2, *The Expansion of an Industry, 1865–1919* (New York: R. R. Bowker, 1975), 483.
42. Shove, *Cheap Book Production,* 8, 17.
43. Tebbel, *A History of Book Publishing,* vol. 2, 487.
44. Ibid., 502.
45. "Cheap Books," *Publishers' Weekly* 71 (9 March 1907): 905.
46. Richard D. Altick, "From Aldine to Everyman: Cheap Reprint Series of the English Classics, 1830–1906," *Studies in Bibliography* 11 (1958): 12.
47. By 1884 the publishers of cheap books were simply called "pirates" to denote their nefarious practices. Shove, *Cheap Book Production,* 18.
48. Tebble, *A History of Book Publishing,* vol. 2, 508–9.
49. The first quote is from Edwin Bjorkman, "Everyman's Library: A Democratic Educational Institution," *Review of Reviews* 44 (December 1911): 755. The second is quoted in R. Farquharson Sharp's *The Reader's Guide to Everyman's Library* (London: Dent, 1932): xl.
50. Percy F. Bicknell, "Classics for the Millions," *Dial* 52 (16 April 1912): 314.
51. On her first visit to the home of one of Main Street's leading citizens, Lewis's protagonist Carol Kennicott notes the "unread-looking sets of Dickens, Kipling, O. Henry, and Elbert Hubbard." Adding Elbert Hubbard, the flamboyant champion of the Arts and Crafts movement in America, was a secondary slap at Main Street—not only did Main Street's denizens buy sets of books they would not read, they even bought sets of questionable authors. Sinclair Lewis, *Main Street* (New York: Harcourt Brace, 1920; reprint ed., New York: Library of America, 1992), 58.
52. See Gordon B. Neavill, "The Modern Library Series and American Cultural Life," *Journal of Library History* 16 (Spring 1981): 242. Neavill cites unpublished interview notes provided by J. C. Furnas from a February 24, 1971, interview with Boni.
53. Floyd Dell, "Introduction" to George Moore's *Confessions of a Young Man* (London: Sonnenschein, Lowrey and Co., 1888; reprint ed., New York: Modern Library, 1918), vii–viii.
54. "Interesting Publishers," *Seven Arts* 2 (October 1917): 808.
55. Louis Kronenberger, "Gambler in Publishing: Horace Liveright," *Atlantic Monthly* 215 (January 1965): 94–95.
56. Gilmer, *Horace Liveright,* 25.
57. Ibid., 26.
58. Dardis, *Firebrand,* 167–68.

59. Alfred Harcourt is an interesting contrast. He published books similar to Knopf's and shared Liveright's marketing panache, yet because he was not Jewish, he is rarely linked to Liveright, Knopf, or Huebsch.
60. Cerf, *At Random*, 57, 41.
61. Edith Stern, "The Man Who Was Unafraid," *Saturday Review of Literature* 24 (28 June 1941): 14.
62. Huebsch tells of John Reed's trying to persuade him to raise "a stink" about cuts in D. H. Lawrence's *The Rainbow*, to which Huebsch added, "I never thought of raising any stink." Quoted in *The Reminiscences of Ben W. Huebsch*, 318.
63. Cerf, *At Random*, 41.
64. Stern, "The Man Who Was Unafraid," 10.
65. Gilmer, *Horace Liveright*, 83.
66. Ibid., 91. Dardis, *Firebrand*, 133–52. Dardis's chapter "The House on Forty-eighth Street" is entirely devoted to the memories of Liveright employees — without exception they were awed by their experiences, some frightened and disturbed, others enlivened and excited.
67. Stern, "The Man Who Was Unafraid," 14.
68. The phrase "parade of vice-presidents" is from Dardis, *Firebrand*, 209.
69. Cerf, *At Random*, 58, 41, 79–80.
70. Liveright's motivation has been debated for years; some say it was to pay off gambling debts, others, to pay off his father-in-law, and still others think it was to finance his Broadway habit. The finances are a little tricky. Cerf had $50,000 invested in the firm and he had borrowed another $50,000 from his family. Klopfer raised $100,000. Then, a year later they bought out Liveright's five-year editorial contract for $15,000 in cash. So the total purchase price was $215,000. See Cerf, *At Random*, 44–55.
71. Ibid., 46.
72. *The Reminiscences of Donald S. Klopfer* (1976), 11, in the Oral History Collection at Columbia University.
73. The first quote is from Dardis, *Firebrand*, 229; the second, from Cerf, *At Random*, 45.
74. Edith Stern, "Random House," *Saturday Review of Literature* 24 (6 December 1941): 18.
75. Bennett A. Cerf, New York, to Waldo Frank, New York, 3 November 1926, RHC.
76. Cerf, *At Random*, 45.
77. *The Reminiscences of Donald S. Klopfer*, 8–9.

Chapter Two

1. Bennett Cerf, *At Random: The Reminiscences of Bennett Cerf* (New York: Random House, 1977), 62.
2. O. H. Cheney, *Economic Survey of the Book Industry 1930–1931* (New York: National Association of Book Publishers, 1931; reprint ed., New York: R. R. Bowker, 1960), 285.
3. "Defense of Advertising," *Publishers' Weekly* 125 (27 January 1934): 383.
4. "An Advertising Catechism," ibid. (13 January 1934): 127–28.
5. "Defense of Advertising," 389.
6. "They Aren't Toothpaste," *Printers' Ink Monthly* 37 (December 1938): 5–6, 34, 36.
7. Tom Dardis, *Firebrand: The Life of Horace Liveright* (New York: Random House, 1995), 119–22.
8. Carolyn Marie Gottneid, "A Study of Book Advertising in the *Saturday Evening Post* from 1899 to 1949" (Master's thesis, University of Minnesota, 1958), 58–66.
9. "Defense of Advertising," 386.
10. "Advertising Campaign for Everyman's Library," *Publishers' Weekly* 78 (17 September 1910): 1017.
11. There are three separate prospectuses in the Random House Collection, none dated but all announcing that the magazine would appear in spring 1930. Apparently the stock market crash curtailed the magazine before it could begin. The quote is from the *American Chronicle* prospectus, RHC.
12. Ibid.
13. *Future* prospectus, RHC.
14. Barbara Ehrenreich and John Ehrenreich, "The Professional–Managerial Class," *Radical America* 11 (March–April 1977): 6–31.
15. Bennett A. Cerf, New York, to Max Schuster, New York, 20 September 1932, RHC.
16. All six boldface titles were from 1935; of the seven other titles listed, six were released in 1934 and one in 1933 (Gertrude Stein's *Three Lives*). Modern Library advertisements, *Nation* 141 (23 October 1935): 481; *New Republic* 84 (23 October 1935): 311.
17. Modern Library advertisement, *Little Review* 12 (May 1929): inside front cover.
18. Modern Library advertisement, *New Masses* 14 (5 March 1935): 24.

19. Belle Becker, "Modern Library's Contest Winners," ibid., 15 (21 May 1935): 23.
20. Modern Library advertisement, ibid., 17 (1 October 1935): 42.
21. Modern Library advertisement, *New Yorker* 1 (13 February 1926): 2. The four "Worst Sellers" were Andreas Latzko's *Men in War*, Marjorie Fleming's *Book*, Ouida's *In a Winter City*, and one of the first Modern Library titles, Maeterlinck's *A Miracle of St. Antony*.
22. Circulation statistics are taken from Helen K. Taylor, "What Magazines Do Book Readers Read?" *Publishers' Weekly* 133 (14 May 1938): 1923. Both "They Aren't Toothpaste" and "An Advertising Catechism" point to the *New York Times Book Review* as the best place to advertise to reach the greatest number of book readers.
23. Eighty-nine Modern Library advertisements appeared in the *New York Times Book Review* from 1925 to 1941.
24. Modern Library advertisement, ibid., 18 November 1928, 31.
25. Aaron Sussman, New York, to Bennett A. Cerf, New York, 4 November 1936, RHC.
26. Aaron Sussman, "See the Pretty Birdie: A Note on Advertising Layout," *Publishers' Weekly* 126 (21 July 1934): 191–92. Sussman recommends listing price only if it is an attention catcher as it was for the Modern Library.
27. See "They Aren't Toothpaste," 6.
28. Modern Library advertisement, *New York Times Book Review*, 10 October 1926, 23.
29. In his sweeping analysis of interwar advertising, Roland Marchand refers to this common strategy as the "Parable of the Democracy of Goods." He is quick to note the "democracy" presented in advertising was implicitly defined "in terms of equal access to consumer products." See Roland Marchand, *Advertising the American Dream: Making Way for Modernity, 1920–1940* (Berkeley: University of California Press, 1985), 217–18.
30. Modern Library advertisement, *New York Times Book Review*, 12 September 1926, 13
31. Ibid., 6 February 1927, 29; 7 August 1927, 15.
32. Ibid., 4 April 1937, 28.
33. Ibid., 10 July 1932, 20.
34. Ibid., 12 July 1931, 17.
35. Bennett Cerf, "The Modern Library and the Price of Books," *Publishers' Weekly* 119 (14 February 1931): 842–43.

36. Modern Library advertisement, *New York Times Book Review,* 26 July 1936, 19.
37. Ehrenreich and Ehrenreich, "The Professional–Managerial Class," 24.
38. Studying changes in professional–middle-class ideology from 1950 to 1985, Barbara Ehrenreich asserts that members of the professional middle class use taste and consumption to promote their status. Richard Ohmann found a similar use of consumption by the same class in the early twentieth century. See Barbara Ehrenreich, *Fear of Falling: The Inner Life of the Middle Class* (New York: Pantheon, 1989), 14; and Richard Ohmann, *Selling Culture: Magazines, Markets, and Class at the Turn of the Century* (London: Verso, 1996), 166–74.
39. Modern Library advertisement, *New York Times Book Review,* 22 January 1933, 24.
40. Ibid., 25 April 1937, 17.
41. O. H. Cheney found no evidence to support the book industry claim that "the automobile, the radio, the movies, cards, outdoor sports—and less intellectual pursuits—have made us less of booklovers than our parents." Cheney, *Economic Survey,* 52–54. Robert L. Duffus was motivated to study the American book trade in part by the charge that Americans were reading less due to modern amusements. Robert L. Duffus, *Books: Their Place in a Democracy* (Boston: Houghton Mifflin, 1930), ix–xiii. The Lynds offer anecdotal support for the charge in *Middletown* by quoting one "rising young lawyer" who was too busy with cards and other social gatherings to read books, in Robert S. Lynd and Helen Merrell Lynd, *Middletown: A Study in American Culture* (New York: Harcourt, Brace, and Co., 1929), 234. Malcolm Cowley scolded publishers for not being more competitive with "golfing and motoring," in "Cheaper and Better Books," *Forum* 84 (September 1930): 167.
42. Rita Felski, *The Gender of Modernity* (Cambridge: Harvard University Press, 1995), 208.
43. Modern Library advertisement, *New York Times Book Review,* 31 January 1937, 24. In interviews and when writing for the book trade in *Publishers' Weekly,* Cerf often used the masculine pronoun for Modern Library readers. Advertisements from the 1940s and 1950s also used the masculine pronoun, perhaps indicating that Cerf, like so many others, had ceased actively questioning gender norms as he had done in the 1920s and 1930s.
44. Carl F. Kaestle et al., *Literacy in the United States: Readers and Reading since 1880* (New Haven: Yale University Press, 1991), 194–95. See also Cheney, *Economic Survey,* 35–38.

45. Janice Radway, *A Feeling for Books: The Book-of-the-Month Club, Literary Taste, and Middle-Class Desire* (Chapel Hill: University of North Carolina Press, 1997), 297, 210–20.
46. Modern Library advertisement, *New York Times Book Review*, 18 November 1928, 31.
47. Ibid., 31 January 1937, 24.
48. For Cerf's assessment of the Modern Library's chief selling points, see his "Modern Library and the Price of Books," 842–43.
49. Modern Library advertisements, *New York Times Book Review*, 22 January 1933, 24; 30 September 1934, 32; 22 September 1935, 22.
50. Ibid., 22 January 1933, 24.
51. Ibid., 4 December 1927, 19; 10 October 1926, 23.
52. Anonymous, "Has America a Literary Dictatorship," *Bookman* 65 (April 1927): 192.
53. Radway, *A Feeling for Books*, 229.
54. Modern Library advertisement, *New York Times Book Review*, 22 September 1935, 22.
55. Cheney, *Economic Survey*, 125–28.
56. Harvard Classics advertisement, *New York Times Book Review*, 26 February 1939, 32.
57. Modern Library advertisement, in ibid., 31 March 1929, 21.
58. For an extended critique of the Book-of-the-Month Club's methods, see Joan Shelley Rubin, *The Making of Middlebrow Culture* (Chapel Hill: University of North Carolina Press, 1992), 98–105; quotation from the Book-of-the-Month Club advertisement, 99.
59. Modern Library advertisements, *New York Times Book Review*, 29 March 1931, 21; 5 August 1934, 13.
60. Ibid., 20 May 1928, 21.
61. Ibid., 22 November 1931, 27.
62. Ibid., 1 October 1933, 24.
63. Ibid., 10 April 1932, 25.
64. "The Modern Library Descriptive Catalogue," November 1925, RHC.
65. This account of Erskine's Great Book Program is from John Erskine, *My Life as a Teacher* (New York: J. B. Lippincott, 1948), 165–75, quotation on 168–69.
66. Mortimer J. Adler, *How to Read a Book: The Art of Getting a Liberal Education* (New York: Simon & Schuster, 1940), viii.

67. Modern Library advertisement, *New York Times Book Review*, 19 May 1940, 32.
68. Rubin illustrates this blending of character and personality in *Making of Middlebrow Culture*, 1–33.
69. Taylor, "What Magazines Do Book Readers Read?," 1922–26.
70. "They Aren't Toothpaste," 55.

Chapter Three

1. Frederic G. Melcher, "The Growth of the Reprint Market," *Publishers' Weekly* 136 (19 August 1939): 509.
2. The term "booming" gained currency in the publishing world in the late 1890s. Initially it was synonymous with book advertising, but it came to describe any promotional activity that smacked of commercialism. See John Tebbel, *A History of Book Publishing in the United States*, vol. 2, *The Expansion of an Industry, 1865–1919* (New York: R. R. Bowker, 1975), 145–46.
3. Malcolm Cowley, "Cheaper and Better Books," *Forum* 84 (September 1930): 167–70.
4. Charles Lee, *The Hidden Public: The Story of the Book-of-the-Month Club* (New York: Doubleday, 1958), 25.
5. Mencken's complaints about the general ignorance of the "booboisie" abound in his writings. For his commentary on publishing and the reading public, see H. L. Mencken, "Diagnosis of Our Cultural Malaise," in *Smart Set Criticism,* ed. William H. Nolte (Ithaca, N.Y.: Cornell University Press, 1968), 2–8. For a similar treatment of the American reading public, see Walter B. Pitkin, "Dollar Books and Thirty-Cent Readers," *Forum* 84 (September 1930): 162–66.
6. Mumford was specifically referring to the chance of a significant "dollar book" market arising in America. Lewis Mumford, "Publishing, Old and New," *New Republic* 64 (1 October 1930): 178.
7. J. George Frederick, "Bookish Snobs," *Independent* 114 (11 April 1925): 416.
8. Robert Duffus cites a figure of $150,000,000 spent on books in his *Books: Their Place in a Democracy* (Boston: Houghton Mifflin, 1930), 4. O. H. Cheney claims $276,000,000 spent for newspapers and another $185,000,000 on magazines in his *Economic Survey of the Book Industry, 1930–1931* (New York: National Association of Book Publishers, 1931; reprint ed., New York: R. R. Bowker, 1960), 339.
9. Duffus, *Books*, 4, 2–3.

10. William S. Gray and Ruth Monroe, *The Reading Interests and Habits of Adults: A Preliminary Report* (New York: Macmillan, 1930), 48.
11. Lee, *Hidden Public,* 27–28.
12. Cheney, *Economic Survey of the Book Industry,* 238.
13. Duffus, *Books,* 128.
14. *The Reminiscences of Donald S. Klopfer* (1978), 12–13, in the Oral History Collection of Columbia University.
15. Bennett Cerf, *At Random: The Reminiscences of Bennett Cerf* (New York: Random House, 1977), 62.
16. Bennett Cerf, "The Reprint—A Vital Force in the Book Publishing Industry," *Printers' Ink* 151 (1 May 1930): 150.
17. For a description of Charles Scribner Jr.'s devotion to the Modern Library during his college years, see his *In the Web of Ideas: The Education of a Publisher* (New York: Scribner's Sons, 1993), 7–10.
18. Granville Hicks, Northampton, to the Modern Library, New York, 26 March 1927, RHC.
19. Ibid., 25 January 1928, RHC.
20. College sales under Crofts's management actually dropped from approximately $34,000 in 1931 to $28,000 in 1932, despite the fact that enrollment went up as young people delayed entry into a severely depressed job market and overall Modern Library sales continued to climb. Bennett A. Cerf, New York, to F. S. Crofts, New York, 14 April 1933, RHC.
21. A series of letters from "The Modern Library, Inc." dated July 1932, each with its own disciplinary emphasis, is located in the "Publicity" file in RHC.
22. Bennett A. Cerf, New York, form letter to college bookstores, July 1932, RHC.
23. Not until 1936 did the trade journal for college bookstores, *College Store,* initiate a "Book Section." Until that time, sales information had focused on beer steins and other sundry merchandise.
24. "A Modern Interview," *College Store* 3 (May 1936): 15.
25. Franklin Spier, New York, to Bennett A. Cerf, New York, 22 April 1936, RHC. The "free publicity in connection with the ad we are running" was prepared in the offices of Spier & Sussman with the "advice and consent" of Random House's editor-in-chief Saxe Commins.
26. "A Modern Interview," 15.
27. Modern Library advertisement, *College Store* 3 (May 1936): 14.
28. Duffus, *Books,* 111.

29. For a full discussion of Scherman and Sackheim's Little Leather Library mail campaign, see Janice Radway, *A Feeling for Books: The Book-of-the-Month Club, Literary Taste, and Middle-Class Desire* (Chapel Hill: University of North Carolina Press, 1997), 159–60.
30. J. J. Hatcher, "Outline of Plan to Sell Modern Library by Mail," undated typescript attached to *Boyd's Catalog of Mailing Lists* no. 97 (1927), RHC.
31. See Joan Shelley Rubin, *The Making of Middlebrow Culture* (Chapel Hill: University of North Carolina Press, 1989), 93–110.
32. Hatcher, "Outline of Plan to Sell Modern Library by Mail," RHC.
33. Rogers Publishing Service mailer, Spring 1931, RHC.
34. Publishers Products Corporation, "How the Multiple-Commission Plan Works with Modern Library Books" [1933], RHC. Date based on number of titles (203) listed in the series and "Chain Selling for Books," *Publishers' Weekly* 123 (1 April 1933): 1126.
35. For a brief account of the "book wars" spawned by the Book-of-the-Month Club, see Lee, *Hidden Public*, 45–59.
36. Quoted in ibid., 49.
37. A brief notice of the pyramid scheme did appear in *Publishers' Weekly*. Even it was designed not to offend booksellers if at all possible by announcing that booksellers could become links in the chain if they so desired. See "Chain Selling for Books," 1126.
38. The Book-of-the-Month Club's first mailing used the list for the New York Social Register, but it had been preceded by a large magazine advertising campaign. Lee, *Hidden Public*, 33.
39. William B. Liebmann, "Random House; Or Fun and Profit in the Search for Excellence," *Columbia Library Columns* 20 (February 1971): 9.
40. Cheney, *Economic Survey of the Book Industry*, 19.
41. Dreiser is quoted in Gilbert Seldes, "The People and the Arts: Bibliomania in the Drugstores," *Scribner's Magazine* 101 (April 1937): 60. For an example of a traditional bookseller's contempt for drugstores, see Ora P. Barclay, "Drug Store Distribution," *Publishers' Weekly* 119 (4 April 1931): 1797.
42. Seldes, "The People and the Arts," 60.
43. There is contradictory evidence on the Modern Library's drugstore distribution. In 1930, Cerf claimed to be selling Modern Library books in drugstores and at newsstands, but in 1934 *Publishers' Weekly* reported that "Modern Library books have never been sold in drug stores." In his thorough business history of the Modern Library, Gordon Neavill found no evidence of drugstore distribution. The American News Company probably placed

some Modern Library books in independent drugstores, but drugstores were never an important distribution point for the series. See Cerf, "The Reprint—A Vital Force in the Book Publishing Industry," 148; "New Display Fixtures for the Bookshop," *Publishers' Weekly* 127 (30 March 1935): 1325; and Gordon Barrick Neavill, "The Modern Library Series" (Ph.D. diss., University of Chicago, 1984), 258–59.

44. The American News Company was a big buyer by 1930, and Modern Library sales manager Emanuel Harper wrote western sales agent Carl Smalley that American News branches received a hefty 45 percent discount (the same as Macy's and Gimbels) instead of the standard 33 ⅓ percent. See Emanuel Harper, New York, to Carl J. Smalley, n.p., 1 June 1930, RHC.

45. Cerf, "The Reprint—A Vital Force in the Book Publishing Industry," 148.

46. See Barclay, "Drug Store Distribution," 1797.

47. *Publishers' Weekly* reported the "biggest single surprise" in the Merchandising Research Division of the U.S. Bureau of Foreign and Domestic Commerce's *National Drug Store Survey* from 1932 was that "the majority of purchasers who buy books in drug stores enter the store with that express purpose." Impulse buys were very rare. See Waldon Fawcett, "Bookselling in Drug Stores," *Publishers' Weekly* 121 (16 April 1932): 1715–16.

48. Sarah Ball, "When Books Sell Themselves," *Publishers' Weekly* 124 (14 October 1933): 1324–25.

49. Modern Library, Inc. form letter, 1 June 1929, RHC.

50. "Sarah Ball en Route to Florida in Trailer," *Publishers' Weekly* 132 (4 December 1937): 2144.

51. Duffus, *Books*, 111.

52. Sinclair Lewis, *Main Street* (New York: Harcourt, Brace, 1920; reprint ed., New York: Library of America, 1992), 217, 226, 169–70.

53. James M. Hutchisson, *The Rise of Sinclair Lewis, 1920–1930* (University Park: Pennsylvania State University Press, 1996), 43.

54. Bennett A. Cerf, New York, to Robert de Graff, Garden City, L.I., 20 November 1933, RHC.

55. Robert de Graff, Garden City, L.I., to Bennett A. Cerf, New York, 23 November 1933, RHC.

56. James L. Crowder, n.p., to Bennett A. Cerf, New York, 11 October 1930, RHC.

57. Donald S. Klopfer, New York, to Carl J. Smalley, n.p., 24 June 1930, RHC.

58. Carl J. Smalley, n.p., to Donald S. Klopfer, New York, 22 June 1930, RHC.

59. Duffus, *Books*, 124–25.

60. This attitude changed slowly over time; it was prevalent in "Is the Cheap Book Worth the Retailer's While?" *Publishers' Weekly* 91 (16 June 1917): 1933–34; and it is the central issue in Ruth Leigh, "How to Merchandise Dollar Books," *Publishers' Weekly* 116 (24 August 1929): 707–9; and "Pushing the Dollar Line," ibid., 710–14. By 1935 it was fairly well settled that dollar lines could help general sales, but there was still some resistance, rebutted by Freeman Lewis in "The Distribution of Reprint Books," *Publishers' Weekly* 127 (30 March 1935): 1313–17.
61. Duffus, *Books,* 124.
62. Leigh, "How to Merchandise Dollar Books," 707–9.
63. "Pushing the Dollar Line," 711.
64. Ibid., 712.
65. Harriet C. Long, "No Book More Than One Dollar," *Publishers' Weekly* 116 (24 August 1929): 715–18.
66. Modern Library advertisement, *Publishers' Weekly* 121 (14 May 1932): 2015.
67. Bennett A. Cerf, New York, form letter to booksellers, 29 December 1930, RHC.
68. Ibid., 6 January 1933, RHC.
69. Duffus, *Books,* 126–27.
70. "Counter Points," *Publishers' Weekly* 122 (16 July 1932): 202.
71. Ibid.
72. Circulation expenses are from "Comparative analysis of Circulation Expenses for first 6 months of 1929 and 1930," typescript, RHC. Matchbook information comes from Diamond Match Company Invoice to Modern Library, Inc., 17 November 1927, RHC.
73. Liebmann, "Random House," 5.
74. "The Gentle Art of Blurbing," *Outlook* 133 (24 January 1923): 164.
75. Roland Marchand, *Advertising the American Dream: Making Way for Modernity, 1920–1940* (Berkeley: University of California Press, 1985), 313–14.
76. "The Gentle Art of Blurbing," 164.
77. See Anonymous, "Confessions of a Blurb Writer," *Bookman* 58 (October 1923): 162–65; and "Sublurbia," *New Republic* 32 (13 September 1922): 61–62.
78. "Sublurbia," 61–62.
79. "The Art of the Book Jacket," *Publishers' Weekly* 117 (1 March 1930): 1139.
80. From the series' inception, a title list was printed on the book jacket. Cerf and Klopfer moved the list to the inside of the jacket in 1926.

81. See John S. Vane E. Kohn, "Some Notes on Book Jackets," *Publishers' Weekly* 132 (30 October 1937): 1732–35. As a bibliographer and collector he discusses the value of keeping jackets that contain pertinent bibliographical information, but he also notes that most book collectors are not likely to foul their shelves with jackets.
82. Belle Rosenbaum, "In Praise of Book Jackets," *Publishers' Weekly* 131 (6 February 1937): 730–31.
83. "The Bargain Market," *Publishers' Weekly* 133 (29 January 1938): 496.
84. This figure is based on George M. Andes, *A Descriptive Bibliography of the Modern Library, 1917–1970* (Boston: Boston Book Annex, 1989).
85. John Steinbeck, on board the *T. S. Drottingholm,* to Bennett A. Cerf, New York, 1937, BCP.
86. Bennett A. Cerf, New York, to John Erskine, New York, 13 October 1926, RHC.
87. Bennett A. Cerf, New York, to William Lyon Phelps, New Haven, 5 October 1926, RHC.
88. William Lyon Phelps, New Haven, to Bennett A. Cerf, New York, 6 October 1926, RHC.
89. Andes, *A Descriptive Bibliography of the Modern Library,* 159, 214.
90. Bennett A Cerf, New York, to Max Eastman, Croton-on-Hudson, 4 November 1937, RHC.
91. Lewis Miller, "Sales Notes Fall 1939 Conference," RHC.
92. Lewis Miller, "Memo to All Salesmen: Random House Publications for Spring and Summer 1940," RHC.
93. Cerf, *At Random,* 55.
94. There is no evidence that either the Macy's or Gimbels book departments operated at a loss, but Cheney reports, "The book department is in many cases unprofitable—in fact, the data shows [sic] that the 'average profit' is a loss." The loss was acceptable, because "there is no question as to the value of a book department for bringing in a good class of shoppers regularly." See Cheney, *Economic Survey of the Book Industry,* 296–98.
95. Scribner, *In the Web of Ideas,* 9.
96. Retail management texts directed at department stores stressed the importance of eye-catching, open displays where attractively packaged merchandise could be handled. Effective displays needed to be supported with posters or show cards especially when price was an important draw, and promotional devices such as contests were recommended. See Paul H. Nystrom, *Retail Store Operation,* 4th ed. (New York: Ronald Press, 1937), 160–

65; and Harold H. Maynard, Kenneth Dameron, and Carlton J. Siegler, *Retail Marketing and Merchandising* (New York: Ginn and Co., 1938), 320–25. For an extended discussion of the development of department store merchandising techniques, see William Leach, *Land of Desire: Merchants, Power, and the Rise of a New American Culture* (New York: Vintage Books, 1993).

97. Between 80 and 90 percent of department store shoppers were women, and most of them came from the middle or upper class. Susan Porter Benson, *Counter Cultures: Saleswomen, Managers, and Customers in American Department Stores, 1890–1940* (Urbana: University of Illinois Press, 1988), 76.

98. Mumford, "Publishing, Old and New," 178.

Chapter Four

1. Edith Stern, "Random House," *Saturday Review of Literature,* 24 (6 December 1941): 18.
2. George M. Andes and Helen Kelly, "Texts of Choice: The Books of the Modern Library," *AB Bookman's Weekly* 84 (27 November 1989): 2082.
3. Frances Lamont Robbins, "Better Than Cards or Calendars," *Outlook* 150 (19 December 1928): 1375.
4. Ibid.
5. For an excellent tracing of changes in the Modern Library's format and design, see Gorden B. Neavill, "The Modern Library Series: Format and Design, 1917–1977," *Printing History* 1 (1979): 26–37.
6. Docket #1277 United States of America before Federal Trade Commission. FTC *v.* Boni and Liveright Order to Cease and Desist. Government Printing Office, dated 23rd day of April, A.D. 1925, RHC.
7. The Modern Library did not shed its imitation leather binding until early 1929. Robbins's comment on the disappearance of the "limp suede" in December 1928 indicates that she probably saw a sample copy of the new balloon-cloth binding before its general release.
8. Steven Heller, "The Master Who Couldn't Draw Straight," *Print* 47 (March–April 1993): 90.
9. Philip Larson, "Hype-Type at the Walker," *Print Collector's Newsletter* 15 (September–October 1984): 121–27. Three of Bernhard's posters appeared in the 1984 Walker Art Center (Minneapolis) exhibit, "The 20th-Century Poster: Design of the Avant-Garde."
10. Heller, "The Master Who Couldn't Draw Straight," 93.
11. Bernhard published two essays on modernism and decoration and he made his living for a time redesigning the homes of wealthy New York patrons.

See Lucian Bernhard, "Modernism in the Home," *House and Garden* 53 (June 1928): 84–85; and idem, "Lady's Bedroom Showing the Contemporary Mode in Furniture and Decoration," *House and Garden* 55 (January 1929): 68–69.

12. Heller, "The Master Who Couldn't Draw Straight," 88.
13. The description of Bernhard's colophon as a "Promethean bringer of enlightenment" comes from the 1992 Prospectus for the Modern Library relaunch, RHC. Neavill also uses a similar phrase in "The Modern Library Series: Format and Design," 28.
14. Geoffrey Ashall Glaister, *The Encyclopedia of the Book*, 2d ed. (New Castle, Del.: Oak Knoll Press, 1996), 5. The term "colophon" originally referred to the concluding statement of a manuscript, and then came to mean an identifying device for trade publishers. In fine-press work, the term always means a brief statement of printing specifics at the end of a book, and I am using the term as it was used in the first half of the twentieth century by trade publishers.
15. "The Cult of the Colophon," *Publishers' Weekly* 112 (6 August 1927): 384–89.
16. Annie Dillard, *An American Childhood* (New York: Harper & Row, 1987), 84.
17. Knopf advertisement, *New Republic* 8 (17 November 1917): ii.
18. T. J. Cobden-Sanderson, *The Ideal Book, or, Book Beautiful: A Tract on Calligraphy, Printing, and Illustration and on the Book Beautiful as a Whole* (Hammersmith: Doves Press, 1900).
19. Geoffrey T. Hellman, "Durable Publisher: Alfred A. Knopf," in *Mrs. de Peyster's Parties and Other Lively Studies from the New Yorker* (New York: Macmillan, 1963), 274.
20. Praise for Knopf's book-manufacturing prowess is omnipresent in the history of American publishing. See Charles A. Madison, *Book Publishing in America* (New York: McGraw-Hill, 1966), 323–24; Hellmut Lehmann-Haupt, *The Book in America: A History of the Making and Selling of Books in the United States* (New York: R. R. Bowker, 1952), 300; John Tebbel, *A History of Book Publishing in the United States*, vol. 3, *The Golden Age between Two Wars, 1920–1940* (New York: R. R. Bowker, 1978), 113–16; and Joseph Blumenthal, *The Printed Book in America* (Hanover, N.H.: University Press of New England, 1989), 89.
21. Alfred Knopf, "A Publisher Looks at Book Design," in *Portrait of a Publisher*, ed. Paul A. Bennett (New York: Typophiles, 1965), 87.
22. Blumenthal, *The Printed Book in America*, 112. Adler's obsessive behavior toward books and printing is well documented in Paul A. Bennett's, *Elmer Adler in the World of Books: Reminiscences of Frederick B. Adams, Jr., John T.*

Winterich, Lawrence McNulty, Al Hine, David Jackson McWilliams, Edward Naumburg, Jr., Philip C. Duschnes, Elmer Adler (New York: Grolier Club, 1964).

23. Quoted in Frederick B. Adams Jr., "Elmer Adler, Apostle of Good Taste," *Publishers' Weekly* 139 (5 April 1941): 1474.
24. Quoted in Blumenthal, *The Printed Book in America*, 109.
25. Cobden-Sanderson, *The Ideal Book*, 6.
26. Bennett Cerf, *At Random: The Reminiscences of Bennett Cerf* (New York: Random House, 1977), 41, 281.
27. Emily Post, *Etiquette: "The Blue Book of Social Usage,"* new and enlarged ed. (New York: Funk & Wagnalls, 1928), 682.
28. Sinclair Lewis, *Babbitt* (New York: Harcourt Brace, 1922; reprint ed., New York: Library of America, 1992), 553.
29. Lawrence F. Abbott, "The Middlebrows," *Outlook* 147 (2 November 1927): 281–82.
30. Lewis, *Babbitt*, 554.
31. Post, *Etiquette*, 3, 66.
32. Cerf, *At Random*, 61–62.
33. Modern Library advertisement, *New York Times Book Review*, 4 December 1927, 19; "New Modern Library Catalog," *Publishers' Weekly* 109 (6 February 1926): 454.
34. "The Modern Library Descriptive Catalogue," November 1925, RHC.
35. "Random House Catalog, Announcement Number Two," Spring 1928, RHC.
36. Cerf, *At Random*, 63.
37. Elmer Adler, New York, to Bennett A. Cerf, New York, 28 August 1928, RHC. Adler used the phrase to remind Cerf of his own dedication to the typographic interests of the firm.
38. For an excellent discussion of the fine-press movement in the United States during this period, see Megan Benton, *Beauty and the Book: Fine Editions and Cultural Distinction in America* (New Haven: Yale University Press, 2000).
39. Bennett A. Cerf, New York, to Manuel Komroff, Paris, 28 October 1926, RHC.
40. Cerf, *At Random*, 77.
41. Bennett A. Cerf, New York, to Edwin Grabhorn, San Francisco, 26 February 1929, RHC.
42. Ibid., 26 November 1929, RHC.

43. See Bennett A. Cerf, New York, to Moira Gibbing, Golden Cockerel Press, Reading, England, 12 February 1930, RHC. "I am sorry to tell you that the recent financial upset in America has very definitely affected the market for press books, particularly the more or less unimportant trifles that most of the presses have been doing as filler-in material, and have been retailing in the region of fifteen to forty-five shillings a copy. I hope that you are not going to do too much of this sort of thing in the coming year. It is easier to sell a book like your edition of The Canterbury Tales for $55.00 a copy than Abyss for $6.00 a copy." Megan Benton asserts that the economic collapse was not the only factor in the decline of American fine printing. More important was "an indiscriminant plentitude in the publishing of fine books and a corresponding laxness in production principles." See Benton, *Beauty and the Book,* 213–14.

44. Bennett A. Cerf, New York, to Richard Ellis, Westport, 28 March 1933, RHC.

45. "Modern Quarters for Modern Enterprises," *Publishers' Weekly* 113 (16 June 1928): 2442.

46. For a detailed description of the professional–managerial class and its relationship to the Book-of-the-Month Club, see Janice Radway, *A Feeling for Books: The Book-of-the-Month Club, Literary Taste, and Middle-Class Desire* (Chapel Hill: University of North Carolina Press, 1997), 221–60; the quotation, 284–85.

47. After the balloon-cloth bindings were introduced in 1929, the books were bound only in red, blue, green, or brown cloth.

48. Donald S. Klopfer, New York, to A. L. Kennelly, New York, 21 February 1931, RHC.

49. Ibid., 9 April 1931, RHC.

50. Donald S. Klopfer, New York, to Bert Wolff, New York, 15 March 1930; 10 December 1930, RHC.

51. Henry Hazlitt, "In Dispraise of Fine Books," *Nation* 132 (20 May 1931): 559–60.

52. Evelyn Harter, "The Bodies of Books," *Bookman* 73 (August 1931): 604.

53. Evelyn Harter, "Little Sixteenmo, the Good Companion," *Publishers' Weekly* 120 (10 October 1931): 1692–93.

54. Emily Newell Blair, "Why I Like Books and Some of the Books I Like," *Good Housekeeping* 84 (February 1927): 51.

55. Emily Newell Blair, *The Creation of a Home: A Mother Advises a Daughter* (Farrar & Rinehart, 1930), 268–69.

56. David Traxel, *An American Saga: The Life and Times of Rockwell Kent* (New York: Harper & Row, 1980), 143–56.
57. Bennett A. Cerf, New York, to Rockwell Kent, Ausable Forks, N.Y., 11 December 1928, RHC.
58. Quoted in Roland Marchand, *Advertising the American Dream: Making Way for Modernity, 1920–1940* (Berkeley: University of California Press, 1985), 148.
59. Rockwell Kent, Ausable Forks, N.Y., to Donald S. Klopfer, New York, 26 January 1929, RHC.
60. Ibid.
61. For an illustration of the invitation, see Cerf, *At Random*, 73.
62. Neavill, "The Modern Library Series: Format and Design," 30–33.
63. Donald S. Klopfer, New York, to Rockwell Kent, Ausable Forks, N.Y., 19 February 1929, RHC.
64. "The Modern Library," *Publishers' Weekly* 115 (9 February 1929): 657–58.
65. Typescript for Radio Book Reviews from *Harper's Magazine*, 28 July to 3 August [1929], RHC.
66. Alexander Woollcott, "Reading and Writing: A Ten-Dollar Shelf," undated typescript [mid- to late 1931], RHC.
67. Cerf, "The Reprint—A Vital Force in the Book Publishing Industry," *Printers' Ink* 151 (1 May 1930): 150.
68. Megan Benton, "'Too Many Books': Book Ownership and Cultural Identity in the 1920s," *American Quarterly* 49 (June 1997): 268–97.
69. F. Scott Fitzgerald, *The Great Gatsby* (New York: Scribner's Sons, 1925), 46. For a satiric look at the use of books as home decoration, see Thomas L. Masson, "Domestic Bookaflage," *Independent* 110 (14 April 1923): 256.
70. Modern Library Advertisement, *New York Times Book Review*, 25 April 1937, 17.
71. Lewis Mumford, "Publishing, Old and New," *New Republic* 64 (1 October 1930): 178.
72. Walter B. Pitkin, "Dollar Books and Thirty-Cent Readers," *Forum* 84 (September 1930): 166.
73. Malcolm Cowley, "Cheaper and Better Books," *Forum* 84 (September 1930): 168.
74. Mumford, "Publishing, Old and New," 178.
75. The following account is from Cerf, *At Random*, 90–93.
76. See *The Reminiscences of Donald S. Klopfer* (1971), 16, in the Oral History Collection at Columbia University; and Cerf, *At Random*, 94.

77. Cerf explains the Adler buyout in a letter to the Nonesuch Press. See Bennett A. Cerf, New York, to Francis Meynell, London, 1 June 1932, RHC. Initially, Random House was a subsidiary of the Modern Library; then in 1936 the roles were reversed, and the Modern Library became a subsidiary of Random House.
78. "Report to O'Neill," 27 June 1933, RHC.
79. Eugene O'Neill to Saxe Commins, 31 May 1933, in Dorothy Commins, ed., *"Love and Admiration and Respect": The O'Neill–Commins Correspondence* (Durham, N.C.: Duke University Press, 1986), 159–60.
80. Carlotta O'Neill to Saxe Commins, 31 May 1933, in ibid., 158.
81. Random House–Modern Library Catalog, Spring 1935, RHC.
82. Modern Library advertisements, *New York Times Book Review,* 27 September 1931, 21; 29 November 1931, 28.
83. "Is the Family Library Doomed?" *Publishers' Weekly* 91 (24 February 1917): 617.
84. F. Scott Fitzgerald, Ashville, N.C., to Bennett Cerf, New York, 23 July 1936, in Andrew Turnbull, ed., *The Letters of F. Scott Fitzgerald* (New York: Scribner's Sons, 1963): 536–37.
85. Rockwell Kent, Ausable Forks, N.Y., to Bennett A. Cerf, New York, 8 June 1939, RHC.
86. Bennett A. Cerf, New York, to Rockwell Kent, Ausable Forks, N.Y., 9 June 1939, RHC.
87. Bennett A. Cerf, New York, to Malcolm Cowley, New York, 31 August 1939 (one letter in a general mailing to book reviewers), RHC.
88. "A Descriptive Catalogue Modern Library Season of 1927–1928," RCH.

Chapter Five

1. Bennett A. Cerf, "The Modern Library and the Price of Books," *Publishers' Weekly* 119 (14 February 1931): 842.
2. Sherwood Anderson, *Poor White* (New York: B. W. Huebsch, 1920; reprint ed., New York: Modern Library, 1926), v–viii.
3. The phrase "modern in spirit" is taken from Bennett Cerf, "The Reprint—A Vital Force in the Book Publishing Industry," *Printers' Ink* 151 (1 May 1930): 148.
4. For two excellent brief histories of the cosmopolitan ideal and its centrality for intellectuals from 1920 to 1950, see Terry Cooney, "New York Intellectuals and the Question of Jewish Identity," *American Jewish History* 80 (Spring 1991): 344–60; and David A. Hollinger, "Ethnic Diversity, Cos-

mopolitanism and the Emergence of the American Liberal Intelligentsia," *American Quarterly* 27 (May 1975): 133–51.

5. Hollinger, "Ethnic Diversity, Cosmopolitanism and the Intelligentsia," 135.
6. Randolph Bourne, "Trans-National America," in *History of a Literary Radical and Other Essays* (New York: B. W. Huebsch, 1920), 278, 297.
7. "The Modern Library," *Publishers' Weekly* 115 (9 February 1929): 657.
8. Bibliographical data were compiled by the author using George M. Andes, *A Descriptive Bibliography of The Modern Library, 1917–1970* (Boston: Boston Book Annex, 1989). Andes's bibliography covers only the Modern Library regular series. My data include Modern Library Giants.
9. "The Modern Library," 657.
10. For a late 1920s Marxist critique of modernism's excesses, see Herman Spector, "Liberalism and the Literary Esoterics," *New Masses* 4 (January 1929): 18–19. See also Paul R. Gorman, *Left Intellectuals and Popular Culture in Twentieth-Century America* (Chapel Hill: University of North Carolina Press, 1996), 140.
11. Bennett A. Cerf, New York, to Edmund Wilson, New York, 18 July 1928, RHC.
12. See Invitation for party to be held on May 21, [1935?] in BCP scrapbook, 1933–1936. When the Book Union had difficulties in 1936, its leaders turned to Klopfer for advice. In addition, Marian Klopfer (Donald's first wife) sat on the board of the Book Union. Donald S. Klopfer, New York, to Victor Gollancz, London, 23 September 1936, RHC.
13. *Publishers' Weekly* 126 (27 October 1934): 1576. See also John Tebbel, *A History of Book Publishing in the United States,* vol. 3, *The Golden Age between Two Wars, 1920–1940* (New York: R. R. Bowker, 1978), 473–74.
14. The group of organizers consisted of Alexander Trachtenberg, A. A. Heller, Ben Huebsch, Roger Baldwin, Heywood Broun, Bennett Cerf, Thomas Coward, Malcolm Cowley, Lewis Gannett, Michael Gold, Alvin Johnson, Freda Kirchway, Alfred Knopf, Corliss Lamont, Robert Morss Lovett, W. W. Norton, and Mary Van Kleeck. Tebbel, *A History of Book Publishing,* vol. 3, 569.
15. Bennett A. Cerf, New York, to Isabel Paterson, New York, 9 June 1932, RHC.
16. For a discussion of Eastman's essay and its impact on the organized left, see Daniel Aaron, *Writers on the Left: Episodes in American Literary Communism* (New York: Harcourt, Brace & World, 1961), 222–23.

17. Donald S. Klopfer, New York, to Max Eastman, Croton-on-Hudson, 16 February 1933, RHC.
18. Max Eastman, *Love and Revolution: My Journey through an Epoch* (New York: Random House, 1964), 547–48.
19. John Strachey, London, to Bennett A. Cerf, New York, 18 February 1937, RHC.
20. Bennett A. Cerf, New York, to Joseph Lesser, New York, 22 July 1942, RHC.
21. Ibid., to Alfred A. Knopf, New York, 24 October 1939, RHC.
22. Ibid., to Joseph Lesser, New York, 18 April 1940, RHC.
23. Joseph Lesser, New York, to Bennett A. Cerf, New York, 12 November 1941, RHC.
24. Bennett A. Cerf, New York, to Joseph Lesser, New York, 20 July 1942, RHC.
25. Joseph Lesser, New York, to Bennett A. Cerf, New York, 21 July 1942, RHC.
26. As an example, see young Malcolm Cowley's reaction to Mann in Hans Bak, *Malcolm Cowley: The Formative Years* (Athens: University of Georgia Press, 1993), 57.
27. Huntington Cairns, "The Modern Library," *Modern Quarterly* 5 (Fall–Winter 1928): 121–23.
28. Hollinger, "Ethnic Diversity, Cosmopolitanism and the Intelligentsia," 133.
29. R. D. Townsend, "A Test of Taste," *Outlook* 129 (14 December 1921): 617.
30. Douglas Waples, *People and Print: Social Aspects of Reading in the Depression* (Chicago: University of Chicago Press, 1938), 7, 13.
31. The general requirements for greatness are: "Truth to human character and experience, gravity and breadth of theme, a freshness of insight which adds to the sum of human understanding, detachment without loss of emotional intensity, and beauty of expression." See Jeannette Howard Foster, "An Approach to Fiction through the Characteristics of Its Readers," *Library Quarterly* 6 (April 1936): 140.
32. Quoted in "College Librarians Round Table," *Bulletin of the ALA* 30 (1936): 683. I have substituted the word *genre* for Foster's *class* so as not to confuse her "class" with Waples's "class." Foster divided two hundred fifty authors into fifteen classes of fiction (such as "adventure," "detective," "romance," and "family"); then she further divided the authors into six cultural levels based on their sophistication to create a ninety-square grid. She studied reading habits to see if readers were more prone to select by class or cultural

level. As an example, the "satiric" class contained Clarence Kelland, Arthur Roche, and George Chamberlain in level one; Tiffany Thayer and Michael Arlen in level two; E. E. M. De La Pasture in level three; John Erskine, Anne Parrish, Christopher Morley, and Robert Nathan in level four; Thomas Macaulay and Lewis Carroll in level five; and Anatole France alone in level six. For her complete findings, see Foster, "An Approach to Fiction," 124–74.

33. Waples, *People and Print,* 206–7. Statistics are based on books borrowed from the St. Louis Public Library in 1934.
34. Sales statistics based on "Modern Library Titles in Order of Sales Popularity Jan–June 1928," RHC.
35. Cerf, "The Reprint—A Vital Force in the Book Publishing Industry," 150. Despite assurances to booksellers, the Modern Library never strictly adhered to the quota.
36. *The Reminiscences of Donald S. Klopfer* (1978), 39, in the Oral History Collection of Columbia University.
37. Bennett A. Cerf, New York, to Whitney Darrow, New York, 31 January 1940, RHC.
38. Ibid., to Alfred A. Knopf, New York, 24 October 1939, RHC.
39. "Suggested Letter to Dodd, Mead & Co.," undated, unsigned—probably Bennett A. Cerf, Spring 1937, RHC.
40. John T. Frederick, "*Of Men and Books:* 'The Classics Are Contemporary,'" *Northwestern University on the Air* 2 (16 January 1943): 4.
41. Ibid.
42. Bennett A. Cerf, New York, to J. Rey Peck, New York, 28 July 1930, RHC.
43. Bennett A. Cerf, New York, to Waldo Frank, New York, 3 November 1926, RHC.
44. Cairns, "The Modern Library," 122.
45. Lewis Gannett, "Books and Things," *New York Herald Tribune,* 3 March 1932, 15.
46. Charles Scribner Jr., *In the Company of Writers: A Life in Publishing* (New York: Scribner's Sons, 1990), 65.
47. Charles Scribner Jr., *In the Web of Ideas: The Education of a Publisher* (New York: Scribner's Sons, 1993), 8.
48. See Cairns, "The Modern Library," 122–23; Gannett, "Books and Things," 15; "Modern Library Best Sellers," *Publishers' Weekly* 125 (13 January 1934): 148; and "The Modern Library at 20," *Newsweek* 14 (16 October 1939): 36–37.

49. Stephan Talty, "Canonizers behind Closed Doors," *New York Times Sunday Magazine*, 6 October 1996, 36.
50. Frederick, *"Of Men and Books,"* 4–5.
51. John F. Baker, "Fifty Years of Publishing at Random," *Publishers' Weekly* 208 (4 August 1975): 25.
52. *Reminiscences of Donald S. Klopfer*, 5.
53. Richard L. Simon, "Try and Stop Them," *Saturday Review of Literature* 33 (23 December 1950): 4–40.
54. Bennett Cerf, *At Random: The Reminiscences of Bennett Cerf* (New York: Random House, 1977), 62.
55. Reminiscences of Donald S. Klopfer: "terrible ham," 63; "charm everybody," 70.
56. Bennett A. Cerf, New York, to Gertrude Stein, Bilignin [France], 8 September 1937, RHC.
57. Sterling G. Slappey, "Authoring Success; A Conversation with Bennett Cerf, Author, Wit, and Co-Founder of Random House," *Nation's Business* 56 (January 1968); reprinted in *Book Publishing: Inside Views*, comp. Jean Spealman Kujoth (Metuchen, N.J.: Scarecrow Press, 1971), 23; Thomas B. Morgan, "The Long Happy Life of Bennett Cerf," *Esquire* 61 (March 1964): 112.
58. Henry May, *The End of American Innocence: A Study of the First Years of Our Own Time, 1912–1917* (New York: Knopf, 1969), 281.
59. The division of labor was never hard and fast. All three owned equal shares of the company, and important decisions were made by the group. See Simon, "Try and Stop Them," 40.
60. This summary of Commins's career is based on Dorothy Commins, *What Is an Editor? Saxe Commins at Work* (Chicago: University of Chicago Press, 1977), 1–26.
61. *Reminiscences of Donald S. Klopfer*, 24.
62. Geoffrey T. Hellman, "Profiles: Publisher; Part II, Big Day for Random," *New Yorker* 35 (16 May 1959): 57.
63. Frederick, *"Of Men and Books,"* 5.
64. A file labeled "Suggestion for New Titles," in RHC, contained William Lyon Phelps "The Fifteen Finest Novels and Short Stories" *Forum* 70 (August 1923): 1817–27, and lists by Arthur Symons, William Lamont, and Edward J. O'Brien, as well as several "Best Books" lists from newspapers and magazines.

65. Granville Hicks, Northampton, Mass., to the Modern Library, New York, 25 January 1928, RHC.
66. Clifford Odets, New York, to Bennett A. Cerf, New York, 20 September 1939, RHC.
67. Edmund Wilson, New York, to Bennett A. Cerf, New York, 28 September 1933, RHC.
68. William Lyon Phelps, New Haven, to Bennett A. Cerf, New York, 9 February 1927, RHC.
69. James T. Farrell, New York, to Bennett A. Cerf, New York, 10 January 1939, RHC.
70. F. Scott Fitzgerald, Ashville, N. C., to Bennett Cerf, New York, 23 July 1936, collected in Andrew Turnbull, ed., *The Letters of F. Scott Fitzgerald* (New York: Scribner's Sons, 1963), 536–37. Heywood Broun, New York, to Bennett A. Cerf, New York, 31 October 1926, RHC; Gertrude Stein, Bilignin, to Bennett A. Cerf, New York, August 1939, RHC; Christopher Morley, Roslyn Heights, N.Y., to Bennett A. Cerf, New York, 31 January 1939 and 4 January 1940, RHC; Alfred Kreymborg, New York, to Bennett A. Cerf, New York, 26 May 1930, RHC.
71. Frederick, *"Of Men and Books,"* 5.
72. Cerf, *At Random,* 63.
73. Ibid., 72–74; the story was retold by Richard L. Simon (with slightly different figures) twenty years later in "Try and Stop Them," 5.
74. Hiram Haydn, *Words and Faces* (New York: Harcourt, Brace, Jovanovich, 1974), 31.
75. List compiled from dozens of letters contained in the "Twelve Against the Gods" file, RHC.
76. Donald S. Klopfer, New York, to Robert Haas, New York, 16 November 1934, RHC.
77. Robert S. Lynd and Helen Merrell Lynd, *Middletown: A Study in American Culture* (New York: Harcourt, Brace, 1929), 76.
78. Henry Holt, *Garrulities of an Octogenarian Editor* (Boston: Houghton Mifflin, 1923), 210–13.
79. Scribner, *In the Web of Ideas,* 8.
80. Ernest Hemingway, Piggott, Ark., to Bennett A. Cerf, New York, 4 January 1930, BCP; William Faulkner, Oxford, Miss., to Bennett A. Cerf, New York, 15 April 1931, BCP.
81. See William Faulkner, Oxford, Miss., to Bennett A. Cerf, New York, 15 April 1931, BCP; Christopher Morley, Roslyn Heights, N.Y., to Bennett A.

Cerf, New York, 10 April 1940, RHC; and John Dos Passos, Provincetown, Mass., to Bennett A. Cerf, New York, 4 July 1937, RHC.
82. Clifford Odets, New York, to Bennett A. Cerf, New York, 13 September 1939, RHC.
83. Bennett A. Cerf, New York, to Malcolm Johnson, Garden City, L.I., 12 May 1938, RHC.
84. Ibid.
85. Although Knopf, from a publisher's standpoint, thought Cather a nearly perfect author (she delivered her books on time, never asked for outrageous advances, and never complained about royalties), her reprint policy cost both Cather and Knopf considerable profits. See Alfred A. Knopf "Publishing Then and Now, 1912–1964," in *Portrait of a Publisher,* ed. Paul A. Bennett (New York: Typophiles, 1965), 39.
86. Alfred A. Knopf, New York, to the Modern Library, New York, 13 November 1925, RHC.
87. To ensure U.S. copyright, works by foreign authors had to be typeset and printed in the United States. In 1904, G. P. Putnam's Sons had published *Green Mansions* in the United States, using sheets from Duckworth and Company's London edition, thus leaving the work unprotected in the United States.
88. Richard Ohmann argues that the professional–managerial class is the crucial market for an author hoping for cultural and financial success. As the nation's primary book-buying public, the professional–managerial class can stimulate high-profile reviews and media attention. Furthermore, once a book begins to receive the right kind of critical attention from educators (also members of the professional–managerial class), they may choose to assign it as reading in college courses. As Ohmann sees it, the process spirals: professional–managerial writers tell stories based on their perceptions that then resonate with professional–managerial editors, readers, and critics to draw the attention of professional–managerial educators. The books are then taught in colleges training the next generation of this class of workers. Over time, this process may lead to canonization. Richard Ohmann, "The Shaping of a Canon: U.S. Fiction, 1960–1975," *Critical Inquiry* 10 (September 1983): 199–223.
89. 1992 Relaunch Prospectus, RHC. Gary Giddins, "Why I Carry a Torch for the Modern Library," *New York Times Book Review,* 6 December 1992, 42.
90. Simon, "Try and Stop Them," 40.
91. James Truslow Adams, *The Epic of America* (Boston: Little, Brown, 1931), 416, 412.

92. Obituary for Arthur Herald Stanley Nelson, *News Tribune* (Tacoma), 3 August 2000.

CHAPTER SIX

1. See Thomas L. Bonn, *Under Cover: An Illustrated History of American Mass Market Paperbacks* (New York: Penguin Books, 1982), 47. For more information on the "Paperback Revolution," see: Frank L. Schick, *The Paperbound Book in America* (New York: R. R. Bowker, 1958); Thomas L. Bonn, *Heavy Traffic and High Culture: New American Library as Literary Gatekeeper in the Paperback Revolution* (Carbondale: Southern Illinois University Press, 1989); and Kenneth C. Davis, *Two-Bit Culture: The Paperbacking of America* (Boston: Houghton Mifflin, 1984).
2. Bennett A. Cerf, London, to Random House, New York, 20 May 1936, BCP.
3. Robert K. Haas and Donald S. Klopfer, New York, to Bennett A. Cerf, London, 1 June 1936, RHC.
4. Bennett A. Cerf, New York, to Richard Walsh, New York, 13 February 1940, RHC.
5. The Grosset & Dunlap outlet figure is from Robert L. Duffus, *Books: Their Place in a Democracy* (Boston: Houghton Mifflin, 1930), 114. The Pocket Books figure is from Thomas Bonn, "Pocket Books, 1938–Present," in *Mass Market Publishing in America,* ed. Allen Billy Crider (Boston: G. K. Hall and Co., 1982), 222.
6. James T. Farrell, "Will the Commercialization of Publishing Destroy Good Writing? Some Observations on the Future of Books," *New Directions* 9 (1946): 9.
7. Ibid., 13, 25.
8. James T. Farrell, "Introduction to Studs Lonigan" in *Studs Lonigan* (New York: Vanguard Press, 1935; reprinted ed., New York: Modern Library, 1938), vii.
9. George Mayberry, "An Open Letter to The Modern Library, Inc., New York City," *New Republic* 109 (8 November 1943): 661. According to Gordon Neavill, when the Modern Library dropped the title, it was still available in a lesser-known edition, a fact that he points to as further proof of the importance of the series in American cultural life, as clearly the most watched reprint series on the market. See Gordon Neavill, "The Modern Library Series and American Cultural Life," *Journal of Library History* 16 (Spring 1981): 248–49.
10. Harry Levin, "Toward Stendhal," *Pharos* 3 (Winter 1945): 71.

11. John F. Baker, "Fifty Years of Publishing at Random," *Publishers' Weekly* 208 (4 August 1975): 26. When Random House moved into a skyscraper in 1969, Cerf remembered, "It broke my heart to leave the old house, and I never stopped believing that we should have kept it for our editorial offices." See *At Random: The Reminiscences of Bennett Cerf* (New York, Random House, 1977), 194.
12. Unless otherwise noted, all sales figures were compiled by the author from charts in Lewis Miller's "Sales Figures" file, RHC.
13. "Notes on Contributors," *New Directions* 9 (1946): x–xi.
14. Quote from masthead of *Pharos* 3. The quarterly managed only four numbers. It was reorganized in 1947 under the title *Direction* and published by New Directions.
15. Sales statistics on Cerf's books are from Thomas B. Morgan, "The Long and Happy Life of Bennett Cerf," *Esquire* 61 (March 1964): 112. Morgan claims sales of ten million books over two decades. All but one of Cerf's highly profitable books were published by his friends and competitors, Richard Simon and Maxwell Schuster.
16. Quoted in ibid., 112.
17. Cowley proposed a *New Yorker* profile of Cerf, but the editors requested he do one on Maxwell Perkins instead. Cowley's profile, originally published in 1944, helped to make Perkins famous. Malcolm Cowley, "Prefatory Note" to *Unshaken Friend: A Profile of Maxwell Perkins* (Boulder, Colo.: Roberts Rinehart, 1985), ix.
18. Geoffrey T. Hellman, "Profiles: Publisher; Part I, Descent from Olympus," *New Yorker* 35 (9 May 1959): 54.
19. Hiram Haydn, *Words and Faces* (New York: Harcourt, Brace, Jovanovich, 1974), 98–99.
20. *Reminiscences of Donald S. Klopfer* (1978), 63, in the Oral History Collection of Columbia University.
21. Cerf, *At Random,* 187.
22. Jason Epstein remembered that, by 1960, Cerf would spend weeks away from the office in pursuit of the activities that brought him personal fame; Jason Epstein, *Book Business: Publishing Past, Present, and Future* (New York: Norton, 2001), 90.
23. Conrad Aiken, Brewster, Mass., to Bennett A. Cerf, New York, 18 November 1943, RHC.
24. Bennett A. Cerf, "Trade Winds: The Case of Ezra Pound," *Saturday Review of Literature* 29 (9 February 1946): 26.

25. Conrad Aiken, Brewster, Mass., to Saxe Commins, New York, 30 June 1945, RHC.
26. Statement attached to a letter from Saxe Commins, New York, to Bernice Baumgarden of Brandt and Brandt agency, New York, 13 July 1945, RHC.
27. Quoted in Robert A. Corrigan, "*What's My Line:* Bennett Cerf, Ezra Pound and the *American* Poet," *American Quarterly* 24 (1972): 101–13.
28. Both the Gannett letter and Cerf's response are reprinted in Cerf, "Trade Winds: The Case of Ezra Pound" (9 February 1946): 26–27.
29. Ibid., 27.
30. Bennett A. Cerf, "Trade Winds: The Case of Ezra Pound," *Saturday Review of Literature* 29 (16 March 1946): 32.
31. The letter from Harrison Smith was one of nearly fifty letters reprinted in ibid.
32. W. H. Auden, New York, to Bennett A. Cerf, New York, 29 January 1946, RHC.
33. Bennett A. Cerf, New York, to W. H. Auden, New York, 31 January 1946, RHC.
34. W. H. Auden, New York, to Bennett A. Cerf, New York, 2 February 1946, RHC.
35. Bennett A. Cerf, New York, to W. H. Auden, New York, 4 February 1946, RHC.
36. Ibid., 6 February 1946, RHC.
37. W. H. Auden, New York, to Bennett A. Cerf, New York, 9 February 1946, RHC.
38. Bennett A. Cerf, New York, to W. H. Auden, New York, 4 March 1946, RHC.
39. W. H. Auden, New York, to Bennett A. Cerf, New York, 6 March 1946, RHC.
40. Cerf, *At Random,* 172.
41. "The Question of the Pound Award, 8 Opinions: W. H. Auden, R. G. Davis, Clement Greenberg, Irving Howe, George Orwell, Karl Shapiro, Allen Tate, William Barrett," *Partisan Review* 16 (May 1949): 512–22; Dwight Macdonald "Homage to Twelve Judges," *Politics* 6 (Winter 1949): 1–2; Robert Hillyer, "Treason's Strange Fruit: The Case of Ezra Pound and the Bollingen Award," *Saturday Review of Literature* (11 June 1949): 9–28; idem, "Poetry's New Priesthood," *Saturday Review of Literature* (18 June 1949): 7–38; and *The Case against the Saturday Review of Literature* (Chicago: Modern Poetry Association, 1949).

42. See C. David Heyman, *Ezra Pound: The Last Rower* (New York: Viking Press, 1976), 217–21; and Corrigan, "What's My Line," 101–13.
43. Saxe Commins played the lead editorial role through World War II, and he was still very active in the Modern Library in the late 1940s, but Stein was a respected editorial voice for the series by the late 1940s. Commins appears to have been primarily occupied with editing anthologies and Modern Library "Basic Books," a set of contracted titles in the Modern Library's regular series by experts that outlined the essentials of various fields of knowledge. When Saxe Commins suffered a heart attack in 1953, Stein assumed primary control of the series until Jason Epstein came to Random House in 1958.
44. In 1930, 7.2 percent of the population between eighteen and twenty-four was enrolled in a college or university; by 1960, it was more than 20 percent. See United States Bureau of the Census, *Historical Statistics of the United States, Colonial Times to 1970*, Part 1 (Washington: D.C., Government Printing Office, 1975): 382–83.
45. Russell Jacoby, *The Last Intellectuals: American Culture in the Age of Academe* (New York: Basic Books, 1987), 14–17.
46. United States Bureau of the Census, *Historical Statistics*, 382.
47. Memo from Lewis Miller to All Salesmen, n.d, RHC.
48. "The Modern Library Announces Modern Library College Editions" [1950], RHC.
49. James Russell, n.p., to Lewis Miller, New York, 2 May 1950, RHC.
50. Lewis Miller, New York, to James Russell, Beverly Hills, 2 May 1950, RHC.
51. Memo from Jess Stein to Bennett A. Cerf, 14 July 1950, RHC.
52. Modern Library advertisement, *Kenyon Review* 12 (Summer 1950): advertising section.
53. James Russell, n.p., to Lewis Miller, New York, 14 August [1950], RHC. Jess Stein did not see the College Editions as exclusively directed to higher education. After a conversation with David Hoffmann, an English teacher in a Philadelphia high school, he sent letters and sample copies to the Boards of Education in New York City, Brooklyn, Austin, Boston, Philadelphia, Providence, Raleigh, and Chicago urging them to consider fifty-five of the titles for use "in the field of English for Grades 7 to 12." Memo from Jess Stein, Random House, to Lewis Miller, Random House, 26 November 1951, RHC; and Jess Stein, New York, to Add B. Anderson, Secretary and Business Manager, Board of Education, Philadelphia, 3 January 1952, RHC. There are eight identical letters included in a folder marked "Board of Education."

54. Memo from Lewis Miller to All Salesmen, n.d., RCH.
55. Illustrated Modern Library advertisement, *Publishers' Weekly* 144 (14 August 1943): 452–53.
56. Bennett A. Cerf, New York, to Harry Abrams, New York, 16 November 1943, RHC.
57. For an excellent discussion of the complicated business maneuverings to establish and maintain the Illustrated Modern Library, see Gordon Barrick Neavill, "The Modern Library Series" (Ph.D. diss., University of Chicago, 1984): 332–57.
58. Cerf, *At Random*, 197.
59. Paperbacks did reduce sales of a few titles in the public domain. Cerf points out that as early as 1943, sales of titles such as *Moby Dick* and *The Scarlet Letter* were being affected by paperback editions, and he cites that as the reason for the launching of Bantam Books, in *At Random*, 195, 202–3.
60. Cerf's "brilliant boy" epithet, in ibid., 201.
61. Epstein, *Book Business*, 47; Schick, *Paperbound Book in America*, 181–87.
62. See Arthur Hale's "Mass Market" column, "Award to Anchor Books," *Publishers' Weekly* 167 (15 January 1955): 237; letters to the editor from Walter Pitkin and Jay Tower, *Publishers' Weekly* 167 (19 March 1955): 1534–35; and Arthur Hale's "Mass Market" column, "What Is 'the Mass Market'?" *Publishers' Weekly* 167 (19 March 1955): 1573.
63. For a description of their manufacture, see "Anchor Books: An Experiment with Serious Books," *Publishers' Weekly* 167 (15 January 1955): 207–8; and Schick, *Paperbound Book in America*, 181–82.
64. Memo from Lewis Miller to All Salesmen, 21 March 1958, RHC.
65. Modern Library advertisement, *New York Times Book Review*, 27 February 1955, 15.
66. "Random House Launches Modern Library Paperback," *Publishers' Weekly* 167 (19 February 1955): 1204.
67. Memo from Lewis Miller to All Salesmen, 21 March 1958, RHC.
68. "You Meet Such Interesting People," *Publishers' Weekly* 174 (3 November 1958): 31. Epstein was not the official chief editor of the series. It was managed by what Gordon Neavill called "an uneasy troika" of Epstein, Morris Philipson, and Jess Stein. By the mid-1960s, Epstein had assumed dominant control over the series. See Neavill, "The Modern Library Series," 469.
69. "Meeting on Modern Library and ML Paperback List for Fall 1959," 5 February 1959, RCH.
70. Memo from Jason Epstein to Bennett A. Cerf, 9 December 1958, RHC.

71. "Modern Library Paperbacks Spring & Fall '59 Advertising" from Sussman and Sugar, New York, to Random House, New York, 15 January 1959, RHC.
72. Epstein, *Book Business*, 4–7.
73. Cerf, *At Random*, 278.
74. Epstein, *Book Business*, 88.
75. When Random House took over Pantheon Books, André Schiffrin was installed as its head. See André Schiffrin, *The Business of Books: How International Conglomerates Took Over Publishing and Changed the Way We Read* (New York: Verso, 2000), 36. Random House was subsequently purchased by RCA in 1966 for $38 million.
76. Baker, "Fifty Years of Publishing at Random," 26–28.
77. Gordon Neavill describes several editorial initiatives contemplated between 1960 and 1967, including replacing old translations, increasing the poetry collections, and one fleeting plan to make Modern Library the single hardbound repository for the impressive combined backlists of Knopf and Random House. Except for the addition of new translations of several Modern Library standards, none of the ideas came to fruition, probably because all concerned saw Vintage as the reprint series with the best future. See Neavill, "The Modern Library Series," 466–90.
78. Memo from Tony Wimpfheimer to Bob Bernstein, Dick Krinsley, Jim Silberman, and Jason Epstein, 9 February 1966, RHC.
79. David Finn, New York, to Sidney Jacobs, New York, 31 January 1966, RHC.
80. Memo from Dick Krinsley to Tony Wimpfheimer, 28 February 1966, RHC.
81. Memo from Jason Epstein to Tony Wimpfheimer, Bob Bernstein, Dick Krinsley, and Jim Silberman, 17 February 1966, RHC.
82. Gordon B. Neavill, "The Modern Library Series: Format and Design, 1917–1977," *Printing History* 1 (1979): 34.
83. Memo from Thomas Lowry to Tony Wimpfheimer, 11 November 1966, RHC.
84. "Dilly" is from a memo from William H. Ryan attached to a draft of proposed contest copy, 25 April 1967, RHC.
85. "Grand Prize Winner of Modern Library Contest Announced," Random House Press Release [February 1968], RHC.
86. "Modern Library Estimated Contributing Margin 1971" attached to memo from Larry Kirshbaum to Donald Klopfer, Bud Baker, Tony Schulte, Bob Gottlieb, André Schiffrin, Jim Silberman, Jason Epstein, Tony Wimpf-

heimer, Jess Stein, Mark Sexton, Dick Krinsley, Dick Liebermann, Howard Stern, Fred Schneebaum, Sidney Jacobs, Jean Pohoryles, Dave Hilliard, Don Singer, Sylvia Bloomberg, Joan Milarsky, 10 February 1971, RHC. Random House's total gross in 1971 was "approaching $100-million a year." See Baker, "Fifty Years of Publishing at Random," 25.

87. Cerf remembered, "Nothing really changed at Random House for a while. I was still there and Donald was still there; we could give advice, take care of our big authors and keep things rolling," but soon Robert Bernstein began to exert full control. See Cerf, *At Random*, 290–91.

88. Lists attached to memo from Larry Kirshbaum to Donald Klopfer et al., 10 February 1971, RHC.

89. Ibid.

90. Memo from Don Singer to Dick Liebermann, 3 August 1971, RHC.

91. As late as 1970, Cerf still believed a market for the clothbound series remained strong, and he asserted that the regular Modern Library "still offers real books, with very attractive bindings and jackets." At the same time, he knew that the series had seen its best days; even though it was still "a beautiful property," it was "no longer a 'must' in all bookstores." Cerf, *At Random*, 202–3.

92. Memo from John Simon to Bennett Cerf, 24 August 1970, RHC.

93. Throughout the 1970s, the College Editions remained in print.

94. The description of the building is from Epstein, *Book Business*, 7; *Reminiscences of Donald S. Klopfer*, 22–23.

95. *Reminiscences of Donald S. Klopfer*, 23.

Epilogue

1. 1992 Relaunch Prospectus, RHC.

2. See Chapter Four for a full discussion of Blair's "volumes *de luxe*."

3. Rick Marin, "Classics Confusion," *Vogue* 183 (April 1993): 270.

4. <http://www.randomhouse.com/modernlibrary/news.html>, 10 October 1998; and <http://www.randomhouse.com/modernlibrary/100discuss.html>, 10 October 1998.

5. David Gates and Ray Sawhill, "The Dated and the Dead," *Newsweek* 132 (3 August 1998): 64.

6. *Ulysses* (no.1 on "The List") was Amazon's second-best seller, followed by *Brave New World* (no. 5) in the seventh position, *Lolita* (no. 4) in the eighth selling spot, with *The Great Gatsby* (no. 2) rounding out the top-ten best-

sellers. David Streitfeld, "'The Best Novels' May Not Be," *Washington Post,* 5 August 1998, A6.

7. See Carolyn Alessio, "These Are the Century's Best English-Language Books? As If!" *Chicago Tribune,* 27 July 1998, Sec. 5, 1; and William Styron, "Talk of the Town: A Modern Library Juror Fesses Up about the Hundred Best Novels," *New Yorker* 74 (17 August 1998): 29.
8. The board consisted of: Daniel Boorstin, A. S. Byatt, Christopher Cerf, Shelby Foote, Vartan Gregorian, Edmund Morris, John Richardson, Arthur M. Schlesinger Jr., William Styron, and Gore Vidal.
9. Louis Menand, "Novels We Love: Why Are Lists So Irresistible?" *New Yorker* 74 (3 August 1998): 5.
10. Styron, "Talk of the Town," 29–30.
11. "Rank Rankings Make the List," *USA Today,* 7 August 1998, 12A.
12. Streitfeld, "'The Best Novels' May Not Be," A6.
13. Quoted in Joanne Kaufman, "Maybe the Next List Will Include a Degree of Difficulty for Each Novel," *Chicago Tribune,* 27 July 1998, Sec. 5, 5.
14. Gates and Sawhill, "The Dated and the Dead," 65; and Christopher Cerf, "End Justifies the Means," *USA Today,* 7 August 1998, 12A.
15. Gerald Early, quoted in Alessio, "These Are the Century's Best English-Language Books?" Sec. 5, 4. Even though Early thought the list was targeting *New Republic* readers, a curmudgeonly *New Republic* commentary sidestepped the whole notion of the list's ranking to assert that the list only shows how few really good novels had appeared in this century. James Wood, "Bookdumb," *New Republic* 219 (17 and 24 August 1998): 14.
16, Streitfeld, "'The Best Novels' May Not Be," A6.
17. Henry Finder was listed on the Modern Library's World Wide Web, "The Modern Library in the News" page, as the person "we actually know (who isn't a Board member)" who has read the greatest number of books on the list. Finder reportedly had read sixty-six of the titles. See <http://www.randomhouse.com/modernlibrary/news.html>, 10 October 1998.
18. Quoted in Alessio, "These Are the Century's Best English-Language Books?" Sec. 5, 4.
19. See Anne Mulrine, "A Novel Idea: The 100 Best Works of Fiction," *U.S. News and World Report* 125 (3 August 1998): 61.

Selected Bibliography

Archives and Oral Histories Consulted

Bennett A. Cerf Papers. Rare Book and Manuscript Library, Columbia University.
Harry Scherman Oral History. *Book-of-the-Month Club Project*. In the Oral History Collection of Columbia University.
Random House Archives. Rare Book and Manuscript Library, Columbia University.
The Reminiscences of Ben W. Huebsch. In the Oral History Collection of Columbia University.
The Reminiscences of Bennett A. Cerf. In the Oral History Collection of Columbia University.
The Reminiscences of Donald S. Klopfer. In the Oral History Collection of Columbia University.
Robert K. Haas Oral History. *Book-of-the-Month Club Project*. In the Oral History Collection of Columbia University.

Books and Articles

Aaron, Daniel. *Writers on the Left: Episodes in American Literary Communism*. New York: Harcourt, Brace & World, 1961.
Abbott, Lawrence F. "The Middlebrows." *Outlook* 147 (2 November 1927): 281–88.
Acocella, Joan. "The Hunger Artist." *New Yorker* 76 (6 March 2000): 68–77.
Adams, Frederick B., Jr. "Elmer Adler, Apostle of Good Taste." *Publishers' Weekly* 139 (5 April 1941): 1473–77.
Adams, James Truslow. *The Epic of America*. Boston: Little, Brown, 1931.
Adler, Mortimer J. *How to Read a Book: The Art of Getting a Liberal Education*. New York: Simon & Schuster, 1940.
Altick, Richard D. "From Aldine to Everyman: Cheap Reprint Series of the English Classics, 1830–1906." *Studies in Bibliography* 11 (1958): 3–24.
"An Advertising Catechism." *Publishers' Weekly* 125 (13 January 1934): 127–30.
Anderson, Sherwood. *Poor White*. New York: B. W. Huebsch, 1920. Reprint ed., New York: Modern Library, 1926.
Andes, George M. *A Descriptive Bibliography of the Modern Library, 1917–1970*. Boston: Boston Book Annex, 1989.
Andes, George M., and Helen Kelly. "Texts of Choice: The Books of the Modern Library." *AB Bookman's Weekly* 84 (27 November 1989): 2073–88.

Bak, Hans. *Malcolm Cowley: The Formative Years*. Athens: University of Georgia Press, 1993.
Baker, John F. "Fifty Years of Publishing at Random." *Publishers' Weekly* 208 (4 August 1975): 25–31.
Ball, Sarah. "When Books Sell Themselves." *Publishers' Weekly* 124 (14 October 1933): 1324–26.
Barclay, Ora P. "Drug Store Distribution." *Publishers' Weekly* 119 (4 April 1931): 1797–98.
Beard, Rick, and Leslie Cohen Berlowitz, eds. *Greenwich Village: Culture and Counterculture*. New Brunswick: Rutgers University Press, 1993.
Becker, Belle. "Modern Library Contest Winners." *New Masses* 15 (21 May 1935): 23.
Bellow, Saul. *Humbolt's Gift*. New York: Viking Press, 1975.
Bennett, Paul A., ed. *Elmer Adler in the World of Books: Reminiscences of Frederick B. Adams, Jr., John T. Winterich, Lawrence McNulty, Al Hine, David Jackson McWilliams, Edward Naumburg, Jr., Philip C. Duschnes, Elmer Adler*. New York: Grolier Club, 1964.
Benson, Susan Porter. *Counter Cultures: Saleswomen, Managers, and Customers in American Department Stores, 1890–1940*. Urbana: University of Illinois Press, 1988.
Benton, Megan. *Beauty and the Book: Fine Editions and Cultural Distinction in America*. New Haven: Yale University Press, 2000.
———. "'Too Many Books': Book Ownership and Cultural Identity in the 1920s." *American Quarterly* 49 (June 1997): 268–97.
Bernhard, Lucian. "Lady's Bedroom Showing the Contemporary Mode in Furniture and Decoration." *House and Garden* 55 (January 1929): 68–69.
———. "Modernism in the Home." *House and Garden* 53 (June 1928): 84–118.
Bicknell, Percy F. "Classics for the Millions." *Dial* 52 (16 April 1912): 313–14.
Bjorkman, Edwin. "Everyman's Library: A Democratic Educational Institution." *Review of Reviews* 44 (December 1911): 755.
Blair, Emily Newell. *The Creation of a Home: A Mother Advises a Daughter*. New York: Farrar & Rinehart, 1930.
———. "Why I Like Books and Some of the Books I Like." *Good Housekeeping* 84 (February 1927): 51.
Bloom, Alexander. *Prodigal Sons: The New York Intellectuals and Their World*. New York: Oxford University Press, 1986.
Blumenthal, Joseph. *The Printed Book in America*. Hanover, N.H.: University Press of New England, 1989.
Bonn, Thomas L. *Heavy Traffic and High Culture: New American Library as Literary Gatekeeper in the Paperback Revolution*. Carbondale: Southern Illinois University Press, 1989.

———. "Pocket Books, 1938–Present." In *Mass Market Publishing in America*, edited by Allen Billy Crider, 218–33. Boston: G. K. Hall and Co., 1982.
———. *Under Cover: An Illustrated History of American Mass Market Paperbacks*. New York: Penguin Books, 1982.
Bourdieu, Pierre. *Distinction: A Social Critique of the Judgement of Taste*. Translated by Richard Nice. Cambridge: Harvard University Press, 1984.
———. *The Field of Cultural Production: Essays on Art and Literature*. Edited by Randal Johnson. New York: Columbia University Press, 1993.
Bourne, Randolph. "History of a Literary Radical." *Yale Review* n.s. 8 (April 1919): 468–84.
———. *History of a Literary Radical and Other Essays*. New York: B. W. Huebsch, 1920.
Brooks, Van Wyck. *America's Coming-of-Age*. New York: B. W. Huebsch, 1915.
Cairns, Huntington. "The Modern Library." *Modern Quarterly* 5 (Fall–Winter 1928): 121–23.
Canby, Henry Seidel. *Definitions: Essays in Contemporary Criticism*. 2d series. New York: Harcourt, Brace and Co., 1924.
The Case against the Saturday Review of Literature. Chicago: Modern Poetry Association, 1949.
Cerf, Bennett A. *At Random: The Reminiscences of Bennett Cerf*. New York: Random House, 1977.
———. "Trade Winds: The Case of Ezra Pound." *Saturday Review of Literature* 29 (9 February 1946): 26–27.
———. "Trade Winds: The Case of Ezra Pound." *Saturday Review of Literature* 29 (16 March 1946): 32–53.
———. "The Modern Library and the Price of Books." *Publishers' Weekly* 119 (14 February 1931): 842–43.
———. "The Reprint—A Vital Force in the Book Publishing Industry." *Printers' Ink* 151 (1 May 1930): 147–50.
"A Cerfit of Riches." *Time* 88 (16 December 1966): 100–8.
Cheney, O. H. *Economic Survey of the Book Industry, 1930–1931*. New York: National Association of Book Publishers, 1931. Reprint ed., New York: R. R. Bowker, 1960.
Cobden-Sanderson, T. J. *The Ideal Book, or, Book Beautiful: A Tract on Calligraphy, Printing, and Illustration and on the Book Beautiful as a Whole*. Hammersmith: Doves Press, 1900.
Colby, F. M. "The Taboo of Culture." *Harper's Monthly* 141 (September 1920): 540–42.
Commins, Dorothy. *What Is an Editor? Saxe Commins at Work*. Chicago: University of Chicago Press, 1978.

Commins, Dorothy, ed. *"Love and Admiration and Respect": The O'Neill–Commins Correspondence.* Durham, N.C.: Duke University Press, 1986.
"Confessions of a Blurb Writer." *Bookman* 58 (October 1923): 162–65.
Cooney, Terry A. "New York Intellectuals and the Question of Jewish Identity." *American Jewish History* 80 (Spring 1991): 344–60.
———. *The Rise of the New York Intellectuals: Partisan Review and Its Circle.* Madison: University of Wisconsin Press, 1986.
Corrigan, Robert A. *"What's My Line:* Bennett Cerf, Ezra Pound and the American Poet." *American Quarterly* 24 (1972): 101–13.
Cowley, Malcolm. *After the Genteel Tradition: American Writers since 1910.* New York: W. W. Norton, 1937.
———. "Cheaper and Better Books." *Forum* 84 (September 1930): 167–70.
———. *Unshaken Friend: A Profile of Maxwell Perkins.* Boulder, Colo.: Roberts Rinehart, 1985.
Dardis, Tom. *Firebrand: The Life of Horace Liveright.* New York: Random House, 1995.
Davis, Kenneth C. *Two-Bit Culture: The Paperbacking of America.* Boston: Houghton Mifflin, 1984.
Dell, Floyd. Introduction to *Confessions of a Young Man,* by George Moore. New York: Modern Library, 1918.
Dewey, John. "The Crisis in Culture." *New Republic* 62 (19 March 1930): 123–26.
Dillard, Annie. *An American Childhood.* New York: Harper & Row, 1987.
Duffus, Robert L. *Books: Their Place in a Democracy.* Boston: Houghton Mifflin, 1930.
———. "An Outline of 'Culture.'" *Bookman* 64 (December 1926): 433–36.
Eastman, Max. *Love and Revolution: My Journey through an Epoch.* New York: Random House, 1964.
Ehrenreich, Barbara. *Fear of Falling: The Inner Life of the Middle Class.* New York: Pantheon, 1989.
Ehrenreich, Barbara, and John Ehrenreich. "The Professional–Managerial Class." *Radical America* 11 (March–April 1977): 6–31.
Epstein, Jason. *Book Business: Publishing Past, Present, and Future.* New York: W. W. Norton, 2001.
Erskine, John. "Culture: The Interplay of Life and Ideas." *Century Magazine* 116 (May 1928): 83–88.
———. *My Life as a Teacher.* Philadelphia: J. B. Lippincott, 1948.
Farrell, James T. *Studs Lonigan.* New York: Vanguard Press, 1935. Reprint ed., New York: Modern Library, 1938.
———. "Will the Commercialization of Publishing Destroy Good Writing? Some Observations on the Future of Books." *New Directions* 9 (1946): 6–37.

Fawcett, Waldon. "Bookselling in Drug Stores." *Publishers' Weekly* 121 (16 April 1932): 1715–16.
Felski, Rita. *The Gender of Modernity*. Cambridge: Harvard University Press, 1995.
Fitzgerald, F. Scott. *The Great Gatsby*. New York: Scribner's Sons, 1925.
Foster, Jeanette Howard. "An Approach to Fiction through the Characteristics of Its Readers." *Library Quarterly* 6 (April 1936): 124–74.
Frederick, J. George. "Bookish Snobs." *Independent* 114 (11 April 1925): 416.
Frederick, John T. *"Of Men and Books:* 'The Classics Are Contemporary.'" *Northwestern University on the Air* 2 (16 January 1943).
Gannett, Lewis. "Books and Things." *New York Herald Tribune,* 3 March 1932, 15.
Gans, Herbert J. *Popular Culture and High Culture: An Analysis and Evaluation of Taste*. New York: Basic Books, 1974.
Gates, David, and Ray Sawhill. "The Dated and the Dead." *Newsweek* 132 (3 August 1998): 64–65.
"The Gentle Art of Blurbing." *Outlook* 133 (24 January 1923): 164.
Gerould, Katherine Fullerton. "The Extirpation of Culture." *Atlantic Monthly* 116 (October 1915): 445–55.
———. "What, Then, Is Culture?" *Harper's Monthly* 154 (January 1927): 190–95.
Giddins, Gary. "Why I Carry a Torch for the Modern Library." *New York Times Book Review,* 6 December 1992, 42.
Gilmer, Walker. *Horace Liveright: Publisher of the Twenties*. New York: David Lewis, 1970.
Glaister, Geoffrey Ashall. *The Encyclopedia of the Book,* 2d ed. New Castle, Del.: Oak Knoll Press, 1996.
Gorman, Paul R. *Left Intellectuals and Popular Culture in Twentieth-Century America*. Chapel Hill: University of North Carolina Press, 1996.
Gottneid, Carolyn Marie. "A Study of Book Advertising in the *Saturday Evening Post* from 1899 to 1949." Master's thesis, University of Minnesota, 1958.
Gray, William S., and Ruth Monroe. *The Reading Interests and Habits of Adults: A Preliminary Report*. New York: Macmillan, 1930.
Hale, Arthur. "Award to Anchor Books." *Publishers' Weekly* 167 (15 January 1955): 237.
———. "What Is 'the Mass Market'?" *Publishers' Weekly* 167 (19 March 1955): 1573.
Harter, Evelyn. "The Bodies of Books." *Bookman* 73 (August 1931): 604–6.
———. "Little Sixteenmo, the Good Companion." *Publishers' Weekly* 120 (10 October 1931): 1692–94.
Hartshorne, Thomas L. *The Distorted Image: Changing Conceptions of the American Character since Turner*. Cleveland: Case Western Reserve University Press, 1968.

"Has America a Literary Dictatorship?" *Bookman* 65 (April 1927): 191–99.
Haydn, Hiram. *Words and Faces*. New York: Harcourt, Brace, Jovanovich, 1974.
Hazlitt, Henry. "In Dispraise of Fine Books." *Nation* 132 (20 May 1931): 559–60.
Heller, Steven. "The Master Who Couldn't Draw Straight." *Print* 47 (March–April 1993): 88–97.
Hellman, Geoffrey T. "Durable Publisher: Alfred A. Knopf." In *Mrs. de Peyster's Parties and Other Lively Studies from the New Yorker*. New York: Macmillan, 1963.
———. "Profiles: Publisher; Part I, Descent from Olympus." *New Yorker* 35 (9 May 1959): 48–92.
———. "Profiles: Publisher; Part II, Big Day for Random." *New Yorker* 35 (16 May 1959): 49–84.
Heyman, C. David. *Ezra Pound: The Last Rower*. New York: Viking Press, 1976.
Hillyer, Robert. "Poetry's New Priesthood." *Saturday Review of Literature* 32 (18 June 1949): 7–38.
———. "Treason's Strange Fruit: The Case of Ezra Pound and the Bollingen Award." *Saturday Review of Literature* 32 (11 June 1949): 9–28.
Hollinger, David A. "Ethnic Diversity, Cosmopolitanism and the Emergence of the American Liberal Intelligentsia." *American Quarterly* 27 (May 1975): 133–51.
Holt, Henry. *Garrulities of an Octogenarian Editor*. Boston: Houghton Mifflin, 1923.
Howe, Irving. "The Idea of the Modern." In *Literary Modernism*. Edited by Irving Howe. Greenwich, Conn.: Fawcett, 1967.
Humphrey, Robert E. *Children of Fantasy: The First Rebels of Greenwich Village*. New York: John Wiley & Sons, 1978.
Hutchisson, James M. *The Rise of Sinclair Lewis, 1920–1930*. University Park: Pennsylvania State University Press, 1996.
Jacoby, Russell. *The Last Intellectuals: American Culture in the Age of Academe*. New York: Basic Books, 1987.
Kaestle, Carl F., Helen Damon-Moore, Lawrence C. Stedman, Katherine Tinsley, and William Vance Trollinger Jr. *Literacy in the United States: Readers and Reading since 1880*. New Haven: Yale University Press, 1991.
Kerfoot, J. B. "The Latest Books." *Life* 70 (23 August 1917): 311.
Knopf, Alfred A. *Portrait of a Publisher*. Edited by Paul A. Bennett. New York: Typophiles, 1965.
Kohn, John S. Van E. "Some Notes on Book Jackets." *Publishers' Weekly* 132 (30 October 1937): 1732–35.
Kronenberger, Louis. "Gambler in Publishing: Horace Liveright." *Atlantic Monthly* 215 (January 1965): 94–104.

Langner, Lawrence. *The Magic Curtain: The Story of a Life in Two Fields, Theatre and Invention.* New York: E. P. Dutton, 1951.
Larson, Philip. "Hype-Type at the Walker." *Print Collector's Newsletter* 15 (September–October 1984): 121–27.
Leach, William. *Land of Desire: Merchants, Power, and the Rise of a New American Culture.* New York: Vintage Books, 1993.
Lee, Charles. *The Hidden Public: The Story of the Book-of-the-Month Club.* New York: Doubleday, 1958.
Lehmann-Haupt, Hellmut. *The Book in America: A History of the Making and Selling of Books in the United States.* New York: R. R. Bowker, 1952.
Leigh, Ruth. "How to Merchandise Dollar Books." *Publishers' Weekly* 116 (24 August 1929): 707–9.
Levin, Harry. "Toward Stendhal." *Pharos* 3 (Winter 1945): 1–72.
Levine, Lawrence. *Highbrow/Lowbrow: The Emergence of Cultural Hierarchy in America.* Cambridge: Harvard University Press, 1988.
Lewis, Freeman. "The Distribution of Reprint Books." *Publishers' Weekly* 127 (30 March 1935): 1313–43.
Lewis, Sinclair. *Babbitt.* New York: Harcourt, Brace, 1922. Reprint ed., New York: Library of America, 1992.
——. *Main Street.* New York: Harcourt, Brace, 1920. Reprint ed., New York: Library of America, 1992.
Liebmann, William B. "Random House; Or Fun and Profit in the Search for Excellence." *Columbia Library Columns* 20 (February 1971): 3–15.
Long, Harriet C. "No Book More Than One Dollar." *Publishers' Weekly* 116 (24 August 1929): 715–18.
Lynd, Robert S., and Helen Merrell Lynd. *Middletown: A Study in American Culture.* New York: Harcourt, Brace and Co., 1929.
Lynes, Russell. *The Tastemakers.* New York: Harper and Brothers, 1954.
Macdonald, Dwight. *Against the American Grain.* New York: Random House, 1962.
——. "Homage to Twelve Judges." *Politics* 6 (Winter 1949): 1–2.
Madison, Charles A. *Book Publishing in America.* New York: McGraw-Hill, 1966.
——. *Jewish Publishing in America: The Impact of Jewish Writing on American Culture.* New York: Sanhedrin Press, 1975.
Marchand, Roland. *Advertising the American Dream: Making Way for Modernity, 1920–1940.* Berkeley: University of California Press, 1985.
Marin, Rick. "Classics Confusion." *Vogue* 183 (April 1993): 268–70.
Masson, Thomas L. "Domestic Bookaflage." *Independent* 110 (14 April 1923): 256–57.

May, Henry F. *The End of American Innocence: A Study of the First Years of Our Own Time, 1912–1917.* New York: Knopf, 1969.
Mayberry, George. "An Open Letter to The Modern Library, Inc., New York City." *New Republic* 109 (8 November 1943): 661.
Maynard, Harold H., Kenneth Dameron, and Carlton J. Siegler. *Retail Marketing and Merchandising.* New York: Ginn and Co., 1938.
Melcher, Frederic G. "The Growth of the Reprint Market." *Publishers' Weekly* 136 (19 August 1939): 509.
Menand, Louis. "Novels We Love: Why Are Lists So Irresistible?" *New Yorker* 74 (3 August 1998): 4–5.
Mencken, Henry Louis. *Smart Set Criticism.* Edited by William H. Nolte. Ithaca, N.Y.: Cornell University Press, 1968.
"A Modern Interview." *College Stores* 3 (May 1936): 15.
Morgan, Thomas B. "The Long Happy Life of Bennett A. Cerf." *Esquire* 61 (March 1964): 112–18.
Mulrine, Anne. "A Novel Idea: The 100 Best Works of Fiction." *U.S. News and World Report* 125 (3 August 1998): 61.
Mumford, Lewis. "Publishing, Old and New." *New Republic* 64 (1 October 1930): 176–78.
Neavill, Gordon B. "The Modern Library Series." Ph.D. dissertation, University of Chicago, 1984.
———. "The Modern Library Series and American Cultural Life." *Journal of Library History* 16 (Spring 1981): 241–52.
———. "The Modern Library Series: Format and Design, 1917–1977." *Printing History* 1 (1979): 26–37.
Nystrom, Paul H. *Retail Store Operation.* 4th ed. New York: Ronald Press, 1937.
Ohmann, Richard. *Selling Culture: Magazines, Markets, and Class at the Turn of the Century.* London: Verso, 1996.
———. "The Shaping of a Canon: U.S. Fiction, 1960–1975." *Critical Inquiry* 10 (September 1983): 199–223.
Opdycke, Mary Ellis. "Laurels for Low-Brows." *New Republic* 39 (2 July 1924): 155–56.
Pitkin, Walter B. "Dollar Books and Thirty-Cent Readers." *Forum* 84 (September 1930): 162–66.
Post, Emily. *Etiquette: "The Blue Book of Social Usage."* New and enlarged edition. New York: Funk & Wagnalls, 1928.
"The Question of the Pound Award, 8 Opinions: W. H. Auden, R. G. Davis, Clement Greenberg, Irving Howe, George Orwell, Karl Shapiro, Allen Tate, William Barrett." *Partisan Review* 16 (May 1949): 512–22.

Radway, Janice A. *A Feeling for Books: The Book-of-the-Month Club, Literary Taste, and Middle-Class Desire*. Chapel Hill: University of North Carolina Press, 1997.
Robbins, Frances Lamont. "Better Than Cards or Calendars." *Outlook* 150 (19 December 1928): 1375.
Rosenbaum, Belle. "In Praise of Book Jackets." *Publishers' Weekly* 131 (6 February 1937): 730–31.
Rubin, Joan Shelley. *The Making of Middlebrow Culture*. Chapel Hill: University of North Carolina Press, 1992.
Sapir, Edward. "Civilization and Culture." *Dial* 67 (20 September 1919): 233–36.
Schick, Frank L. *The Paperbound Book in America*. New York: R. R. Bowker, 1958.
Schiffrin, André. *The Business of Books: How International Conglomerates Took Over Publishing and Changed the Way We Read*. New York: Verso, 2000.
Scribner, Charles, Jr. *In the Company of Writers: A Life in Publishing*. New York: Scribner's Sons, 1990.
———. *In the Web of Ideas: The Education of a Publisher*. New York: Scribner's Sons, 1993.
Seldes, Gilbert. "The People and the Arts: Bibliomania in the Drugstores." *Scribner's Magazine* 101 (April 1937): 60–64.
Selzer, Jack. *Kenneth Burke in Greenwich Village: Conversing with the Moderns, 1915–1931*. Madison: University of Wisconsin Press, 1997.
Sharp, R. Farquharson. *The Reader's Guide to Everyman's Library*. London: Dent, 1932.
Shove, Raymond Howard. *Cheap Book Production in the United States, 1870–1891*. Urbana: University of Illinois Library, 1937.
Showerman, Grant. "Liberal Culture in Action." *Nation* 110 (31 January 1920): 134–136.
Simon, Richard L. "Try and Stop Them." *Saturday Review of Literature* 33 (23 December 1950): 4–40.
Slappey, Sterling G. "Authoring Success: A Conversation with Bennett Cerf, Author, Wit, and Co-Founder of Random House." In *Book Publishing: Inside Views*. Compiled by Jean Spealman Kujoth, 17–29. Metuchen, N.J.: Scarecrow Press, 1971.
Spector, Herman. "Liberalism and the Literary Esoterics." *New Masses* 4 (January 1929): 18–19.
Steadman, J. M., Jr. "Affected and Effeminate Words." *American Speech* 13 (February 1938): 11–18.
Stern, Edith. "The Man Who Was Unafraid." *Saturday Review of Literature* 24 (28 June 1941): 10–14.

———. "Random House." *Saturday Review of Literature* 24 (6 December 1941): 18–21.

Styron, William. "Talk of the Town: A Modern Library Juror Fesses Up about the Hundred Best Novels." *New Yorker* 74 (17 August 1998): 29–30.

"Sublurbia." *New Republic* 32 (13 September 1922): 61–62.

Susman, Warren I. *Culture as History: The Transformation of American Society in the Twentieth Century.* New York: Pantheon, 1984.

Sussman, Aaron. "See the Pretty Birdie: A Note on Advertising Layout." *Publishers' Weekly* 126 (21 July 1934): 187–95.

Talty, Stephan. "Canonizers behind Closed Doors." *New York Times Sunday Magazine,* 6 October 1996, 36.

Tanselle, G. Thomas. "The Little Leather Library Corporation's 'Fifty Best Poems of America.'" *Papers of the Bibiographical Society of America* 62 (1968): 604–7.

Taylor, Helen K. "What Magazines Do Book Readers Read?" *Publishers' Weekly* 133 (14 May 1938): 1922–26.

Tebbel, John. *A History of Book Publishing in the United States.* Vol. 2, *The Expansion of an Industry, 1865–1919.* New York: R. R. Bowker Co., 1978.

———. *A History of Book Publishing in the United States.* Vol. 3, *The Golden Age between Two Wars, 1920–1940.* New York: R. R. Bowker Co., 1978.

"They Aren't Toothpaste." *Printers' Ink Monthly* 37 (December 1938): 5–37.

Townsend, R. D. "A Test of Taste." *Outlook* 129 (14 December 1921): 617–18.

Traxel, David. *An American Saga: The Life and Times of Rockwell Kent.* New York: Harper & Row, 1980.

Turnbull, Andrew, ed. *The Letters of F. Scott Fitzgerald.* New York: Scribner's Sons, 1963.

United States, Bureau of the Census. *Historical Statistics of the United States, Colonial Times to 1970.* Washington, D.C.: Government Printing Office, 1975.

Waples, Douglas. *People and Print: Social Aspects of Reading in the Depression.* Chicago: University of Chicago Press, 1938.

Ware, Caroline F. *Greenwich Village, 1920–1930: A Comment on American Civilization in the Post-War Years.* Boston: Houghton Mifflin, 1935.

Williams, Raymond. *Keywords: A Vocabulary of Culture and Society.* New York: Oxford University Press, 1985.

Wood, James. "Bookdumb." *New Republic* 219 (17 and 24 August 1998): 14.

Young, Stark. "No Culture but the Opera." *New Republic* 65 (14 January 1931): 346–47.

Index

Abbott, Lawrence F., 95–96
Abrams, Harry, 160
Adams, Frederick J. Jr., 94
Adams, James Truslow, 7, 8, 140–41
Ade, George, 22
Adler, Elmer, 42, 94–95, 198n. 22; and Modern Library catalog, 97–98; and Modern Library format and design, 50, 89–92, 97–98, 102, 109, 112, 118; and Random House, 98, 100, 114, 116, 202n. 77
Adler, Mortimer, 60–62
"An Advertising Catechism," 39, 63
Aiken, Conrad, 151–52
Altick, Richard D., 24
Amazon.com, 173
America's Coming-of-Age (Brooks), 15
American Chronicle, 42
The American College Dictionary, 165
American dream, 7–8, 140, 181n. 21
American Institute of Graphic Arts "Fifty Books," 94
American Library Association, 60
American Mercury, 28
American News Company, 72, 193n. 43, 194n. 44
Anchor Books, 142, 161–63, 165
Anderson, Margaret, 44
Anderson, Sherwood, 12, 46, 68, 74, 84; on Modern Library, 120–21, 130, 146
Andes, George, 88, 177n. 5, 203n. 8
Angelo, Valenti, 83
Ann Veronica (Wells), 68
An Anthology of Famous English and American Poetry (Benét), 151–56
Apocryypha (Goodspeed), 163
April Twilights (Cather), 94
Arlen, Michael, 205n. 32
Armed Services Editions, 143

Arnold, Matthew, 4–5, 7, 180nn. 15, 16
Arts and Crafts movement, 26, 90, 98, 185n. 51
Arundel (Roberts), 138
Atherton, Gertrude, 30, 32
Atlantic Monthly, 20, 31, 63, 71
Auden, W. H., 153–155, 164
Austen, Jane, 172
The Autobiography of Alice B. Toklas (Stein), 135
The Autobiography of Benjamin Franklin (Franklin), 160

Babbitt (Lewis), 42, 95–96
Baldwin, Roger, 203n. 14
Ball, Sarah, 73–74, 81
Ballyhoo, 6, 9, 31, 41, 86, 174; defined, 81–83
Balzac, Honoré, 117
Bantam Books, 144–145, 156, 161, 163, 165, 213n. 59
Barnes, A. S., 160
The Basic Writings of Sigmund Freud (Freud), 140
Baskin, Leonard, 163
Baudelaire, Charles, 28
Beach, Sylvia, 133
Beecher, Henry Ward, 80
Beerbohm, Max, 176
Bell, Daniel, 156
Bellman, 20, 23
Bellow, Saul, 8
Ben Hur (Wallace), 65
Benét, William Rose, 151
Bennett, Arnold, 113, 173
Benton, Megan, 200n. 43
Bernhard, Lucian, 98, 100–101, 116, 118, 197n. 11; and Modern Library format and design, 89–91, 107–8, 172, 175, 198n. 13

227

The Best Russian Short Stories, 20, 44
"Best sellerism," 56–57
"Best Society," 96–97
Best, Marshall, 136
Beyond Good and Evil (Nietzsche), 28
Beyond Life (Cabell), 46
Bicknell, Percy, 26
Black Oxen (Atherton), 30
Blair, Emily Newell, 104–6, 172
Bloomingdale's, 86
Blue Ribbon Books, 75, 117, 136
Blumenthal, Joseph, 83, 94, 117–18
Blurbs, 81–82
Bodenheim, Maxwell, 151
Bollingen Prize for Poetry, 155
Boni & Liveright: and anti-Semitism, 12; character of firm, 29–31, 33–35; early years, 18–20; and Jewish publishers, 10, 12, 33, 35; and Modern Library, 18–20, 27, 33–34, 36, 82, 84, 88; and Modern Library format and design, 88, 107–8, 118
Boni, Albert, 13–15, 60, 65, 176; and Little Leather Library, 17–19, 36; and Horace Liveright, 18–19, 30; and Modern Library founding, 18–19, 28, 42, 172
Boni, Charles, 14, 17, 65
Book booming, 19n. 2
Book clubs, 6, 78. *See also* Book-of-the-Month Club
Book jackets, 81–83. *See also under* Modern Library
Book Union, 123, 203n. 12
Bookman, 55–56, 71, 82, 103–4
Book-of-the-Month Club, 53–54, 61, 100–1, 181n. 24, 200n. 46; advertising, 40, 56–58, 190n. 58, 193n. 38; critics on, 2–3, 55, 71; distribution, 69, 71; Modern Library, relationship to 17, 115–16, 160; and Random House, 135–36, 144
Books: advertising and promotion, 31, 38–41, 49, 63–64, 78–79; distribution, 64–67, 71–73, 75–76; format and design, 93–95, 102–5, 111–13, 117–18, 144, 166, 170, 172; as merchandise, 9–10, 14, 39, 77–78, 82, 112–13, 145–46. *See also* Paperback books; Reprint books
Books (Duffus), 7–8
Books Are Bullets (Cerf), 149
Bookstores: and Anchor Books, 162; availability, 67; and Book-of-the-Month Club, 71; and Modern Library, 27, 65, 72–73, 76–81, 85, 87, 99, 130, 193n. 37; and Modern Library College Editions, 159; and reprint books, 24–25, 27, 77. *See also* College bookstores
Boorstin, Daniel, 216n. 8
Borzoi Books, 40, 88, 93–94, 98, 138
Borzoi Pocket Books, 128, 139
Boswell, James, 35, 116
Bourdieu, Pierre, 178n. 7, 179n. 13
Bourne, Randolph, 4, 14–17, 28–29, 63, 120–21
Bowen, Elizabeth, 167
Boyd, Ernest, 31
Brave New World (Huxley), 173
Brodzky, Horace, 107, 109
Brooks, Van Wyck, 12, 15–16, 19–20, 178n. 12
The Brothers Karamozov (Dostoyevsky), 58, 140
Broun, Haywood, 135, 203n. 14
Bryant, Louise, 14
Buck, Pearl, 84, 122, 144
Buddenbrooks (Mann), 125
Bunyan, John, 134
Burt, A. L., 19, 25
Butler, Samuel, 20, 22, 46, 68, 122
Byatt, A. S., 216n. 8

Cabell, James Branch, 46
Cairns, Huntington, 126, 130
Caldwell, Erskine, 84, 122
Calverton, V. F., 123, 126
Camus, Albert, 165
Canby, Henry Seidel, 178n. 12

Candide (Voltaire), 100, 105, 116
Canterbury Tales (Chaucer), 122
Capote, Truman, 169
Carey-Thomas Award, 161
Carnegie, Dale, 148
Carroll, Lewis, 168, 205n. 32
The Case against the Saturday Review of Literature, 155
"The Case of Ezra Pound" (Cerf), 153
Catch-22 (Heller), 169
Cather, Willa, 13, 94–95, 208n. 85; and Modern Library, 138, 165, 167
CEA Critic, 158
Cendrars, Blaise, 104
Censorship, 11, 31–32, 186n. 62
Century Club, 13
Century Magazine, 28
Cerf, Bennett: as bibliophile, 98, 115; at Boni & Liveright, 31–35; as businessman, 9–10, 38, 65, 81, 86, 98, 128, 134–36, 154; cultural ambitions, 9–10, 71, 98; Donald Klopfer, relationship with, 35, 132, 150; on Alfred Knopf, 12, 32, 95; on Horace Liveright, 12, 32, 35, 135; on Modern Library, 74–78, 106, 112–13, 117–19, 130–31, 215n. 91; on Modern Library audience, 52, 72–76, 160, 163–64, 167, 175; Modern Library, purchase of, 35–37; on paperbacks, 143–44; personality of, 33, 35, 132–33, 149–50; politics of, 123–24, 153–55; and Ezra Pound, 152–56; profiles of, 132, 149–50; as promoter, 40, 54, 63, 67–68, 77–81, 150–51; publishers, negotiations with, 125, 128–29, 135, 137–38; on publishing, 12, 67; and Random House, 98–101, 113–16, 148, 151, 164–65, 169; *Saturday Review of Literature*, 149; "Trade Winds," 149, 153–55; *What's My Line?*, 149
Cerf, Christopher, 173–74, 176, 216n. 8
Chamberlain, George, 205n. 32
Chappell, Warren, 94
The Charterhouse of Parma (Stendhal), 134, 146–48

Chase, Stuart, 42
Cheap books, 23–26, 50–51, 77, 185n. 46, 195n. 60. *See also* Dollar books
Cheney, O. H., 56, 189n. 41, 191n. 8, 196n. 94; on book advertising, 38–39; on book distribution, 72
Chesterton, G. K., 16
Chicago Daily News, 55
Cimino, Harry, 104
Citizen Tom Paine (Fast), 135
"Civilized minority": characteristics, 41–43, 45–46, 49, 167; Modern Library and, 53, 74, 119, 125, 134, 156, 167, 142; and professional-managerial class, 43
Class: books and reading, 25, 50–52; as marker of taste, 88, 95–98, 162
Classics of the Western World, 60
Clean Books League, 32
Cobden–Sanderson, T. J., 94–95, 101, 104
Collected Tales and Plays of Nikolai Gogol (Gogol), 169
College bookstores, 65, 68–69, 157–58, 192n. 23
College English, 158, 163
College Store, 68, 192n. 23
Colleges and universities, 156, 186n. 46, 195n. 60
Colophons, 91–93. *See also under* Modern Library
Columbia University, 5, 60, 84
Columbia University Oral History Project, 132
Commager, Henry Steele, 153
Commentary, 163
Commins, Dorothy, 133–34
Commins, Saxe, 31, 192n. 25; as Modern Library editor, 131, 133–34, 142, 151–52, 212n. 43; and Eugene O'Neill, 114–15, 133
Communist Party, 85, 124
The Comprehensive Anthology of American Poetry, 58
"Confessions of a Blurb Writer," 82
Confessions of a Young Man (Moore), 20, 28

Confessions of Nat Turner (Styron), 169
Confucius, 54
Les Conquérants (Malraux), 134
Cooper, James Fenimore, 26
Copeau, Jacques, 16
Copyright law, 11, 23–24, 208n. 87
Cosmopolitanism, 43, 120–22, 126–28, 202n. 4
Council on Books in Wartime, 143
The Counterfitters (Gide), 128, 139
Covici-Friede, 35, 103, 133
Coward, Thomas, 115, 203n. 14
Coward–McCann, 115
Cowley, Malcolm, 123, 178n. 8, 203n. 14, 204n. 26; on Bennett Cerf, 150, 210n. 17; on Modern Library, 8; on publishing, 65, 189n. 41
Crime and Punishment (Dostoyevsky), 157
Croft leather, 36, 89, 103, 118
Crofts, F. S., 68, 192n. 20
Crowder, James L., 75–76
"Cult of the Colophon," 93
Culture: Arnoldian, 4–5, 7, 16, 180nn. 15, 16; "genuine" or "organic," 4–6, 9–10, 20, 29, 38, 42–43, 50, 63; highbrow–lowbrow, 4, 16, 42, 178n. 12, 180n. 15; Modern Library as, 8–10, 20, 38, 50, 63; "spurious" or "false," 4, 6, 42
cummings, e.e., 30

Dali, Salvador, 160
Dardis, Tom, 19
Darwin, Charles, 68, 168
Day, Clarence, 148
De La Pasture, E. E. M., 205n. 32
Death Comes for the Archbishop (Cather), 138
The Decameron (Boccaccio), 103, 122
Dell, Floyd, 14, 28
Deluxe editions, 93, 105, 145, 166, 172. See also Limited editions
Dent, J. M., 25–26
Department stores, 65, 85–86, 196nn. 94, 96, 197n. 97

Dewey, John, 5, 68, 84, 168
Dial, 14, 20
Diana of the Crossways (Meredith), 20
Dickens, Charles, 26, 45, 185n. 51
Dillard, Annie, 8, 93
Dinesen, Isak, 115, 167
Direction, 210n. 14
The Divine Comedy (Dante), 45
Dodd, Mead, 129
Dodge, Mabel, 14
A Doll's House (Ibsen), 19
Dollar books, 77–78, 145, 191n. 6, 195n. 60. See also Cheap books
Don Quixote (Cervantes), 122
Donnelley, R. R., 100
Dos Passos, John, 8, 84, 122–23, 137, 140
Dostoyevsky, Fyodor, 2, 19–20, 45, 122, 162, 168
Doubleday Company, 148
Doubleday, Doran, 136, 138, 144, 161
Doubleday, Page and Company, 11, 182n. 3
Douglas, Norman, 46, 68
Doves Press, 94
Dr. Eliot's Five-Foot-Shelf. See Harvard Classics
Dr. Seuss, 165
Dracula (Stoker), 34
Dreiser, Theodore, 11, 14, 44, 46, 54, 169; and Liveright, 30, 32–33; on publishing, 72–73
Dreyfus affair, 13
Droll Stories (Balzac), 78, 122
Drugstores, 67, 72, 76, 193n. 43, 194n. 47
Du Maurier, Daphne, 148
Dubliners (Joyce), 68
Duckworth and Company, 208n. 87
Duffus, Robert, 66, 76–77, 189n. 41, 191n. 8; on culture, 6–8, 70
Dutton, E. P, and Sons, 25, 41, 71
Dwiggins, W. A., 94
Dynamo (O'Neill), 133

Earle, Edward Meade, 84
Eastman, Max, 14, 85, 123–24, 203n. 16
Edman, Erwin, 84

Index

Ehrenreich, Barbara, 43, 189n. 38
Ehrenreich, John, 43
Eliot, T. S., 8, 13, 30, 151
Elliot, Paul, 135
Ellis, Havelock, 84, 89
Ellis, Richard, 100
Emerson, Ralph Waldo, 80
Emma (Austen), 172
An Enemy of the People (Ibsen), 19
The Epic of America (Adams), 140
Epstein, Jason: and Anchor Books, 161;
  on Bennett Cerf, 210n. 22; and
  Modern Library, 163–65, 167, 169,
  212n. 43, 213n. 68
Ernst, Morris, 113
Erskine, John, 4–5, 60–61, 63, 205n. 32
Esquire, 132, 149
Evergreen Review, 164
Everybody's Autobiography (Stein), 135
Everyman's Library, 19, 25–27, 41, 90–91,
  146

Farrar & Rinehart, 136
Farrar, John, 136
Farrell, James T., 123, 135, 144, 146–151,
  173
Fast, Howard, 135
Fathers and Sons (Turgenev), 163
Faulkner, William, 8, 30, 84, 115, 122,
  137, 162, 167
Faust (Goethe), 134
Federal Trade Commission, 89
The Federalist Papers, 84
Fellows of the Library of Congress, 155
Fielding, Henry, 162
Finder, Henry, 216n. 17
Fine press movement, 94, 98–101, 199n.
  38, 200n. 43
Finn, David, 167
Fitzgerald, F. Scott, 84, 112, 117, 128, 135
Flaubert, Gustave, 122
Fletcher, John Gould, 151
Foote, Shelby, 216n. 8
Ford, Ford Madox, 113
Forster, E. M., 167

Foster, Jeannette Howard, 127, 204n. 32
Four Famous Greek Plays, 122
France, Anatole, 12, 19–20, 122, 205n. 32
Frank, Waldo, 30, 32, 129
Franklin Square Library, 24
Frederick, J. George, 66, 72
Free (Dreiser), 46
Free French, 148
Freud, Sigmund, 12–14, 30, 129
Friede, Donald, 31, 35
Fujita, Neil, 165
Fuller, Richard, 80
Future, 42

Galdone, Paul, 83
Galsworthy, John, 16
Gannett, Lewis, 130, 152–55, 203n. 14
Gans, Herbert J., 179n. 13
Gautier, Theophile, 28
General reader, 3, 20, 101–2, 184n. 34
Gentlemen Prefer Blondes (Loos), 30
Georgian Press, 100
Gerould, Katherine Fullerton, 180n. 15
Ghosts (Ibsen), 19
GI Bill, 156
Giddens, Gary, 140
Gide, André, 128, 139, 165, 167
Gilmer, Walker, 11, 31, 33
Gimbels, 1, 9, 85–86, 194n. 44, 196n. 94
Gish, Dorothy and Lillian, 31
Gissing, George, 135
Glaspell, Susan, 14
God's Little Acre (Caldwell), 44, 130
Godoff, Ann, 174
Goethe, Johann Wolfgang von, 134
Gold, Michael, 123, 203n. 14
Golden Cockerel Press, 99
Goldman, Emma, 13–14, 133
Gone with the Wind (Mitchell), 49
The Good Earth (Buck), 130, 144
Good Housekeeping, 104, 112, 172
Goodspeed, Edgar, 163
Gordimer, Nadine, 173
Gorki, Maxim, 12, 16
Grabhorn Press, 100

Grabhorn, Edwin, 100
Graff, Robert de, 75–76, 125, 136, 143–44
Graves, Robert, 115
Great Depression, 42, 51–52, 95, 127, 177n. 5; and limited editions, 100, 113; and Modern Library advertising, 41, 51–52; and Modern Library sales, 2, 65
The Great Gatsby (Fitzgerald), 128, 131, 139
Great Modern Short Stories (Cerf), 162
Green Mansions (Hudson), 46, 68, 138, 160, 208n. 87
Greenwich Village, 2, 12–18, 54, 133–34, 183nn. 6, 12; and Modern Library, 20, 27, 29, 107
Gregorian, Vartan, 216n. 8
Grosset & Dunlap, 19, 25, 27, 67, 144, 161; distribution, 72, 144
Guinzburg, Harold, 136
Gulliver's Travels (Swift), 122, 134, 162

Haas, Robert, 115, 131, 133–36, 143
Haldeman-Julius, 40
Hammett, Dashiell, 146
Hapgood, Hutchins, 31
Harcourt, Alfred, 40, 133, 186n. 59
Harcourt, Brace and Company, 63, 136
Hardy, Thomas, 16, 20, 68
Harper Bros., 11, 24, 136, 144
Harper's Bazaar, 53
Harper's Magazine, 174; *Radio Book Program*, 111
Hart, Henry, 123
Hart, Moss, 169
Harter, Evelyn, 103, 105–6
Harvard Classics, 49, 53, 61, 111, 176; advertising, 40, 54, 57, 59, 69; as culture, 2, 6, 8
Hatcher, J. J., 69–70
Haydn, Hiram, 150
Hays, Arthur Garfield, 36
Hazlitt, Henry, 103, 105, 112
Heap, Jane, 44
Heller, A. A., 203n. 14
Heller, Joseph, 169

Heller, Steven, 90
Hellman, Geoffrey, 150
Hellman, Lillian, 31
Hemingway, Ernest, 8, 30, 122, 130, 137
Henry, O., 185n. 51
Herbst, Josephine, 123
Hersey, John, 167, 169
Hicks, Granville, 45, 68, 121, 123, 134
Highbrow, 2, 4, 15–16, 21–22, 96, 178n. 12, 179n. 14, 180n. 15; and "civilized minority," 42; Modern Library as, 74, 76
Hillyer, Robert, 155
The History of Tom Jones (Fielding), 61, 122, 157, 162
Hitchcock, Curtice, 136
Hobson, Thayer, 136
Holladay, Polly, 14, 17
Hollinger, David, 120–21, 126
Holmes, Oliver Wendell, 80
Holt, Henry, 137
Horace, 54
Horizon, 42
How to Read a Book (Adler), 60–62
How to Win Friends and Influence People (Carnegie), 148
Howe, Irving, 156
Howells, William Dean, 28
Hubbard, Elbert, 185n. 51
Hudson Review, 163
Hudson, W. H., 46, 68, 138
Huebsch, Ben W., 15, 17, 186n. 62, 203n. 14; anti-Semitism, 12–13; and Jewish publishers, 10, 12–13, 31–33, 35, 186n. 59
Hugo, Victor, 116–17
Human Being (Morley), 135
Human Nature and Conduct (Dewey), 68
Hutchisson, James M., 75

Ibsen, Henrik, 17, 19–20
The Ideal Book (Cobden-Sanderson), 94
Iliad (Virgil), 122
In a Winter City (Ouida), 188n. 21
In Cold Blood (Capote), 168

In Quest of the Perfect Book (Orcutt), 104
In the Sweet Dry and Dry (Morley), 31
Independent, 20, 22, 184n. 34
Institute for Advanced Studies, 84
Intellectuals, 13, 42, 131–33; and cosmopolitanism, 120, 202n. 4; as Modern Library market, 8, 20, 27–28, 38, 43, 101, 105, 119, 126–27, 140–41; Modern Library, reaction against 147, 151; and modernism, 122–24
Intelligentsia. *See* Intellectuals
International Publishers, 123
Irving, Washington, 13
Ivory Soap, 78

Jacobs, Sidney, 166
Jacoby, Russell, 156
James, Henry, 2, 134
Jane Eyre (Brontë), 157
Jeffers, Robinson, 115, 151
Jester, 34
Jewish publishers, 10–13, 32, 35, 136, 186n. 59
John Day, 144
John Reed Clubs, 124
Johnson, Alvin, 203n. 14
Joyce, James, 12, 44, 54, 68, 113, 133
Julian (Vidal), 169

Kafka, Franz, 165, 167–68
Kauffer, E. McKnight, 160
Kaufman, Beatrice Bakrow, 31
Kazin, Alfred, 156
Kelland, Clarence, 205n. 32
Kelly, Helen, 88
Kelmscott Press, 94
Kennedy, Joseph, 148
Kennelly Paper Company, 102
Kent, Rockwell, 50, 83, 105–12, 116–18; *Candide,* 100, 105, 116; *Moby Dick,* 100, 116, 135
Kenyon Review, 158, 162–63
Kerfoot, J. B., 22
Kipling, Rudyard, 19–20, 185n. 51
Kirchway, Freda, 203n. 14

Kirshbaum, Larry, 169
Klopfer, Donald: as businessman, 9–10, 38, 65, 81, 86, 98, 128, 134–36; as bibliophile, 98, 131–32; Bennett Cerf, relationship with, 35, 132, 150–51; on Saxe Commins, 133; cultural ambitions, 9–10, 71; on Horace Liveright, 37, on Modern Library, 74–76, 170; on Modern Library audience, 74–76, 167, 175; Modern Library production, 102–3, 106–7, 109, 111, 133; Modern Library, purchase of, 35–37; personality of, 132–33, 150; politics of, 123–24; as promoter, 67; and Random House, 98–101, 113–15, 148, 164; and Twelve Against the Gods of Publishing, 136–37
Klopfer, Marian, 123
Knopf, Alfred, 17, 94–95, 133, 136, 148, 161, 203n. 14, 208n. 85; and book design, 94, 97, 118; and Jewish publishers, 10–13, 31–33, 182n. 3, 186n. 59; Modern Library, negotiations with, 125, 128, 138–39; and Random House, 165, 169, 214n. 77; trademark, 40, 88, 93, 98. *See also* Borzoi Books; Borzoi Pocket Books
Knopf, Blanche, 12, 136
Komroff, Manuel, 31, 99
Kreymborg, Alfred, 14, 30, 151
Krinsley, Dick, 166
Kronenberger, Louis, 30

Ladies' Home Journal, 40, 63
Lamont, Corliss, 203n. 14
Lamont, William, 206n. 64
Landmark Books, 165
Lane, Allan, 143
Langner, Lawrence, 14, 18–19
Larrabee, C. B., 39
Latzko, Andreas, 188n. 21
Laughlin, James, 149
Lawrence, D. H., 12, 68, 186n. 62
Leaves of Grass (Whitman), 100
Leigh, Ruth, 77

Lenin, Vladimir Il'ich, 45, 124
Lerner, Max, 153
Lesser, Joseph, 125
Lessing, Doris, 173
Levin, Harry, 147
Levine, David, 168
Levine, Lawrence, 14, 179n. 13
Lewis, Oscar, 167
Lewis, Sinclair, 14, 27, 30, 42, 74–75, 95
Liberal Club, 14, 17, 33
"Libraries," 19, 23–27, 126, 165
Library of Congress, 7
Liebmann, William B., 81
Life, 20, 22, 63
Life and Death of a Spanish Town (Elliot), 135
The Life of Samuel Johnson (Boswell), 116, 122
Life with Father (Day), 148
Limited editions, 99–101, 114–15. See also Deluxe editions
Limited Editions Club, 160
Linscott, Robert, 153
Lippincott, J. B., and Co., 11
Little Leather Library: and Albert and Charles Boni, 17–19; distribution, 17, 24, 67, 69, 193n. 29; and Modern Library, 18–20, 115
Little magazines, 3, 17, 31, 149
Little Review, 44
Little, Brown & Co., 136, 144
Little-Blue-Books, 40
Liveright, Inc., 114
Liveright, Horace, 2, 10–11, 18, 95, 129, 176, 186n. 59; anti-Semitism, 12–13; Albert Boni, relationship with, 18–19, 30; censorship, 31–32, 114; marketing, 31, 40; Modern Library, sale of, 34–37; publishers, relationship with, 32, 135, 138
Liveright, Otto, 18
London, Jack, 11
Longwell, Daniel, 136
Loos, Anita, 30
Lovett, Robert Morss, 203n. 14

Lowbrow, 4, 15–16, 21–22, 96, 178n. 12
Lowry, Thomas, 167–168
Luce, J. W., 19
Lucian Leuwen (Stendhal), 134
Lugosi, Bela, 34
Lynd, Helen Merrell, 137, 189n. 41
Lynd, Robert S., 137, 189n. 41
Lynes, Russell, 179n. 13

Macaulay, Thomas, 205n. 32
Macdonald, Dwight, 155, 179n. 13
MacLeish, Archibald, 151
Macmillan and Co., 36, 136
Macrae, John, 71
Macy's, 1–2, 85–86, 194n. 44, 196n. 94
Mad Magazine, 93
Mademoiselle Fifi and Twelve Other Stories (Maupassant), 19
Maeterlinck, Maurice, 19–20, 188n. 21
The Magic Barrel (Malamud), 163
The Magic Christian (Southern), 168
The Magic Mountain (Mann), 78, 125
Magnificent Ambersons (Tarkington), 173, 176
Main Street (Lewis), 27, 65, 74–75
Malamud, Bernard, 163
Malraux, André, 115, 134
The Maltese Falcon (Hammett), 130
Man's Fate (Malraux), 134
Mann, Thomas, 125–26, 167–69, 204n. 26
Manutius, Aldus, 91, 103–04
Marchand, Roland, 188n. 29
Marius the Epicurean (Pater), 126
Marjorie Fleming's Book (Macbean), 188n. 21
Married (Strindberg), 19
Marx, Karl, 12, 124, 154; in Modern Library, 45, 85, 122, 153
Mass production, 6–8, 111–13, 140–41, 146
Masses, 14, 28, 133
Masters, Edgar Lee, 74
Maugham, W. Somerset, 134, 169
Maupassant, Guy de, 19–20
May, Henry, 8, 13, 132

Mayberry, George, 146–48, 151
The Mayor of Casterbridge (Hardy), 20
Melcher, Frederic G., 65
Melville, Herman, 13, 100
Memoirs of Jacques Casanova (Casanova), 122
Mencken, H. L., 28, 31, 66, 191n. 5
Meredith, George, 16, 20
Messner, Julian, 31, 36
Metropolitan Museum of Art, 105
Meynell, Francis, 99
Michener, James, 167, 169
Middlebrow culture, 3–4, 54, 96, 178n. 11, 179n. 13
Millay, Edna St. Vincent, 14
Miller, Lewis, 85, 157, 159, 162–63
A Miracle of St. Antony (Maeterlinck), 19, 188n. 21
Les Misérables (Hugo), 116
Moby Dick (Melville), 100, 116, 157, 213n. 59
Modern Library: advertising, 20–22, 38, 41, 43–64, 69–71, 78–79, 97, 112, 118, 131, 158, 162–64, 175–76, 188n. 23; bindings, 27, 36, 89, 103, 111–12, 117–18, 197n. 7, 200n. 47; and Boni & Liveright, 18–19, 34, 36; Book-A-Month Plan, 65, 70, 71; book jackets, 81–83, 167, 195n. 80; catalogs, 60, 97–98, 116, 178n. 6; chain selling, 65, 70–71, 193n. 37; and classics, 54–55, 61, 122; college market, 65, 67–69, 156–59, 161, 192n. 20, 212n. 53; colophon design, 89–91, 105, 107–8, 118, 167, 172, 198n. 13; contests, 44–45, 65, 80–81, 168; copyright, 19, 135; critics on, 2, 8, 22–23, 29–30, 89, 103–5, 111, 113, 126, 130–31, 146–49, 152–55; demise, 143, 168–171; and department stores, 1–2, 85–86; distribution, 65, 67–81, 85–87, 193n. 43; endpapers, 89, 91, 105, 107, 109–10, 118; fiftieth anniversary, 142, 168; format and design, 27, 50–51, 88–93, 97–98, 101–13, 116–19, 165–67, 170–72, 177n. 5; founding, 2, 18–19, 42; and gender, 53–54, 107, 189n. 43; Illustrated Modern Library, 159–61, 166, 213n. 57; introductions, 28, 83–85, 120, 123, 130; as loss leader, 1, 86; mail order sales, 65, 69–71, 83; manufacture, 102, 106, 109, 111, 133; Modern Library College Editions, 142, 157–59, 161–63, 212n. 53, 215n. 93; Modern Library Giants, 116–17, 129, 140, 151, 159, 163; Modern Library Paperbacks, 142, 161–5; modernity of, 19–20, 27–30, 47–48, 53, 90–91, 107, 119, 122, 125–26, 166, 168, 171; "One Hundred Best Twentieth-Century Novels" list, 173–76; popularizer, 27, 129–31, 139–40; price of, 1, 18, 22, 49–52, 86, 102, 111–13, 116–17, 119, 157, 159–60, 172; promotional materials; 65, 81, 86, 93; publishers, negotiations with, 125, 128–29, 137–38; and Random House, 71, 98–99, 101, 114–16, 145, 165, 169–70, 202n. 77; as reading guide, 55–56, 59–61, 172; rebirth, 140, 172; reprint fees, 129, 135, 138; reputation, 8–9, 72, 130–31, 140, 146–49; rural sales, 74–76; sale of, 35–37, 186n. 70; sales, 2, 36, 56, 119, 127–28, 130, 159, 162–63, 168–69, 192n. 20; title page design, 89–90, 92, 97–98, 118; title selection, 19–20, 34, 113, 119–141, 146–48, 157, 162, 167, 169–70, 176
Modern Quarterly, 2–3, 126
Modernism, 182n. 2; and gender, 107; and Jewish publishers, 12–13, 17, 31–33; Modern Library as purveyor of, 29, 75, 122, 125, 142, 176; Modern Library format and design, 90, 107; and politics, 122–23, 203n. 10
Moore, George, 20, 28
Moore, Marianne, 151
Moran, Thomas, 104
Morley, Christopher, 31, 135, 137, 205n. 32
Morris, Edmund, 216n. 8

Morris, William, 26, 90–91, 94
Morrison, Toni, 173
Morrow, William, & Co., 136
Mourning Becomes Electra (O'Neill), 133
Mrs. Dalloway (Woolf), 54
Mumford, Lewis, 6, 30, 66, 87, 112
Munro, George, 24, 26

Nathan, George Jean, 31
Nathan, Robert, 205n. 32
Nation, 3, 22, 103–4, 133; as advertising medium, 20, 43, 46, 63, 138, 164
National Association of College Stores, 68, 158
National Drug Store Survey, 194n. 47
National Gallery of Contemporary Art, 105
Neavill, Gordon B., 167, 177n. 5, 193n. 43, 209n. 9, 213n. 68, 214n. 77
Nelson, Arthur, 141
New American Library, 162
New Criticism, 155
New Directions, 149
New Directions, 149
New Journal, 168
New Masses, 3, 42, 44–46, 133
New Republic, 3, 5, 14, 22, 133, 180n. 15; as advertising medium, 20–21, 43, 46, 164; on Modern Library, 146, 216n. 15; on publishing, 71, 82
The New Spirit (Ellis), 89
New York Evening Mail, 23, 28
New York Evening Post, 23
New York Herald Tribune, 130
New York Herald Tribune Books, 83, 152–53
New York Review of Books, 168
New York Times, 1, 23, 82
New York Times Books Review, 8, 52; as advertising medium, 46–49, 62–63, 161–62, 164, 188n. 22
New York Times Sunday Magazine, 130–31
New York Tribune, 34
New Yorker, 94, 149–50, 173, 210n. 17; as advertising medium, 43, 46, 174–75

Newsstands, 72–73, 76, 193n. 43
Newsweek, 130, 173
Nietzsche, Friedrich, 12; in Modern Library, 19–20, 22, 28, 122, 153
Nonesuch Press, 99, 114
Norman, Charles, 152
Northwestern University, *Of Men and Books,* 131
Norton, W. W., 136, 203n. 14
Novels of Henry James (James), 26

O'Brien, Edward J., 206n. 64
O'Hara, John, 167, 169
O'Neill, Carlotta, 115
O'Neill, Eugene, 30, 44, 133; and Random House, 114–16, 145
Odets, Clifford, 115, 123, 134, 137
Odyssey (Homer), 122
Of Human Bondage (Maugham), 61, 78, 134, 140
Of Mice and Men (Steinbeck), 130
Ohmann, Richard, 189n. 38, 208n. 88
Old Corner Bookstore, 80–81
Opdycke, Mary Ellis, 179n. 12
Oppenheim, James, 12
Oppenheimer, George, 136
Orcutt, William Dana, 104
Orczy, Baroness, 126
Origin of Species (Darwin), 68
Ouida, 188n. 21
Our Crowd (Birmingham), 12
Outlook, 20, 82, 95, 126–27, 184n. 34
Oxford Standard Authors, 103
Oxford World Classics, 146

Paine, Thomas, 13, 135
Pantheon, 165, 214n. 75
Paperback books: effect on Modern Library, 118, 142, 144, 156, 161–62, 166, 170, 172, 177n. 5; effect on publishing, 145, 147; growth of, 143–44; quality or "egghead," 139, 142, 161–62, 165, 170. *See also under* Modern Library
Parrish, Anne, 205n. 32

Partisan Review, 121, 162–63
Pater, Walter, 126
Paterson, Isabel, 124
Pell, Arthur, 36–37
Penguin Books, 143, 156
Perkins, Maxwell, 210n. 17
Personal History (Sheean), 61
Pfleiderer, Otto, 12
Pharos, 147–49, 151
Phelps, William Lyon, 16, 84, 134, 206n. 64
Philipson, Morris, 213n. 68
The Philosophy of David Hume (Hume), 169
The Philosophy of Plato (Plato), 45
The Philosophy of Santayana (Santayana), 84
Pickford, Mary, 31
The Picture of Dorian Gray (Wilde), 19, 172
Pierce, "Cap," 136
The Pilgrim's Progress (Bunyan), 134
Pisan Cantos (Pound), 155
Pitkin, Walter, 112
Plato, 7, 162
PM, 152
PMLA, 158, 163
Pocket Books, 35, 75, 136, 148; effect on Modern Library, 143–44, 156, 161–62, 170
Pocket Book of War Humor (Cerf), 149
Poe, Edgar Allan, 13
Poetry: A Magazine of Verse, 155
Politics, 155
Poor People (Dostoyevsky), 19
Poor White (Anderson), 46, 120, 130
Portrait of the Artist as a Young Man (Joyce), 54
Post, Emily, 95–96
Pound, Ezra, 113, 121; *An Anthology of Famous English and American Poetry*, 151–56
Pride and Prejudice (Austen), 157
Priester Match Company, 90
The Prince (Machiavelli), 61
Printers' Ink, 39–40, 63–64, 67, 106, 112

Professional–managerial class, 69, 139, 156, 200n. 46, 208n. 88; and "civilized minority," 43; as consumers, 53, 86; and Modern Library editors, 133–34; politics of, 43, 54, 109; and reading, 101–2; tastes, 53, 119, 125–27, 175, 189n. 38
Proust, Marcel, 2, 44, 47, 140
Psychology: A Simplification (Commins), 133
Publishers Lunch Club, 12, 136–37
Publishers' Weekly, 1, 39, 81–82, 93–94, 117; advertisements in, 20, 78–79; on cheap books, 24, 26; on Modern Library, 19, 65, 73–74, 97, 101, 111, 122, 130, 160; on reprints, 77–78
Putnam's Sons, 208n. 87
Pynson Printers, 94, 97, 100

Radcliffe College, 173
Radway, Janice, 3, 9, 56, 178n. 13, 181n. 24; on reading, 101–3
Rahab (Frank), 129
The Rainbow (Lawrence), 186n. 62
Random House Dictionary of the English Language, 165
Random House: and Bantam Books, 144–45, 161; and fine presses, 98–101, 114–15, 145; early years, 71, 88, 98–101; growth of, 115–16, 142, 148–49, 164; mergers, 125, 133, 136, 164–65; and Modern Library, 9, 71, 98–99, 101, 114–16, 145, 162–63, 165, 169–70, 202n. 77; offices, 101, 148, 164, 170, 210n. 11; operations, 133–34; public ownership, 164–65, 214n. 75; and trade publishing, 113–116; unionization of, 123
Ransom, John Crowe, 151
Readers and reading, 53–54, 65–66, 68–69, 75–76, 101–5, 111, 165–66, 191n. 8
Rebecca (Du Maurier), 148
The Red and the Black (Stendhal), 122, 134
The Red Lily (France), 19

Reed, John, 14, 28, 30, 133, 186n. 62; in Modern Library, 44–45
Renault, Mary, 167
Reporter, 164
Reprint books, 23–26, 77–78, 99, 113, 143–46, 161
The Republic (Plato), 7, 162
The Return of the Native (Hardy), 68
Review of Reviews, 20
Reynal & Hitchcock, 136
Reynal, Eugene, 136
Richardson, John, 216n. 8
Rinehart Editions, 156–57, 159
Rinehart, Stanley, 136
Robbins, Frances Lamont, 89
Roberts, Kenneth, 137–38
Roche, Arthur, 205n. 32
Rogers, Bruce, 98, 160
Rolland, Romain, 16
Rolls Royce, 105
Roscoe, Burton, 31
Rose, Stuart, 136
Rosenbaum, Belle, 83
Rubin, Joan Shelley, 3, 58, 178n. 11, 179n. 13
Ruder & Finn, 165–67
Russell, Bertrand, 84
Russell, James, 159
Russian Revolution, 20, 44, 106

Sackheim, Maxwell, 17, 115, 193n. 29
Saint Joan (Shaw), 104
Sanctuary (Faulkner), 78
Sapir, Edward, 5–6, 8, 43
Saroyan, William, 84
Saturday Evening Post, 40, 63
Saturday Review of Literature, 63, 149, 153, 155
The Satyricon (Petronius Arbiter), 122
The Scarlet Letter (Hawthorne), 45, 84, 157, 213n. 59
Scherman, Harry, 135–36; and Little Leather Library, 17, 67, 69, 115, 193n. 29; and Book-of-the-Month Club, 17, 69, 115
Schiffrin, André, 214n. 75

Schlesinger, Arthur Jr., 154, 216n. 8
Schopenhauer, Arthur, 12, 19–20
Schuster, Maxwell, 43, 69, 133, 136, 210n. 29
Scott-Moncreiff, C. K., 147
Scribner, Charles, Jr., 8, 130, 137, 192n. 17
Scribner's Sons, 26, 128, 130, 136, 144
Seldes, Gilbert, 72
The Selected Works of Thomas Paine (Paine), 135
Self-culture, 60–61, 63, 70, 178n. 11
Seltzer, Thomas, 20, 28, 31
Seven Arts, 14–15, 29–30
Sewanee Review, 158
Shakespeare Head Press, 99
Shaw, George Bernard, 17, 20, 104, 138
Sheean, Vincent, 61
Signet Classics, 172
Simon & Schuster, 35, 41, 43, 136, 144, 148
Simon, John, 169
Simon, Richard, 31, 34–35, 40, 133, 136, 210n. 15; on Donald Klopfer, 132
Sinclair, Upton, 11
Sister Carrie (Dreiser), 169
Six Plays by Clifford Odets (Odets), 61, 137
Six Plays by Corneille and Racine, 45, 122
Smalley, Carl, 76
Smiley, Jane, 176
Smith & Haas, 115
Smith College, 68
Smith, Harrison, 115, 133, 136, 153
Smith, T. R., 28, 31
Society for the Suppression of Vice, 31
Soldiers Three (Kipling), 19
Sons and Lovers (Lawrence), 44, 68
Sontag, Susan, 8
South Wind (Douglas), 46, 68
Southern, Terry, 164
Spier & Sussman, 47, 192n. 25
Spiral Press, 94, 99, 117
Spoon River Anthology (Masters), 74
Springfield Republican, 23
Standardization, 5, 8, 56, 112
Star Dollar series, 75, 144
Stark, Daniel, 106
Steffens, Lincoln, 13–14

Stein, Gertrude, 30, 115, 122, 132, 135, 187n. 16
Stein, Jess, 156, 212n. 43, 213n. 68; and Modern Library College Editions, 142, 158, 212n. 53
Steinbeck, John, 84, 122–23
Stendhal, 133–34, 147–48
Stern, Edith, 32–33
Stevens, George, 136, 151
Stevenson, Robert Lewis, 19–20
The Story of a Lover (Hapgood), 31
Stowe, Harriet Beecher, 80
Strachey, John, 124
Strindberg, August, 19–20
Studs Lonigan (Farrell), 146
Studies in Pessimism (Schopenhauer), 19
Styron, William, 169, 173, 176, 216n. 8
"Sublurbia," 82
Sumner, John, 31
Sun Dial Library, 75
Susman, Warren I., 181n. 21
Sussman, Aaron, 31, 47
Sutter's Gold (Cendrars), 104–5
Swann's Way (Proust), 47, 58, 78, 140
Swift, Jonathan, 134, 162
Swinburne, Algernon Charles, 28
Symons, Arthur, 28, 206n. 64
Sze, Mai–Mai, 163

Tarkington, Booth, 176
Tebbel, John, 24
Ten Days That Shook the World (Reed), 44–45
"A Test of Taste," 126
Thackeray, William, 162
Thayer, Tiffany, 205n. 32
Theatre Guild, 15
Theatre Guild Anthology, 138
The Theory of the Leisure Class (Veblen), 44
"They Aren't Toothpaste," 39–40, 63
Three Lives (Stein), 135, 187n. 16
Three Soldiers (Dos Passos), 140
Thucydides, 169
Thurber, James, 168

Thus Spake Zarathustra (Nietzsche), 19, 89
Tide, 145
Time, 149
Tolkien, J. R. R., 167
Tolstoy, Leo, 16–17, 28, 116
Tono-Bungay (Wells), 134
Tortilla Flat (Steinbeck), 84
Trachtenberg, Alexander, 203n. 14
"Trade Winds," 149, 152, 154–55
"Trans-National America" (Bourne), 120–21
The Travels of Marco Polo (Marco Polo), 122
Treasure Island (Stevenson), 19
Turgenev, Ivan, 16, 135
The Turn of the Screw (James), 134
Twain, Mark, 13, 16, 26
Twelve Against the Gods of Publishing, 136–37, 148
Twelve Men (Dreiser), 54

U.S. News and World Report, 176
Ulysses (Joyce), 113–15, 140, 173
United Diamond Works, 36
United Office and Professional Workers Union, 123
University of Pennsylvania, 133
The Unsocial Socialist (Shaw), 20
Updike, Daniel Berkeley, 98
Updike, John, 169
USA Today, 174

Van Doren, Mark, 42
Van Kleeck, Mary, 203n. 14
Vanity Fair (Thackery), 162
Veblen, Thorstin, 45
Vidal, Gore, 169, 216n. 8
Viking Press, 33, 136
"Village Virus," 74–75
Villard Mansion, 148, 164
Villiard, Oswald Garrison, 20
Villon, Francois, 122
Vintage Books, 142, 161–62, 165
Vogue, 53, 172
Voltaire, 122

Walker, Jimmy, 32
Waples, Douglas, 127, 204n. 32
War and Peace (Tolstoy), 116–17, 140
War in the Air (Wells), 19, 22
Ward, Lynd, 83
Washington Square Book Shop, 14, 17–19
Washington Square Players, 15, 17, 20
The Way of All Flesh (Butler), 20, 46, 68
The Way of Chinese Painting (Sze), 163
Weeks, Edward, 31
Wells, H. G., 19–20, 22, 68, 134
What's My Line?, 149
Whitman Candy Company, 17, 24
Whitman, Walt, 100
Whittier, John Greenleaf, 80
Wilde, Oscar, 19–20, 172
Wilder, Thornton, 173
Wilderness (Kent), 105, 117
"Will the Commercialization of Publishing Destroy Good Writing?" (Farrell), 145

Williams College, 131
Williams, Raymond, 180n. 16
Wilson, Edmund, 113, 122, 134
Wimpfheimer, Tony, 165–66
Winesburg, Ohio (Anderson), 68
Wisconsin Library Association, 78
The Wisdom of Confucius (Confucius), 61
Wolf, Blanche, 12, 136
Wolff Estates, 102
Woollcott, Alexander, 11
Woolf, Virginia, 2, 54, 84
Woolsey, John, 114
Works of Plato (Plato), 122
World's Great Thinkers, 85
Wright, Cuthbert, 14
Wright, Willard Huntington, 28

"Young Intellectuals," 14, 178n. 8, 179n. 13
Young, Stark, 5

Zola, Emile, 12–13, 122
Zuleika Dobson (Beerbohm), 173, 176

Jay Satterfield was born in Lincoln, Nebraska. He received his B.A. from Grinnell College, an M.A. in Library and Information Science and an M.A. and a Ph.D. in American Studies from the University of Iowa. He was granted a research fellowship from the Bibliographic Society of America and was the recipient of the Seashore Dissertation Fellowship and the Alexander Kern Dissertation Travel Award from the University of Iowa. *"The World's Best Books": Taste, Culture, and the Modern Library* is his first book. Mr. Satterfield is the Head of Reader Services at the Special Collections Research Center at the University of Chicago Library. He lives in Chicago with his wife, Jennifer, and son, Evan.

www.ingramcontent.com/pod-product-compliance
Lightning Source LLC
Chambersburg PA
CBHW020648230426
43665CB00008B/349